KNOWLEDGE
AND
POWER

in a South
Pacific Society

D1430074

1,2,5,6

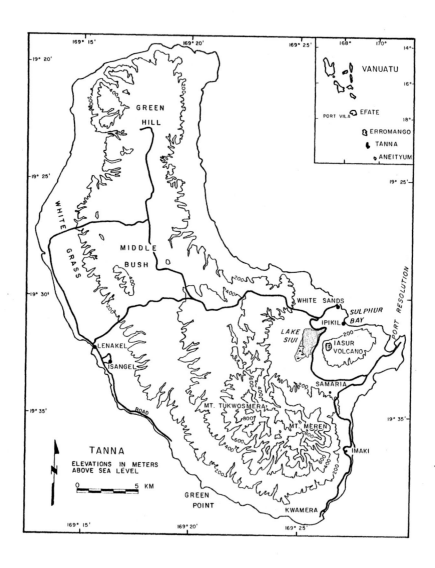

VANUATU

PORT VILA EFATE

ERROMANGO

TANNA

ANEITYUM

GREEN HILL

WHITE GRASS

MIDDLE BUSH

WHITE SANDS

SULPHUR BAY

IPIKIL

LAKE SIUI

IASUR VOLCANO

LENAKEL

ISANGEL

PORT RESOLUTION

SAMARIA

ROAD

MT. TUKWOSMERA

MT. MEREN

IMAKI

TANNA

ELEVATIONS IN METERS
ABOVE SEA LEVEL

0   5 KM

N

GREEN POINT

KWAMERA

KNOWLEDGE AND POWER

in a South Pacific Society

Lamont Lindstrom

SMITHSONIAN INSTITUTION PRESS
WASHINGTON AND LONDON

Library of Congress Cataloging in Publication Data

Lindstrom, Lamont, 1953–
    Knowledge and power in a South Pacific
society / Lamont Lindstrom.
        p.   cm. — (Smithsonian series in
ethnographic inquiry)
    Includes bibliographic references and index.
    ISBN 0-87474-365-6 (cloth). — ISBN
0-87474-357-5 (paperback)
    1. Tanna (Vanuatu people)—Politics and
government. 2. Tanna (Vanuatu people)—
Psychology. 3. Cargo movement—
Vanuatu. 4. Language and culture—
Vanuatu. I. Title. II. Series.
DU760.L54   1991
    306'.0899595—dc20   90-53172

For Elsa Katiri and Carla Maui

SMITHSONIAN SERIES IN ETHNOGRAPHIC INQUIRY

Ivan Karp and William L. Merrill, Series Editors

Ethnography as fieldwork, analysis, and literary form is the distinguishing feature of modern anthropology. Guided by the assumption that anthropological theory and ethnography are inextricably linked, this series is devoted to exploring the ethnographic enterprise.

Contents

Preface

This book applies a discursive model of knowledge and of power to a South Pacific society: to Tanna, an island of southern Vanuatu. It is—in the original sense of the word—an essay; an attempt to extend Michel Foucault's writings on discourse, knowledge, and power to a remote South Pacific society around the backside of the globe from Foucault's own theoretical targets. Foucault's oeuvre comprises vivid analyses of a number of European institutions and cultural practices (clinics, prisons, sexuality), as well as important theoretical statements. Many commentators have celebrated the richness of Foucault's work, although some have suggested that its brilliant singularity makes it "difficult to integrate" into ordinary research concerns and methodologies (Hamilton 1985:9). The integration attempted here, I think, will show its considerable relevance for making sense of systems of knowledge and power in Melanesia. I draw especially on Foucault's 1970 lecture "The Order of Discourse" (1981) (sometimes translated as "The Discourse on Language"); I have also learned much from Bourdieu's economic analyses of language (e.g., Bourdieu 1977).

My wife and I first arrived in Vanuatu (then the New Hebrides) in February, 1978. These were exciting times. National political parties had recently coalesced and were contending for power in this period before independence—an independence that came, finally, on July 30, 1980. The Vanuaaku Party had just declared a People's Provisional Government on the islands and in the villages of its supporters. In response, opposition parties in some places ripped down its new flags and uprooted its flagpoles. Moreover, the British and the French, who together had ruled this "condominium" colony since 1906, continued the bickering and squabbling that had characterized their relations during the previous seven decades. The competition now was to determine which would influence the country after its independence. My application for a residence permit to do anthropological research on Tanna was not surprisingly delayed by Franco-British suspicions and worries about loose anthropologists camped out in island hinterlands that were rapidly slipping from administrative control. I am grateful that we at last did receive permission to come to the capital, Port Vila. By April, we were welcomed on Tanna by the island's first national (ni-Vanuatu) District Agent, who had been appointed to succeed his departing European predecessors.

Wading the last few yards to the beach from the small launch that was transporting passengers and cargo ashore from the inter-island ship *Nalkutan*, I carried certain baggage. In addition to mosquito nets, boots, notebooks and pencils, portable typewriter, antimalarial tablets, shower bucket, wife's adopted kitten, and all that marks a novice anthropologist, I also had with me a research proposal. This was a plan to study the relative degree of engagement in the developing, cash economy of the various religious groups on the island, an idea that traces its genealogy back to Max Weber's spirit of capitalism and the Protestant ethic, to the relationship between ideology and economic behavior. I arrived on Tanna with an interest in what people did with money, and in the island's various religious ideologies and associations. The population includes Presbyterians, assorted traditionalists who follow what in Vanuatu is called *kastom*, and supporters of the John Frum movement—a local group I wrongly presumed to be an exemplar of the Melanesian "cargo cult."

I immediately found myself in trouble. First signs of this were the question of where we would live. I had thought to prospect about somewhat and choose an area that would serve the goals of my research. I was wrong about this. Our village, Samaria, was picked out for us long before we had even arrived in the country. I also began to notice that some people avoided talking seriously with us and, furthermore, that islanders often refused to talk with each other as well. The naivete of my appreciation of what anthropology is all about began to dawn on me. I wanted economic and religious data. To get this, I knew I needed a "methodology." What I had in mind was a little participant observation, rounding up a clutch of informants for interviews, a couple of questionnaires and surveys—in short, the usual anthropological "tool kit."

Tanna forced me to recognize that none of these tasks is simple. Anthropology is not an innocent or neutral technique for learning another culture. Nor is a culture wide open and free, like a text or poem that anyone might casually pick up and read. Rather, much of culture is unshared and unevenly distributed among people of a society, and a set of conditions and procedures work hard to keep it so. These conditions and procedures are discursive. They regulate the ways in which people exchange and learn cultural knowledge in talk. This has obvious, and sometimes ominous, implications for anthropology. *All* anthropological methods for "learning," "gathering," or "collecting" cultural data, when it comes right down to it, are kinds of talk, and that talking is always regulated and controlled. People who are empowered by the fact that they know something that others do not have an interest in protecting this unshared culture. Power structures, and cultures in general, survive through time only if discursive rules and conditions successfully reproduce the existing distribution of local knowledge and conversational competencies.

The hidden task that any anthropologist faces—no matter what his or her research interest—is to figure out the rules and conditions that govern talking and access to knowledge in a society. Landing on an island and asking, "tell me about your economy and religion" is not enough. An anthropological endeavor, if successful, depends on first penetrating the local discursive order that establishes differential conversational positions and functions, the ordinary times and places to talk, certain truths and falsities, domains of knowledge and regions of ignorance, the wise and the silent. I gradually, often painfully, figured out Tanna's order of discourse—at least enough of it that I was able to work through it, and sometimes around it, to learn something about my original research concerns. I have written elsewhere about some of these more ethnographic findings (see References).

My original interest in counting pigs, coffee trees, and sewing machines, and measuring cash income and expenditure lost much of its flavor as I found myself both plagued and teased by Tanna's startling conversational order. I had waded ashore into a field of knowledgeable talk—a talk controlled by copyrights and authorities, regulated means of inspiration, communicative roads and meetings, secrets and revelations, dangerous questions and even more dangerous answers, powerful nonsense, commentary and exegesis, and ridicule, truth, and lies. Furthermore, people's own interests and attentions were focused here. Controlled conversation maintains local relations and structures of power, especially among the competing religious and political groupings on the island.

In this book, I describe this discursive order itself that sustains the island's culture, both shared and unshared. Traveling, as it were, with Foucault to the South Seas, I approach Tannese culture as an organized "mode of information" to describe, in this, discursive procedures that regulate the production, the circulation, and the consumption of knowledge statements. These procedures reproduce certain conversational subjects and objects through time. In so doing, they also maintain local regimes of power and knowledge.

A word about language: the writings of post-structuralist theorists are not always remarkable for elegance and clarity of style (Sturrock 1979:15–16). Occasionally, the novelties, densities, and seeming inconsistencies of this writing follow from a theoretical concern to evade—even to shatter—the "tyranny of the signifier." Old language represses new truth. Foucault, however, is a "hyperactive" pessimist (Dreyfus and Rabinow 1983:264). Any new language, however random or devious, carries its own dangers. Take, for example, the word "discourse." This purposely blurs together three levels of meaning: the act of talking itself; a body of knowledge content that is talked about; and a set of conditions and procedures which regulate that talking. Available anthropological synonyms for all this, such as "cultural domain," immediately come to mind. The post-structuralist term "discourse," however, has supplanted anthropology's "culture." Although "culture," for anthropology, is a comfortably neutral term, it has long carried a negative charge within the philosophical, literary, and critical theories out of which post-structuralism has emerged. I, too, adopt some of this language (e.g., "subjectification," "disjunction," "statement") because I believe, in the end, a new way of talking does cast different light on familiar anthropological concerns. Die-hard anthropologists, however, every time they come across "discourse," may substitute for it some form of their word "culture."

Second, I also use an economic metaphor for the conversational interplay of knowledge, a metaphor I borrow from Bourdieu (1977) and Collins (1975). I do this as a shorthand that captures what I believe to be important political, economic, and powerful aspects of knowledge. An economic metaphor also captures local Melanesian sensibilities. People in these islands commonly treat knowledge as a commodity—something that can be bought and sold. Again, where I talk about knowledge "production," readers might prefer to substitute words like formulation or inspiration, as they might dialogue, communication, or teaching for knowledge "exchange," and hearing or listening for knowledge "consumption." Whatever one's taste in metaphors for conversation, the point is that "it is through talk that people construe their cultural worlds, display and recreate their social orders, plan and critique their activities, and praise and condemn their fellows" (Frake 1980:334).

A conversational model of society, although perhaps less familiar than are its tropic alternatives—the organic, the mechanistic, the systemic—speaks directly to some of the main characteristics of Melanesian societies. If we start with the assumption that culture is an organization of knowledge that demands regulated talk, I believe we can begin to form a new understanding of many of the familiar constructs of Melanesian anthropology. I discuss big-men, oratory, and consensus; decision-making meetings and moots; song, dance, and myth; personhood and shared place; courts and schools; magic and medicine; ancestors, cargo cults, and the desire for the new; controlled mobility and a longing to travel; the inspirational impact of dreams and of the drinking of kava; Christianity and development; episodic time and the new man; shame, lies, and the rule of law; and other aspects of everyday life in the Southwestern Pacific. Although I describe Tanna's mode of information in particular, this has much in common with those of other Pacific societies. I mean this book to be comparative, and I cite examples of parallel discursive practices elsewhere in the Pacific.

More than this, I suggest that the workings of Tanna's mode of information tell us much about our own. That often foretold post-industrial global village of the information age perhaps has important features in common with the real villages of the South Pacific. For me, this is one of the most attractive claims of anthropology: to understand one's own social condition by juxtaposing it with that of others. Some might find my discovery of a knowledge economy in a preindustrial society to be rather suspicious. Anthropology pursues its object in terms of its current interests. When these interests aimed at savage origins, we found evolutionary forebears in Melanesia practicing primal social forms. When these interests led toward the history of diffused civilization, we followed the Kava and Betel People into these islands, remnant heliolithic migrants. When we banked our interests in Economic Man, we discovered him there too, busily exchanging pigs, and latterly copra, coffee, and cash for prestige and political power. Now, as talk about our emerging "information society" increases in volume, it is not surprising to recognize that in Melanesia a knowledge economy has always been operating.

Still, there is good reason to compare Melanesian modes of information with our own. If modernism tended to find its principal "other" in the cultures of Africa and the Orient, post-modernism might look with profit to the Pacific. Here are people who define humanity by the capacity to talk. A Tannese child—a *iapou* ("mute")—is not fully human until it says its first word. These are people who understand their societies as "worked out through talk" (Sack 1985:17). These are people who deny historical continuities, desiring disjunctions instead. Islanders know that they live in information societies. They realize the power of talk. They recognize both the value and the danger of knowledge.

Acknowledgments

This book was written with the generous support of the East-West Center's Area Studies Fellowship Program. I would like to thank both the Center's Office of Open Grants and Student Affairs and its Institute of Culture and Communication, in which I was a guest. My interests in discourse, knowledge, and power developed during several fieldtrips to Tanna (which varied in length between a couple of weeks and 22 months) during 1978–1979, 1982, 1983, 1985, 1987, 1988, and 1989. A number of institutions and programs supported research in Vanuatu, including the University of Tulsa and its Henry Kendal College of Arts and Science, the Vanuatu Cultural Centre, the East-West Center, Fulbright and the Council for the International Exchange of Scholars, the National Endowment for the Humanities, the Wenner-Gren Foundation for Anthropological Research, the English-Speaking Union of the United States, Phi Beta Kappa, the Department of Anthropology, University of California at Berkeley, and the Department of Anthropology, Research School of Pacific Studies, Australian National University.

For encouragement and criticism during the writing and for publication assistance, I would like to thank Elizabeth Christopher, Wimal Dissanayake, Daniel Goodwin, Mary Huber, Janet Keller, John Kirkpatrick, John Larcom, Gordon Lester-Massman, George Marcus, Fred Myers, cartographer Frieda Odell, Dale Phelps, K. S. Rajyashree, Michael Shapiro, Glenn Shive, Theresa Slowik, several anonymous reviewers, and especially Geoffrey M. White. I, not they, of course am responsible for the argument as presented and any infelicities of style.

For anthropological companionship, inspiration, and assistance in Vanuatu, I also thank Joel Bonnemaison, Ken and Anne Calvert, Charles de Burlo, Miriam Dornoy-Vurabaravu, Ellen Facey, Roger and Uhlee Goucke, James Gwero, Michael and Judy Heath, Kirk and Claudia Huffman, Bill and Margaret Rodman, Jim Shiffer, Phillip Shing, Jeff Siegel, Matthew Spriggs, Bob and Myrna Tonkinson, Darrell Tryon, and especially my wife Cynthia Frazer. Finally, I acknowledge both my gratitude and my large debt to the people of Tanna—I wish I could name you all here—who provide always warmhearted welcomes and generous assistance, not to mention excellent conversation.

1

Knowledge and Power

Iou, Masta Mataru	I, Master Mataru
iakamara ia wok u.	I live for this work.
Iakaman wok u	I follow the work
pen Iamerika.	away to America.
Iahamreirei wok me pam.	We understand none of the work.
Pwah in u Aisak Wan	Let Isaac One here
rahatin pen ia ket ia Is.	teach it from the gate in the East.

—JOHN FRUM HYMN

It was the cool season of 1957 when people on Tanna began to build offices for Americans. Following local methods of construction, they felled trees for house post and rafter, wove wild cane into walls, and plaited coconut leaves for thatch. They varied the local custom when they outfitted these small buildings with unusual furniture. In each they arranged a table and chair. Once constructed and furnished, the offices stood vacant waiting for Nampas, a leader of the John Frum movement. People made ready to celebrate the day when Nampas, escorting an American, would arrive to install him in the office and open it for business. Americans, everyone knew, were arriving regularly by submarine.

These were local supporters of the John Frum movement of East Tanna, headquartered at Sulphur Bay. John Frum is a spiritual

1

"newsman" who links the island with the outside world, particularly America. The John Frum movement is a classic example of the so-called Melanesian "cargo cult." Since these Pacific Islands were colonized, Europeans encountered a variety of cults, movements, excitements, and paroxysms across the region (Burridge 1969; Lawrence 1964; Worsley 1968). As in millenarian movements elsewhere, island prophets commonly foretold world reversal, the retreat of European colonials, and the return of the dead. Islanders reorganized their marriage patterns and other social institutions, and turned to ritual practice in order to hurry the advent of the new age. They put into play marathon dancing, trance, and magical sympathies between objects, awaiting fulfillment of prophesy. In the 1940s, the massive influx of military materiel during the Pacific War found its way into cult mythologies, reworking the theme of the return of the dead. The ancestors now were to come back home with planeloads and shiploads of "cargo," consisting of industrially produced European goods.

Typical functionalist accounts of Melanesian cargo cults point to the cognitive utility of these beliefs as a way of explaining and making existential sense of recent transformations in social life, sparked by the incorporation of these remote islands into worldwide political and economic systems (e.g., Burridge 1969). Or, cults function as a local form of organized protest in reaction to the penetration of colonial authority and the establishment of new political inequalities (Worsley 1968). Or, cults occur as a release and expression of a rising spring of psychological tensions fed by rapid social change (Schwartz 1973). John Frum was and is all of that. But my interest in the movement is that it reveals, clearly, the relation between knowledge and power in Melanesia. The interplay of the production and control of John Frum knowledge, on the one hand, and power, on the other, points to more general connections between knowledge and power within Tanna's culture, and within our own. The place to start an investigation of this sort is with John Frum talk. How are people variably able to talk in this way about John Frum? And how are people able to hear and to take as true what gets said?

John Frum talked first in 1941 to villagers near Green Point on the island's west coast (Bonnemaison 1987:465–499; Brunton 1981; Gregory and Gregory 1984; Guiart 1952, 1956a, 1956b). Here, a shadowy figure appeared in the night and made a number of interpretive and prescriptive statements about island traditions and appropriate relations with European missionaries and colonialists. Partly because of his continuing value within island talk, John Frum's identity still remains a mystery. This mystery is part of his long-lived attractiveness. The Tannese commonly see, sometimes talk with, and even may go so far as to claim to have sex with ancestral ghosts and other spirits, and it was no accident that John Frum appeared at a kava-drinking clearing. Leading men of the past are buried around the circumferences of these spaces where their descendents meet daily to prepare and drink the Pacific drug kava (*Piper methysticum*).

John Frum's continuing visits, in this sense, are no different from many other ghostly appearances on the island. The colonial administration at the time, however, was convinced that a conspiracy of local men dressed one of themselves in long trousers, a white shirt, and a hat to declaim spookily from one of the darker corners of the kava clearing. It was perplexed, however, that John Frum continued to appear even after the several men who were accused of playing the part were arrested and exiled to northern islands in the archipelago. American Army intelligence officers, a few years later, also investigated the possibility that John Frum was, in reality, a Japanese provocateur.

There is also a minor body of exegesis about the name John Frum. Is it derived from John the Baptist? Is it John *Broom*—the instrument that would sweep the whites off the island? Is it John from America? Is it John Brown, the American emancipationist (cf. Schwartz 1962:356)? Is Frum related to *urumun*, a word for spirit medium? Whatever his name, and whether or not adroit intellectual entrepreneurs conjured up this drama and personated John Frum to serve their particular ends, John Frum has since come to take his place among an assemblage of didactic ancestors and island culture heroes. Fairly soon after his successful performance in the west, Nampas and several other men from East Tanna began, gradually, to appropriate the figure of John Frum and to control the production of his talk. They did this initially by contriving for him several sons (Guiart 1956b:159).

The joint British and French colonial government was much concerned to repress the dilating circulation of these lies. For a time, the colonial administration forbade any conversation about John Frum, or even the mention of his name (Bonnemaison 1987:469).

European District Agents on Tanna tried and punished a number of people for spreading "rumors" of John Frum. To further silence John Frum's spokesmen, the government removed them from the island's field of conversation. The talk went underground until Nampas and other organization authorities returned home from a final sentence of exile in 1956.

The following year, leaders of local villages who supported the wider movement took initiative at a number of kava-drinking grounds scattered across the island. They organized office buildings. At Isina kava-drinking ground, Tain and his son Nouata directed the building crew. When everything was ready, Tain sent word to Nampas. Tain killed pigs, harvested his yams, and invited supporters to a dance in order to celebrate properly the coming of his American. Local dancing, which begins in the cool of the night, usually persists past midnight, past false dawn, to conclude only when the sun fully rises, marks all important events on the island. This event was particularly special. People danced two consecutive nights. More than this, their dance was animated and novel. They formed long chains that snaked across Isina kava-drinking ground, men and women joined together. In the more staid traditional style, men dance alone in the prestigious center of the clearing, separated from a periphery of revolving women.

Nampas arrived and secretly installed the American in his office. Men prepared and drank kava to celebrate. The American's invisibility proved his power. He would, everyone knew, soon invest them all with the hat of wisdom. Although invisible, the American was hungry. That first night, Nouata brought pork—taken hot from an earth oven—to his office. The office, placed at the edge of a cliff to overlook Iasur volcano, which steams across the valley, stood out of the way of kava-drinking ground and surrounding hamlets. Nouata returned with bones.

Tain and his son Nouata were "wire-men," people of the red cross. Wires, radios, telephones, and other metaphoric communication devices are common throughout the history of Melanesian millenarian movements. A decade before, moreover, some Tannese had helped string American military telephone wires across Efate Island. Others in the John Frum movement identified themselves as men of custom, people of the black cross (see Bonnemaison 1987:496–497).

Whereas those of the black cross claim the right to ascertain the truth of island traditions, those of the red cross control the importation of powerful, alien knowledge. Tain managed an information terminus, one of which was located in every kava-ground at which people accepted the wisdom of John Frum organization leaders. Knowledge, transmitted over the invisible "wires," originated in America, passed through Honolulu, through Sulphur Bay, to then diffuse out to scattered local groups on Tanna. Some arriving information took the form of song. If Tain or his sons, sometimes in the office with their American, received a song across the wire, they summoned local supporters, drank kava, and taught everyone its words and tune.

Every Friday, each local group, or "team," traveled to Sulphur Bay on the coast. Teams from kava-drinking grounds around East Tanna congregated on this day, John Frum's sabbath, to sing their repertoires and thus demonstrate received knowledge. At Isina, songs continued to arrive "by wire." Cane houses generally last five years or so. During these years, until his death, Tain the wire-man periodically killed and roasted pigs to feed his American.

A second interpretation of the events at Isina currently circulates. That first night, Kamuti, latterly a member of a rival church and thus an enemy of John Frum, crawled up to the office and peered through chinks in the cane walls hoping to catch a glimpse of the American. He saw Nouata eating pork.

Over the succeeding 30 years, neither of these opposing truth statements has achieved what might be called popular self-evidence. People today differ in their acceptance of the versions, and in evaluations of the truth. Pig bone data alone are not sufficient to verify the American for sceptics. Nor are they sufficient to undermine the truth of his habitation of the office for believers. Wider conversational relations, not detached evidence, establish what counts on the island as the truth or the lie.

CODE/CONTENT

Here are a number of statements about Americans, about pork, and about wisdom. What are we to make of them? At one time they circulated orally, in a conversation I shared with several friends on the slopes of a Melanesian volcano. That conversation consisted of commentary on events people recalled to have taken place at Isina kava-drinking ground in the late 1950s. The present textual form of the conversation and its extended epigrammic situation here at the head of Chapter One, is an effect of its appropriation by anthropological practice. It is thus akin to many similarly descriptive statements elsewhere in the archives of Melanesian ethnography. Fieldwork, translation, and textualization manage to transform cross-cultural conversation into useful anecdote—"from my field notes" as the typical attribution goes.

Beyond a simple packaging of alien talk recalled from fieldwork, the anthropological desire is to make something of this. How might we approach what the Tannese said they said and did at Isina in order to capture not only an anecdotal text but a cross-cultural message as well? Two theoretical strategies are commonly applied to exotic statements such as this. Both are concerned with the Saussurean dialectic between signifier and signified. On the one hand, structuralism accounts for a statement by investigating something about its encoding. On the other, "cultural hermeneutics" (Geertz 1983:5) accounts for a statement in terms of its meaningful content.

Although signified content does not exist without signifying code (and pretty much *vice versa*), structuralism and hermeneutics start at opposite ends of the interrelationship between a text's encoding and its content. Structuralism is principally concerned with relations between the mutually conditioning elements of a code, or the relationship of signifiers to other signifiers. The meaningful content carried by a code is theoretically secondary and, in this sense, "dominated" by the signifiers. Meanings are made multiple, labile, and convertible insofar as they are arranged and organized by the operation of codes. A culture's statements about "totems," for example, "constitute codes making it possible to ensure, in the form of conceptual systems, the convertibility of messages" (Lévi-Strauss 1966:90). Codes vary much less than do meaningful contents: to reveal human nature, "to explain the noticeable frequency of certain sociological solutions, not attributable to particular objective conditions, appeal must be made to form and not content" (Lévi-Strauss 1966:95).

A structuralist calculus of the events at Isina might begin by exposing the obvious dualism that correlates the symbolic elements found there:

Codes

> black cross/red cross
>
> house/office
>
> traditional nupu dance/novel snake dance
>
> center/periphery
>
> Tanna/America

In this decomposition, the totality of the various encoded elements (crosses, dances, buildings, etc.) adds up to a dualistic opposition. This underlying structural form remains constant. Meanings, conversely, are convertible. Surface elements such as black cross/red cross may be rewritten house/office. Conceivably, any other pair of symbolic elements (taro/potato?) could potentially be drawn upon to substitute for existing symbols. We might, furthermore, search for other elements that stand between and "mediate" the underlying opposition: wires, submarines, John Frum, pork. These, too, are convertible insofar as each occupies a homologous position within the structure as a whole. This analysis, finally, depends little on a subject's point of view. We can crack the code without bothering much about Nampas's and Tain's subjective understanding of crosses, Americans, offices, or other content of their statements.

Whereas structuralism decodes, hermeneutics interprets. The signifier/signified seesaws. On this side, the problem is what a text says. The aim is to elucidate content rather than code—a reading (the deeper and thicker the better) of the meaning of a text, or statement, achieved by situating this in the horizons of understanding of its speaker. "The whole point of a semiotic approach to culture is . . . to aid us in gaining access to the conceptual world in which our subjects live so that we can, in some extended sense of the term, converse with them" (Geertz 1973:24). Geertz's (1983:5) "understanding of understanding" demands hunting down deep meaning, not deep structure.

Should we pursue a hermeneutic reading of the events at Isina, we would need to situate Nampas's and Tain's statements within intersubjective horizons of understanding. What, for example, are the traditional meanings of pork, of food exchange, of red/black contrasts, and of the sexual organization of dance? What, moreover, are the locally construed understandings of World War II? The John Frum movement absorbed a number of wartime symbols: red crosses from the doors of the ambulances that carried American wounded, returned from Guadalcanal, down from Bauer Airfield to Army and Navy hospitals in Port Vila; wires from military communication networks; offices; submarines. How has this borrowed symbolic content mutated on Tanna? To grasp the meaning of a statement (e.g., "The American is in his office"), we would have to ground this in a detailed ethnographic exposition of Tannese systems of significance.

My purpose in introducing this simple opposition between Lévi-Strauss's structuralism and Geertz's cultural hermeneutics (see Boon 1982:137–147) is to excuse this essay from being neither. Instead, I attempt to follow Foucault into a theoretical space beyond any teetering domination of the signifier or the signified—beyond symbolic codes, on the one hand, and meanings, on the other. Foucault "has sought to avoid the structuralist analysis which eliminates notions of meaning altogether and substitutes a formal model of human behavior as rule-governed transformations of meaningless elements; to avoid the phenomenological project of tracing all meaning back to the meaning-giving activity of an autonomous, transcendental subject; and finally to avoid the attempt of commentary to read off the implicit meaning of social practices as well as the hermeneutic unearthing of a different and deeper meaning of which social actors are only dimly aware" (Dreyfus and Rabinow 1983:xxiii—xxiv).

Structuralist calculus and hermeneutic readings both make something important of Tannese statements. Slipping, here, between the poles of code and content in no way wants to undermine the claims of either, but to get beyond the signifier/signified code/content couplet in order to analyze Tannese talk about America and submarines on other grounds.

This book is, in its aim, unlike other ethnologic attempts to make something of Melanesian culture. This is not ethnography—an interpretation of the content, the ontology of Tannese cultural understanding. It does not attempt to account for the content of island talk in terms of transcendental subjects; nor does it interpret the infrastructural, political, or other functions of a given belief or idea, important as these may be. Neither is this a structuralist decypherment of the underlying code frameworks which carry that cultural meaning. In fact, I do not much care about the details of what the Tannese say, nor about the structures in which they encode what they say. My intent, instead, is to read between "the lines" in order to uncover local procedures that manage the practice of saying itself: conditions that govern the making, circulation, and hearing (consumption) of island talk.

This is a different task than Lévi-Strauss's calculation of the universal foundations of communication, or Geertz's figuring how to "converse" with the subjects. My project is first simply to describe the practice of Tannese talk, as apparent in island conversational events (see Foucault 1972:27). I locate a number of discursive and nondiscursive procedures and conditions that govern the formulation, deployment, and consumption of what I will call "knowledge statements" or sometimes, "truth statements." These discourse control procedures and conditions are detailed in Chapters Three, Four, and Five. Second, I analyze the relationship of this conversational practice to island orders of truth and power—to what, following Foucault, might be termed the subjectification and domination of those who talk. These conversational procedures carry a charge. The cultural conditions that make our talking possible both empower and subdue us as we talk. And they feed directly into more institutional structures of social inequality.

Certain relations of conversational inequality, for example, appear in the manipulation and control of information during the events at Isina kava-drinking ground. Nampas and Tain's leadership depended on their production and exchange of John Frum messages. People who consumed this knowledge became their followers. John Frum statements spoke to people's interests, including their desire to acquire American wisdom and wealth, by reforming and articulating these interests as questions. Cult leaders expressed ruling desires in a particular kind of talking about offices, Americans, submarines, dances, and songs. Complementary knowledge statements proposed answers to the questions thus articulated. Nampas and Tain knew what to do and organized followers to do it. Nampas suggested the building of offices. He guided the said Americans from submarines to install them in new office buildings near kava-drinking grounds around the island. Metaphorically, he strung the wires.

In the local village market, Tain controlled the further exchange of John Frum knowledge statements, mediating between Nampas and America on the one hand, and his co-residents on the other. With his American at work in the office, Tain operated a procedure for the production of additional choral statements. The wires brought in new songs. Tain knew how to know. He managed the production of information embodied in cult song as well as the transmission of this to others in ritualized instruction; to celebrate the reception of every song, his pupils made special preparations and drank kava.

At Isina, John Frum's answers met people's desire to know. These answers, in large part, were about knowledge itself. Typical Melanesians, the Tannese value knowledge as a source of power. People knew that the official American would produce new wisdom. The wires, stretching to America, transmitted some of this information. Within the John Frum organization, relation to the means of knowledge production and circulation defined a hierarchy of status. Nampas and other cult leaders at organization headquarters managed knowing how to know. Information transmission wires converged at Sulphur Bay. At local village terminals, wire-men managed the further transmission of incoming statements to their fellow islanders. A parallel structure ordered the circulation and consumption of more traditional knowledge. Men on the side of the black cross claimed rights to manage the production and exchange of knowledge recognized to be "customary."

This John Frum discourse achieves some awareness of its own practice: in its evaluations, it recognizes the political weight of knowledge, and of the procedures that regulate knowing. In statements about official Americans, people assert the patent effects of information exchange in constituting social relations of power: the wise are powerful; knowledge is a resource (Rubinstein 1981:163–164). As elsewhere in Melanesia, restricted knowledge (technological and otherwise) is part of the recognized requisite capital that supports the production of material goods (Lawrence 1964:29–30). People attempt purposely to control those procedures that order the production, circulation, and consumption of knowledge statements. They economize information.

In this, they define themselves to be a kind of information society—this a conceit increasingly familiar to us "post-moderns" in the process of inventing the post-industrial order. On Tanna, where the media of information production, storage, circulation, and consumption are only recently and still uncommonly literate, the information society is grounded in talk. The compass of island conversation circumscribes a social order; the content of conversation sustains a culture; the duration of conversation is history; the discursive rules and conditions of conversation, which work to limit who can converse thereby making the practice of conversation unequal, bring into being relations of domination among people who talk together (cf. Collins 1975:113–114, 146–147).

A notion of society as a "conversational economy" invites the restatement of received anthropological understandings of "culture," e.g., culture consists of "whatever it is one has to know or believe in order to operate in a manner acceptable to its members, and do so in any role that they accept for one of themselves" (Goodenough 1964:36)—how, in Geertz's word, to "converse" with the natives by learning a set of more-or-less shared cultural codes and contents. But defining a culture to be neutral codes and meaningful contents is inadequate. The problem is also to investigate the practices by which cultural code/content comes to be *shared*. Culture is not reproduced innocently or by accident. The continued existence and purview of commonalities in cultural knowledge, in fact, require a political accounting.

Shared culture, in the sense of codes and beliefs held in common, was afoot during the events at Isina (events not atypical in the history of Tanna). People, acting in keeping with encoded dualism and a more-or-less shared system of significations, joined together, gathered materials to build an office, collected and prepared food, and danced. Common cultural knowledge of this sort organizes and expresses individual and group interests. We can understand Isina in these terms by situating events within local horizons of understanding. This, of course, is the hermeneutic claim: in order to figure the course of people's social interaction as well as the meanings they invest in that behavior, one must grasp the culture they share.

Through time, however, people produce and reproduce their common cultural codes and contents in interpersonal conversational practice. This practice is never disinterested. From this perspective, culture is better defined as a body of conversationally managed statements, rather than "acceptable" common knowledge. Culture both requires and informs relations of domination among those who take part in its conversations. Conversational inequalities do not result simply from the fact that people reify culturally constituted social relations and definitions and, in so doing, mystify the means of knowledge production, as well as the interests knowledge serves, so that the social origins of cultural products thereby escape immediate apprehension. We need to go beyond a Marxian approach to notice that culture, as an economy of information, does not just conceal or mystify power, it makes power possible. The continued existence of culture itself, shared or otherwise, depends on the interested conversational production, circulation, and consumption of knowledge statements. Reproduction of shared culture depends on people talking; and talking unavoidably produces power and inequalities.

Anthropological hermeneutics has established a cross-cultural dialogue in part to denature reality. It presents alternative cultural formulations that can challenge the certainties established within our own system of cultural knowledge. This cross-cultural denaturing makes use of a relativist comparison of cultures. Such comparison exposes knowledge as "merely" differently situated cultural interpretations, not reflections, of reality. Whether words and concepts objectively reflect reality is at least now questionable.

This comparative technique, however, has sometimes tended to lend cultural systems a spurious internal neutrality. A cultural definition of reality, for those who consume this (be they native or anthropological observer) often appears neutral and innocent. Accountings of this sort, moreover, may posit a cultural system to be an adaptive mechanism that reproduces a particular society in an environment from generation to generation. Shared culture is made to serve supposedly common interests, needs, or functions whether these are ecological, psychological, or sociological. We make shared cultural knowledge neutral, in this fashion, when we characterize it as a means of human adaption; when we calculate it to be a surface level reflection of profound, atemporal cognitive universals; or when we interpret, in empathetic description of religious significations, the reasons why people in one society believe in ghosts and submarining Americans.

However functional, code-governed, or meaningful it may be, as a conversationally regulated body of knowledge statements, culture is always freighted with interests. Everywhere there is inequality of access to the means of cultural knowledge production, and to the means of its deployment. A culture may indeed adapt a society to a particular environment; but it also maintains orders of truth and power within that society. A religious belief in ghosts or Americans may make interpretive sense in terms of some profound horizon of understanding or in terms of certain systems of rationality; but it also promotes the conversational domination of those who best know these truths and thereby manage ghostly power. Cultural order is political order; its economy of knowledge is an economy of power. The very fact that a culture is shared, at least in part, testifies to its dangers.

We might say that those of us who manage the production and deployment of cultural knowledge pose both the serious questions and the ruling answers. Knowledge producers give answers in response to the existing organization of individual desires and interests. Responding to islander desire for wealth and wisdom, Nampas produced official Americans and exchanged this knowledge with others. Those people who invent or colonize a new body of knowledge that articulates known interests and tenders answers that further those interests, bring into being new conversational relations of power between knowledge producer and consumer. With his John Frum knowledge, Nampas established novel communicative relations of political inequality and directed the behavior of his believing supporters. He enunciated the answers about America and about wisdom and thus, at Isina and elsewhere on Tanna, organized an active, social response to pressing interests. Folks built offices for him to staff.

Nampas to a degree also shaped the questions: What do we want? Who can help us? How can we become wise? Control of the questions—even more than control of the answers—maintains existing social inequalities in that such control helps frame and make sense of felt desire. This sort of talk makes you know what you feel and, moreover, sometimes works to make you feel in the first place. Whereas a number of answers may compete within a knowledge market, and thus encounter and struggle with sceptics, management of how people talk about desire and interest represses both the production and the consumption of alternative cultural knowledge. Knowledge statements that articulate *answers* are often self-evidently interested, unshared, or ideological. They easily generate their own sceptics. Statements that articulate or adumbrate *questions*, on the other hand, maintain and extend less witting, more shared knowledge. By producing talk that defines and ranks desire, the powerful set the conversational agenda and, by this means, establish inequalities more difficult to perceive or challenge.

Shared culture is more than neutral commonalities of code and content; it is the by-product of communicative practices within particular modes of information. An analysis of knowledge statements (such as "The American is in his office") that situates these bits of shared culture within orders of conversational practice complements alternative theoretical approaches. The same statement, of course, might also be decoded structurally or read hermeneutically. Being suspicious of how culture comes to be shared, however, attunes one to issues of knowledge and power.

A discursive analysis of culture is perhaps especially apposite given increasingly noisy characterizations of present-day advanced capitalism as a new sort of "information society." In the market of quasi-evolutionary social and economy theory, the value of this body of speculation is on the rise. "The term 'mode of information' designates the new language experiences of the twentieth century brought about for the most part by advances in electronics and related technologies" (Poster 1984: preface). Poster supposes that "reason has become, in history, a form of power in a way that it perhaps was not before the eighteenth century" (1984:13).

Maybe so—but premodern social orders also presume conversational economies of power, in that they presume the existence of "shared culture." It is useful to keep in mind, here, Derrida's (1976:106) criticism of Lévi-Strauss's assumptions of preliterate innocence—assumptions that continue to echo today. Writing, of course, provides a technology by which powerful elites may more closely record, survey, and control, but all the dangers of discourse do not appear with literacy. Nor do they begin with modernity. Terdiman has noted that, "under the transformed conditions of social existence in the nineteenth century, signs and discourses increasingly become exchange values. They are offered, desired, and acquired; they circulate and are consumed" (1985:43). But so do they circulate, and are consumed, on Tanna. There is no garden of benign language in the premodern lower reaches of the evolutionary ladder.

Every language is a preexisting system of symbolic choices in which people discover themselves; and all talking is regulated by preexisting rules and conditions of discourse. All talk inflicts "violence," in Derrida's terms (1976:101); all modes of information impose a framework of power. Anthropological analyses of nonwestern information systems, such as Tanna's, usefully cross-examine the claims of post-structuralist theories of discourse, as well as the evolutionary claims of those soothsaying a coming information society.

These claims have been both, for the most part, based in the Western experience.

In applying Foucault's concept of "discourse" to a South Pacific society, I both ignore and expand aspects of his approach. Discourse on Tanna is conversation. As such, much of Foucault's oeuvre, concerned as it is with tracing the "genealogy" (i.e., history) of textually stored and circulated European knowledge, cannot bear upon the island's oral mode of information. Furthermore, to outline the sort of power that inheres in vocal discourse, I must stretch the post-structuralist agenda so that it speaks to a non-textualizing society, to a mode of information in which statements circulate conversationally and knowledge is stored only in memory.

MODE OF INFORMATION

Individuals born into a social order are not free to chat at will. Rather, each faces extant cultural rules and practices of discourse. The least of these practices are linguistic rules of grammar and semantic detail. More critically, a number of discursive conditions also exist that maintain and reproduce the conversational order. Any person's position and capacities vis-a-vis his fellow conversationalists depend on his situation within what Foucault calls an "order of discourse." This consists of (1) a finite body of shared codes and knowledge content (a "culture," or "subculture"); and (2) a set of discursive procedures, apparatuses, and institutional arrangements that regulate the "practice" of that knowledge. Following Poster (1984:164), we might also call a discursive order a "mode of information," or the ways of knowing that sustain both shared and unshared culture and relations of power. In more anthropological terms, these are cultural rules that govern who talks, how one talks, and what is sayable.

Knowledge

The content of a "culture" consists of a view of the world that people learn and sustain in discourse, or in shared talk. Culture (shared knowledge) is "that of which one can speak in a discursive practice"; it is "the space in which the subject may take up a position and speak of the objects with which he deals in his discourse"; it is "the field of coordination and subordination of statements in which concepts appear, and are defined, applied and transformed" (Foucault 1972:182–183). Sustaining culture, people talking together constitute "domains of objects, in respect of which one can affirm or deny true or false propositions" (Foucault 1981:73). "We must conceive discourse as a violence which we do to things, or in any case as a practice which we impose on them" (1981:67).

If conversation carries and maintains cultural knowledge, the compass of the known turns back to restrict the paths discourse takes: "There is no knowledge without a particular discursive practice; and any discursive practice may be defined by the knowledge that it forms" (Foucault 1972:183). Culture includes knowledge of "subjects," or of the recognized, available ways to be human—what anthropology tends to call "personhood." In conversation, people gradually become the sorts of people they know to be locally possible and authentic.

Power

As conversation deploys and sustains cultural content, or knowledge, so does it bring into being and maintain ratios of power between conversational "subjects," between the people who talk together. Semantically, we are frequently led to construe "power" as an entity, a right, or a commodity (Foucault 1980:88). Power fills us as does wonder, awe, or hope; it grows and declines; we give it, take it, or lose it; we possess a lot or a little. Anthropology generally avoids being embarrassed by these everyday fashions of talking about power (see Fardon 1985:7–8). Dodging metaphoric commodification, it commonly defines power as an aspect of social relationships. One of the individuals involved, more than any other, influences group decisions and directs joint action. The powerful manage or influence the behavior of others. Power is not a commodity; rather, we know power only in its social relational effects on ourselves and on others. Measures of social power are ratios (Elias 1984:251; cf. Foucault 1983:221); one is powerful by virtue of another being powerless. A Robinson Crusoe enjoys power only when he finds his Friday.

Foucault latterly identified his major problem to be the constitution, in discourse, of the human subject (1980:97). An order of discourse "subjectifies" or "subjugates" all who talk in its terms (Dreyfus and Rabinow 1983:186–187). Here, he echoes the anthropological concern with "enculturation" or "socialization"—how one becomes human by learning a culture. As such, Foucault (1980:98) locates an inherent "power" within all of conversational practice:

> Power is not to be taken to be a phenomenon of one individual's consolidated and homogeneous domination over others, or that of one group or class over others. What, by contrast, should always be kept in mind is that power, if we do not take too distant a view of it, is not that which makes the difference between those who exclusively possess and retain it, and those who do not have it and submit to it. Power must be analysed as something which circulates, or rather as something which only functions in the form of a chain. It is never localised here or there, never in anybody's hands, never appropriated as a commodity or piece of wealth. Power is employed and exercised though a net-like organisation. And not only do individuals circulate between its threads; they are always in the position of simultaneously undergoing this power. They are not only its inert or consenting target; they are always also the elements of its articulation. In other words, individuals are the vehicles of power, not its points of application.

Foucault's power, here, might be called sub-institutional, as it inheres in the simple details of living one's life according to the dictates and expectations of local culture. Power, therefore, not only represses, it "expresses." It brings into being certain kinds of people with particular desires and pleasures it then serves.

Given a concern with how people are turned into subjects (with enculturation), Foucault (1980:97) suggests:

> Let us not, therefore, ask why certain people want to dominate, what they seek, what is their overall strategy. Let us ask, instead, how things work at the level of on-going subjugation, at the level of those continuous and uninterrupted processes which subject our bodies, govern our gestures, dictate our behaviours etc.

Foucault's investigation into subjectivity is less concerned with what might be called conversational domination (why individuals and groups have power over others) than it is with subjugation/subjectification (how the subject, endowed with certain rights and desires, and illumed with cultural truths, appears as a peculiarly construed individual) (Foucault 1980:96). All conversationalists are equally subjugated, in this sense, be they big-man or small, capitalist or worker, wise man or ignoramous.

An emphasis on conversational subjugation discounts and, in fact, makes rather pitiful, the power of those people who dominate the workings of a mode of information—the production and deployment of culture. It also discounts the social impotence of those people who merely consume cultural knowledge. Enthralled in a mode of information, those individuals who operate its machinery are less its bosses (i.e., authors of cultural texts) than they are its secretaries, schooled in xerography.

Here Foucault makes the author disappear. A person has no independent privilege to invent culture: "The author is not an indefinite source of significations which fill a work; the author does not precede the works, he is a certain functional principle by which in our culture, one limits, excludes and chooses" (1979:159). Certain modes of information require "authors" as one sort of useful subject. "Authors" function to control the cultural content of conversation in order to exclude alternative knowledge. To do a genealogical analysis of Western discourses (i.e., European culture), we must see through authors and Western beliefs in the reality of individual creativity and in the personal origins of meaning: "It is a matter of depriving the subject (or its substitute) of its role as originator, and of analyzing the subject as a variable and complex function of discourse" (1979:158).

In his genealogical analyses of the West, Foucault also makes subjective desire disappear. Desire does not exist naturally. Human interests, too, are discursively produced within a social order. In depriving a person of "natural" creativity, we likewise deprive him of any natural subjective interests or desires that his creativity serves. Interests, instead, appear parthenogenetically within orders of discourse, within particular cultural traditions.

I must make reappear and reprivilege the individual Tannese "author" in order to investigate those ratios of power that form within the island's mode of information. We see Nampas formulating his submarining Americans, and Tain dictating his statements of song wisdom; we also see their neighbors and followers taking these statements as wisdom. A revivification of "author," on Tanna, is perhaps doubly perverse in that the Tannese themselves generally fail to recognize him in the first place. Unlike Foucault, however, they do not

send the author packing in order to dethrone the sovereign individual. Instead, island discourses appoint a stand-in for the regulatory
function that authors serve in the West. Island ancestors and other
local *authorities* replace individual *authors* as the culturally recognized
fount of meaning and knowledge; and inspiration, discursively, takes
the place of creativity. Nampas and Tain receive knowledge from
authoritative sources—rather than authoring this themselves—along
various channels of information transmission, including their invisible "wires." Nonetheless, authority and inspiration, like authors and
creativity in the West, set limits and exclusions on island talking and
likewise protect and maintain ruling understandings of the world—
the island's discursive order.

I acknowledge, but then set aside, conversational subjugation on
Tanna in order to turn back to the level of grosser, interpersonal
domination located within and alongside this subjugation. People,
although subjected, may still dominate (see Taylor 1986:87–90; Walzer 1986:63–67). The successful operation of any cultural system,
that subjugates individuals so that they become proper Frenchmen,
Americans, or Tannese, both depends upon and engenders relations
of domination among these individuals. In a genealogical analysis of
subjugation, the identity of who, exactly, "authors" knowledge and
who oversees the workings of the local mode of information is not
important. For the people who do the talking and listening, however,
this may matter very much. It mattered, for example, for Nampas. It
mattered for Tain. It mattered for their fellow islanders who, in consuming American knowledge, became their collaborators in shared
cultural codes and contents.

Access to cultural knowledge and to its practice is rarely equal or
open to all. A mode of information subjugates individuals differently
and distributes conversational functions and positions unevenly.
Conversational practice establishes individual cultural incompetence
as well as competence. Discursive procedures regulate who may
speak and who may not—who is conversationally qualified, and
who is disqualified. They "ensure the distribution of speaking subjects into the different types of discourse and the appropriation of
discourses to certain categories of subject" (Foucault 1981:64).
Power, if it is not in anybody's "hands," is at least sometimes in their
mouths. Some of these mouths speak; others remain silent. Some are
perceived to articulate truths; some utter falsehoods. The knowledge

statements of some circulate and are clearly heard; others vanish into power's hush.

Discourse

I am concerned only with *conversational* domination. Power to converse, of course, is not the only power that inheres within human relationships. Nevertheless, it is in and by talking that people define and in part reproduce their economic positions, physical reputations, and other personal qualifications that situate them within other planes of inequality. The task consists "of not—of no longer—treating discourses as signs (signifying elements referring to contents or representations) but as practices that systematically form the objects of which they speak" (Foucault 1972:49; see also, Collins 1975:115; Foucault 1983:217–218):

> Discursive practices are characterized by the delimitation of a field of objects, the definition of a legitimate perspective for the agent of knowledge, and the fixing of norms for the elaboration of concepts and theories. Thus, each discursive practice implies a play of prescriptions that designate its exclusions and choices (Foucault 1977:199).

Discourse, then, is the practice in which people reproduce relations of power (both subjugation and domination), at the same time as they sustain shared culture. Or, as Terdiman (1985:54) summarizes, "discourses are the complexes of signs and practices which organize social existence and social reproduction." Reproduction of a discursive order—of a mode of information—continues as long as people talk only about what they know and only with what they know. This requires certain mechanisms of conversational control. Discourse, which "carries" knowledge, desire, and power (Foucault 1981:64), must be regulated lest this load is transformed in the carrying.

Although power and cultural knowledge exist and survive in discursive practice, their inhabitation of this practice must be such that it rarifies and limits alternative varieties of understanding (Foucault 1981:73). Discourse is potentially dangerous. People affirm structures of power and ruling knowledge and desire through their discourse; they might also, however, by talking in a different way, transform existing relations of inequality. Successful reproduction of ratios of power depends, therefore, on riding close herd on conversation:

> In every society the production of discourse is at once controlled, selected, organised and redistributed by a certain number of procedures whose role is to ward off its powers and dangers, to gain mastery of its chance events, to evade its ponderous, formidable materiality (Foucault 1981:52).

Reproduction of culture and ruling power structures depends on the effectual operation of a mode of information—on a set of discursive control procedures that work to prevent the emergence, in conversation, of alternatively possible subjective knowledges, personal desires, and ratios of power.

Foucault (1981), describing orders of discourse in the West, categorizes various procedures of discourse control: some of these are rules and conditions established within a discourse itself; others are grounded in the material limitations of a mode of information (see also Collins 1975:116–117). As such, conversational control procedures include both discursive practices and nondiscursive structures and conditions. On Tanna, for example (see Chapters Three, Four, and Five), procedures that regulate talk include a discursive insistence on inspiration (rather than creativity); rules that give people variable rights to ask questions; and other rules that control the public revelation and repetition of certain sorts of knowledge statements. Island conversational control procedures also consist of various nondiscursive, material conditions. These include, for example, the historical situation of public clearings in the forest where important conversation takes place; private "roads" from village to village along which information circulates; and differential handicaps on individual mobility. The totality of these rules, practices, and conditions regulates the content, distribution, and reproduction of island culture. It also positions people unequally within the local conversational order, qualifying them with different rights and opportunities to produce, circulate, and consume cultural knowledge.

In short, people are subjectified with different conversational powers, given the workings of a mode of information. "Discourse is the power which is to be seized" (Foucault 1981:53; see Collins 1975:135–136). By controlling (or operating) the conversational

means by which culture comes to be shared—by which it is produced, deployed, and circulated—people create and maintain structures of domination among themselves. Thus, discourse

> is an asset—finite, limited, desirable, useful—that has its own rules
> of appearance, but also its own conditions of appropriation and
> operation; an asset that consequently, from the moment of its exis-
> tence (and not only in its 'practical applications'), poses the question
> of power; an asset that is, by nature, the object of a struggle, a
> political struggle (Foucault 1972:120).

Whereas all participants in a mode of information are the "subjects" of their culture (of ruling discourses), not all seize its power
equally. At the level of subjugation, discourse contrives and reproduces knowing, desiring persons. At the level of domination, those
same persons possess unequal competences to participate in conversation. While the ultimate consequence of their conversational practice, given cultural constitution of knowledge, persons, and desire, is
to reproduce systems of subjugation, its immediate effect is to reproduce structures of domination. *Contra* Foucault, power of this sort *is*
localized. By conversing, people maintain shared culture. Moreover,
personal management of the mode of information, the discourse control procedures that regulate the conversational production, exchange, and consumption of culture, creates and maintains power
within the power, localized interpersonal domination within diffuse
networks of subjugation.

CONVERSATIONAL DISCOURSE

The unit, or "function," of discourse is the "statement" (Foucault
1972:80, 87; Dreyfus and Rabinow 1983:53–54). Culture, in this
view, consists of a field of knowledge statements that people produce,
circulate, and consume in a more-or-less unified knowledge market,
or society. This approach purposely overlooks a statement's claim to
truth, or the breadth of its content. A knowledge statement has no
use value, or truth value, in itself; it has potential exchange value
only. Culture must take some materially exchangeable and consume-
able form, e.g., written or oral statements. Cultural knowledge con-

sists of the sum of these statements that people deploy in their conversations (Foucault 1972:182).

Oral knowledge statements are especially prominent on Tanna which, like other Melanesian societies, until recently possessed no written, printed, or electronic means of discoursing. The materiality of most statements on the island is entirely verbal. Given this, there is perhaps too much textism in post-structuralist approaches to discourse (see Ong 1982:10–15, 168–169). Despite Derrida's (1976) jeremiad against "phonologism" (a theoretical focus on the voice that leads to the exclusion and abasement of writing), and his countermove to privilege "writing" as metaphor for language, it seems to me that the tropes of post-structuralist theory run heavily along alphabetical lines. These bookish figurations are not surprising. In the West, authors and amanuenses discourse in written form. To (de)construct a genealogy of Western orders of discourse, one must read texts. Textualism "privileges literature as the mode of discourse in which the process of signification that produces the world of subjects and objects can be experienced" (Shapiro 1984:394). On Tanna, however, people just talk. If, for Derrida, thinking is always writing, for Nampas it is just talk (see Ong 1982:77; Tyler 1986:131). The non-print materiality of island discourse necessitates different kinds of control procedures; analogously, post-structuralist theory requires a clearer apprehension of non-textualizing, conversational orders of discourse.

Within Tanna's mode of information, speakers occupy the position that authors do elsewhere, and hearers that of readers. People talk rather than write, listen rather than read, pursue rhetoric rather than literature. The discourse people practice is face-to-face. Their texts, to which we turn in order to overhear their statements, and cultural knowledge in general, are enunciations. Although text-like songs, spoken formulae, recipes, lists, genealogies, and oral narratives exist, people store such verbal formulations in memory rather than in manuscript. Knowledge statements, which are anchored only to interested and contextualized personal memory, more easily drift about. "Even the most standardised segments of oral sequences never become so standardised, so formulaic, as the products of written man. Reproduction is rarely if ever verbatim" (Goody 1977:118).

It is difficult, however, for me to erase completely pen and ink metaphors and to stand lingual ones in their place. Although rubbing out textual tropes and "writing in" vocal ones might better figure discursive practice on Tanna, the fact is that I must textualize this practice in order to describe it. Within anthropology's own "mode of information," Tanna exists only as text. Anthropology cannot avoid textualizing its object in order to move that object from there to here, or from then to now (Clifford 1983:131). A textualizing discipline itself, anthropology is only able to describe practices of conversational discourse to the extent that it possesses a means to write statements down. Consequently, a number of figurative textual tropes will still be readable, here, through my erasure marks.

The vocality, rather than the chirography, of Tannese discourse has further consequences for the analysis of discursive practice (see Barth 1987:75). It is obviously difficult to trace the genealogy of a discursive order the knowledge statements of which circulate vocally. The present study, therefore, cannot avoid being basically synchronic rather than genealogical in character. Western literate discourses did not penetrate Tanna until 1774 when James Cook dropped anchor at what he named Port Resolution, a harbor on the southeast coast of the island. Cook and his successors, according to their own lights, produced a body of statements in order to know the island. They also, where they were interested, wrote down statements they perceived Tannese men and women to say. In order to overhear these island statements of the past, we thus must rummage through the lumber rooms of this explorational discourse, or missionary discourse, or fringe-capitalist discourse, or colonial discourse, or anthropological discourse.

These five conversations, which have heard, selected, and textualized island statements over the past two hundred years, form what might be called a historical statement cartel. External, Western discourses appropriated island conversation as they textualized this; one can hear no Tannese voice that is not dependent on the cartel. The surviving knowledge statements purchased from this discursive monopoly are hand-me-down, even tawdry goods. Needless to say, those island statements that contemporary oral historical endeavor manages to capture are equally suspect. If one wanted to pursue a genealogy of island knowledge, he must draw upon these five alien literatures. It is a good guess, however, that they tell more about themselves than about Tanna. Reading them, we might construct something of the genealogy of exploratory or anthropological talk, but only indirectly and hesitantly that of the appearance, growth, and variation of discourses on Tanna.

Genealogy of any non-print discourse is obviously difficult to undertake. Foucault, however, once proposed a concomitant sort of inquiry he labeled "critical" (see Dreyfus and Rabinow 1983:105). Whereas this "applies to the systems that envelop discourse, and tries to identify and grasp these principles of sanctioning, exclusion, and scarcity of discourse" (Foucault 1981:73), genealogical description, which alternates with and complements critical, asks "how did series of discourses come to be formed, across the grain of, in spite of, or with the aid of these systems of constraints; what was the specific norm of each one, and what were their conditions of appearance, growth, variation" (1981:70).

My purpose, therefore, is critical more than genealogical. I describe the practices that envelop and control knowledgeable island conversation, rather than the appearance and growth of such discourses in time. I am less interested in the knowledge content of local talk, than in the procedures that regulate cultural enunciation, circulation, and audibility—in the conditions under which people talk. My aim is not to explain the details of what people are saying (why Americans? why offices? why submarines?), nor to read cultural content as some reflex of economic or other social or natural functions. Rather, I describe the rules and conditions that regulate island conversations, no matter their messages. What must a person do in order to produce, deploy, and consume knowledge? How does culture become shared? How does shared culture effect power?

I will, however, repeat island statements I textualize from several Tannese discourses, including the local disciplines of medicine, magic, and geography as well as John Frum and Christian doctrine. I acquire these statements from secondhand accountings of the island and from my own field research. As I, too, appropriate Tannese statements in textualizing them, this knowledge also must be reflexively suspect. Maintain suspicion. I repeat these knowledge statements to illustrate the regulatory procedures of their production, circulation, and consumption rather than, more genealogically, to comment on the rarity of their content, or on how islanders of the past managed to clear a discursive space for their original enunciation.

Tannese society is a field of conversation; its culture inheres in a mode of information whose conditions and procedures bring into being and reproduce power inequalities among people who talk together. A culture, such as Tanna's, is only realized so that it is shared and persists through time insofar as its mode of information and its conversations remain under control. The survival of shared culture presumes the regulation of conversation, as well as relations of inequality among those who converse. Beyond structuralist decodings and hermeneutic interpretings of cultural conversation, we must consider its dangers as well.

2

Knowing Tanna

Nipin riti fwe tui
iahamara reraha mhamamwur
ti nari riti u,
nari ia tiprena.
Nermama ia tina me
hapwah saimwanraha
hapwah ti nari u
kini kinua dola mine frank.
Aue aue nakur imwak,
waet man nomo ia
save gud long hem.
Kitaha sanapwah nari u
kaha rinara i.
Iema asori riti riuan triri pen
kitaha ia kwopun amasan riti,
fwe ia tina usapa.
Kitaha sapikosi mha
Ierminu sakitaha.
i gud yumi evriwan
saesi pen in apa.

A time long ago
we lived badly toiling
at these things,
things of the earth.
People of the world
abandon their practice
abandon for this thing
one calls dollar and franc.
Alas alas people of my place,
only white men
understand it.
We abandon that which
grandfather lived by.
No big-man will lead
us to a good place,
to the wonderful land.
Let us not refuse
our Lord.
It's good we everyone
follow him only.

—CHRISTIAN STRING BAND SONG

27

Tanna is an island world of discourse. The sea, which surrounds the conversational field, impedes but does not of course prevent the transmarine circulation of information. People both import and export knowledge from the surrounding world information system, although this overseas trade is imbalanced. Islanders consume more foreign knowledge than they export. This deficit in their balance of knowledge exchange has much to say about the relative effects Tanna's and the world's modes of information have upon one another (see Chapter Six). The insularity of the discursive field, however, serves to turn people inward toward one another. The vocality of discourse also limits overseas knowledge commerce. Tannese, until recently, discursed only in person. This restricts access to exotic knowledge. Foreign travel is the principal means of access to nonindigenous discourses, save for those that missionaries and other foreign knowledge brokers deliberately bring to the island. Insularity bears upon the expanse of conversation, its content, and its procedures; it defines, in this regard, a recognizable although not monistic Tannese society, a culture, and a power regime.

After sketching a Tannese ethnography and also local theories about knowledge and learning, this chapter introduces several domains of powerful knowledge on the island. Talking about this sort of knowledge most obviously delineates and sustains relations of domination. As Dreyfus and Rabinow note, Foucault's approach is "not concerned with everyday speech acts. . . . Rather, Foucault is interested in just those types of speech acts which are divorced from the local everyday background so as to constitute a relatively autonomous realm" (1983:47–48). This is "serious" talk—that is, statements in which "an authorized subject asserts (writes, paints, says) what—on the basis of an accepted method—is a serious truth claim" (1983:48). These are conversations in which "methods allow privileged speakers to speak with authority beyond the range of their merely personal situation and power" (Dreyfus and Rabinow 1983:48).

The most powerful knowledge statements on Tanna are serious rather than common; their truth claims special rather than mundane; their discursive practice conspicuous rather than ordinary. Everyday knowledge statements, such as "it's raining," carry less charge than ones such as "American wisdom will arrive by wire." Nampas's and Tain's talk about American offices was serious in this manner. In addition to John Frum talk, I focus on other domains of serious island discourse including conversations about health and illness, about controlling natural conditions and forces, and about claims to land, place, and to a personal identity.

Less serious, ordinary, or everyday talk is, from this point of view, more ephemeral in its effects on those who are doing the talking. Depending on the knowledge involved, all talk is not equal in either its conversational consequences or its social duration. People may enunciate some knowledge statements perhaps once only; others they repeat again and again, sons after their fathers:

> We may suspect that there is in all societies, with great consistency, a kind of gradation among discourses: those which are said in the ordinary course of days and exchanges, and which vanish as soon as they have been pronounced; and those which give rise to a certain number of new speech-acts which take them up, transform them or speak of them, in short, those discourses which, over and above their formulation, are said indefinitely, remain said, and are to be said again (Foucault 1981:56–57).

Some knowledge circulates throughout all social conversation. This sort of shared culture, including linguistic codes, makes conversation itself possible. On the other hand, some knowledge circulates within restricted markets, usually inaudible to all but a few people.

Cultural knowledge that anyone can talk about—and, in fact, that anyone *must* talk about within broad discourses for a culture to be shared—belongs to all. Everyone but the culturally eccentric or naive has rights and access to this knowledge. The conversational procedures that order the circulation of these cultural basics enforce their near universal distribution. Educative and socialization practices work to impress every person's memory. In addition to language itself, shared culture includes central concepts, interests, and rules at several levels according to which people talk, and talk sense. Individual inequalities in the distribution of this knowledge are temporary. Particular adults, for example, may know more than particular children. They sometimes find some power in the role of transmitting knowledge to the puerile. Insofar as education succeeds in its task, however, core cultural knowledge is eventually generalized.

Other knowledge is socially more restricted in its distribution, and discourse control procedures work to keep it that way. To acquire knowledge that serves his or her interests, a person must talk with those who know. This sort of powerful knowledge, knowledge with conversational exchange-value, is typically organized into what Foucault (1981) has termed "doctrines" and "disciplines." These structures consist of both bodies of knowledge content, and sets of procedures and conditions that work to keep that content under control.

Doctrines and disciplines most obviously affect conversation by regulating who can talk about what. The final part of this chapter focuses on conversational qualifications on Tanna. In addition to the internal regulations of a given discipline or doctrine that qualify some people to talk knowledgeably but disqualify others, a person's abilities to talk seriously depend as well upon his or her subjective situation within other appurtenant discourses, and on his or her possession of necessary conversational resources. Bourdieu (1977:651) has called these resources one's "linguistic capital." They include a person's sex, age, cash and other material property, class and educational backgrounds, and so on. Not everyone has equal qualifications, resources, and opportunities to speak seriously. As Bourdieu notes:

> Among the most radical, surest, and best hidden censorships are those which exclude certain individuals from communication (e.g., by not inviting them to places where people speak with authority, or by putting them in places without speech). One does not speak to any Tom, Dick or Harry; any Tom, Dick or Harry does not take the floor (1977:648–649; see also Collins 1975:119, 134–136).

Only those people who know the secrets of how to phrase a knowledge statement in appropriate disciplinal or doctrinal terms, and who also possess the right and opportunity to do so, will be heard.

Powerful Tannese doctrines include talk about John Frum, about Christianity, and about "custom." Important island disciplines include three that I will call "medicine," "magic," and "geography." In following chapters where I describe the discursive regulation of knowledge production, circulation, and consumption, I refer principally to doctrinal and disciplinal knowledge of this sort. When I speak of conversational domination, I locate this mostly within talk about serious doctrinal and disciplinal matters.

TANNA

Anthropology's own discourse has invented the "standard" ethnography. Demonstrating the actuality of the cultural object, these ethnographic statements represent a selected culture's ecological, demographic, linguistic, social structural, economic, and historical dimensions. It is through reading such knowledge statements that we know something anthropological about Tanna. I present here only a sketch of the island's culture, language, and history. More extensive description is provided by Adams (1984); Bastin (1980); Bonnemaison (1987); Brunton (1990); Gregory, Gregory, and Peck (1978); Guiart (1956b); Humphreys (1926); Lynch (1978); MacClancy (1983); and Wilkinson (1979).

Tanna, to begin, lies at 19° latitude and 169° longitude in the southern district of Vanuatu. This archipelago was once, before its independence on July 30, 1980, the New Hebrides, a condominium colony that France and Great Britain administered jointly. Tanna is high and volcanic, about 26 kilometers wide by 40 long at its points of greatest expanse, a total area of 561 km² (Carney and MacFarlane 1979:1). The land rises to a central plateau, called Middle Bush, and further ascends in the south to several peaks that top off just over a thousand meters. In the southeast squats a small Stromboli-type cinder cone volcano, Iasur, which erupts fitfully every five minutes or so as it has done at least since Cook logged it in August of 1774. After each eruption, columns of volcanic ash and particulates rise several thousand feet. Carried by the whim of prevailing winds, this precipitates in a black, dry, fertilizing rain on garden land, village, and sea.

The northwest quadrant of the island lies in a rain shadow, sheltered by the mountains from prevailing southeasterlies. The landscape here is one of bare, rolling hill and plain covered with "white grass," hibiscus, and wild cane. The rest of the island is thickly forested, the bush magnified by towering banyan trees. Rain comes unevenly over the year. There are two main seasons: a wet, warm, and humid time that lasts from November to May; and a cool and dry spell from April to October. The climate is almost subtropical. Average temperatures range from 20 to 27 degrees Celsius, although nights during the dry season are sometimes very cool, dropping as low as 12 degrees. The rainfall, running off the central plateau and southern heights, has etched and carved the land. Deep ravines meander down to the sea. In the East, creeks flow into Siui, a lake with no outlet, trapped at the foot of the cinder volcano.

Tanna's population, in 1979, was 15,397 (Government of Vanuatu 1984:4), and is currently estimated to be nearing 20,000. In this essay, I generalize from knowledge statements produced and circulated in limited conversation with a small percentage of this population; mine is thus an extrapolated knowledge of the island's mode of information as a whole. Most of the knowledge statements I heard and wrote down are from the Kwamera (Nɨninɨfe) language area. The two thousand speakers of Kwamera live along the southern and southeastern coasts of the island (Lindstrom 1983; 1986). More specifically, I talked most frequently with about a hundred Kwamera speakers who live in the hills and valley back of Port Resolution.

Islanders speak four other related Austronesian languages. The grammars of all Tanna languages are very similar. They differ primarily in lexicon. Although Kwamera is the most dissimilar of the lot, Tryon (1976:158–160) estimates its cognate ratio with White Sands language to the north to be 50% and, with the neighboring language of the Southwest, 62%. Most islanders are multilingual and have a choice of codes in which to phrase their statements. A common pattern in bilingual conversation is for each participant to speak his or her own language while hearing and processing the language of the other. Moreover, almost everyone save for a few older women is competent in Bislama (i.e., Beach-la-mar), the Pidgin English lingua franca of the archipelago (see Camden 1977; Guy 1974). This linguistic diversity overlies an island-wide sameness in cultural knowledge and in the control procedures that regulate discourse. Within the bounds of these shared cultural contents and codes, however, people frequently produce opposing knowledge statements within contentious talk.

Slash-and-burn subsistence agriculture continues to provide almost all of day-to-day island nourishment. Staple crops include yam, taro, manioc, sweet potato, banana, plantain, *Hibiscus edulis* and other edible greens, and a wide range of other native and introduced fruits, nuts, and vegetables. In the course of a year, families clear, burn, plant, and tend several garden plots generally located near where they live. In southeast Tanna, land is plentiful. People may garden on their own lands, or ask permission to use land belonging to their neighbors if its location is more convenient. Frequent falls of volcanic ash make garden land very fertile. People often replant after a very short fallow period of three or four years, and sometimes do not bother to allow land to lie fallow at all. In addition, they raise pigs, fowl, cattle, horses, and goats. Occasional hunting (for fruit bats and birds), fishing, and reef gathering add to island diet.

The Tannese today need cash to purchase a number of imported goods and services. These include cloth and clothing, automobiles and fuel, hurricane lamps and kerosene, simple agricultural tools, luxury feast foods such as rice, tinned fish, and liquor, and overseas travel and local transport. Much of a family's income goes toward education. The national school system charges fees that many people are troubled to pay. Although the Christian missions established rudimentary schools early on in the nineteenth century, it was not until the middle 1960s that the British and French at last funded a primary education system on the island. In southeast Tanna, most children study a few years at anglophonic or francophonic primary schools located within walking distance of their villages. Less than half, however, graduate to senior primary schools, where most students board during the week. Of these, less than ten percent go on to secondary institutions. Those children who do must leave the island. There is still no high school on Tanna, although one has been promised for a number of years.

If islanders were not still engaged in a functioning subsistence economy, they would be called poor. Through sale of cash crops and occasional wage labor, the average family only earns a little over US$500 a year. People earn cash for school fees and to purchase imported goods by producing copra, coffee, kava, and vegetables for sale, and by engaging in wage labor either on Tanna (working mostly for local government) or abroad (see Bastin 1985). The European Economic Community has funded a large coffee plantation in north Tanna that hires labor periodically. Government cooperatives purchase and store island copra and coffee crops for sale overseas. Gardeners sell their kava and vegetables in local markets (particularly near the government center at Lenakel), or ship this up to markets and stores in the capital, Port Vila. Small, interisland ships call at the island several times a month, transporting cargo and passengers. In addition, small planes make a couple of flights a day between Port Vila and Tanna, carrying local people and also a few intrepid tourists who come to see Iasur volcano and, perhaps, to stay a few days at one of the two seaside tourist "bungalows," if these happen to be in operation.

Islanders live in scattered villages and hamlets. In the southeast, most of these are small with populations of less than 70 residents. The village, however, is not the center of the cultural landscape. This is, instead, the kava-drinking ground: a circular clearing of approximately 10–50 meters in diameter. These clearings, swept bare of grass and weeds in counterpoint to the surrounding bush, are everywhere shaded by at least one magnificent banyan tree. In addition to kava-drinking, clearings serve as dance grounds and are the appropriate space for public debate, decision-making, and exchange of both material goods and information. Whereas gardens and bush are the principal loci of private conversation, and the village the locus of everyday public discourse, the kava-drinking ground is a theater for more polemic talk.

Villages and hamlets, composed of a scattering of houses, fruit trees, and decorative plants, occupy surrounding arcs of these central kava-drinking clearings. Whereas in the past, men often slept apart in a makeshift men's house on their kava-drinking ground, today parents and children together make up the residential unit (Humphreys 1926:44). The customary house resembles a peaked roof, without walls, set directly onto the ground. Nowadays, people practice an architectural eclecticism and build an assortment of rectangular or ovoid houses with wild cane or woven bamboo slat walls they thatch with wild cane, sugarcane, and coconut fronds. A few men, with jobs in the capital, have recently constructed houses of cement block and aluminum sheeting. Every family owns two or more houses. It uses one primarily for cooking and its others for sleeping and storage. Low internal walls sometimes divide a house into several sections. Over the life cycle of a family, people use these separate places of rest as older sons and daughters move to sleep apart and men separate from women during their times of pregnancy or menstruation. Generally, people live out-of-doors and only occupy their houses to shelter from rain, wind, or the night. Nearby are earth ovens: heaps of water-polished volcanic stones that people heat and cover with leaves and dirt to bake *nifar*, the local feast food that is "pudding" of grated taro, yam, manioc, sweet potato, or banana mixed with coconut milk, greens, and meat.

Feasts and food exchanges are common. Feasting marks important events in a person's life cycle, including birth, naming, a boy's circumcision, a girl's first menses, marriage, and death. Life cycle exchange has a simple dualistic structure. The family of the person concerned presents pigs, kava, mats, baskets, bark skirts, blankets, lengths of imported cotton cloth, *nifar*, cooked and raw taros, yams, and other staple foods to the family of one of his mother's brothers, or the family of one of his wife's brothers. Sometime later, the exchange will be reversed, and the same kinds and numbers of goods will be returned. People seek balance in their transactions of goods and persons. Marriage, adoption, and murder all demand the eventual return of a second person. Tannese marriage is of the sort commonly called "sister-exchange." Cross-cousins (actual fathers' sisters' children and mothers' brothers' children, if possible) are the ideal brides and grooms. To marry, a man must give a sister or promise his future daughter to his wife's family. Similarly, a family's adoption of a child makes it liable to return a child in future. The subtraction of a person from his family by murder also obligates the murderer to come up with a replacement.

To fund a particular ceremonial exchange, a person receives support from his kin and neighbors. Village co-residents—the men who drink kava together at one clearing—are for the most part members of local "name-sets" that regulate individual rights to surrounding lands. The members of each of these lineage-like structures control finite sets of male and female personal names with which, recycling appellatives over the generations, they nominate their successors (Bonnemaison 1987:70, 163–165, 230–235, 382–386; Lindstrom 1985). Although people entertain notions of patrilineal descent and parenthood, and symbolize kinship with the metaphor of shared blood, they formally recruit additional local group members through naming rather than by the facts of birth. A child only belongs to the name-set of his father if he receives an appropriate name from that set. Adoption, which is very frequent, is thus the naming of another man's son. Of the people I know best on Tanna, only slightly more than half received names from their fathers. The rest were named by other men who happened to have more names than children, although these were in the main their father's brothers, and thus typically also members of the same name-set.

Nomination, therefore, rather than descent determines the basis of each individual's social identity, and his membership in a group localized at one of the island's kava-drinking grounds. The inconsequence of descent for the constitution of local land-controlling groups renders island genealogy very shallow. Few people recall the details of their ancestry beyond the grandparental level.

Every male name is simultaneously a personal appellation and a title to property including land, magical stones, and positions of control along certain "roads," or formalized exchange relationships, that link neighboring local groups. Each boy child receives, along with his name, rights to drink kava at a particular kava-drinking ground, rights to live in its peripheral hamlets, and rights to a number of plots of garden and coconut plantation land near that kava clearing. As is common in Melanesia, people take into account numerous personal and structural factors in choosing where actually to live. A person's name, however, indicates a nomenclaturally proper place of residence. Daughters receive name-set appellatives with no property entailments. They live with parents, or with whomever gave them their names (adopted them), until they marry when they generally move to their husband's village.

Local name-sets in the southeast part of Tanna tend to be small, comprising fifteen or fewer named male adults. Each, however, is tied into a hierarchy of larger structures (Bonnemaison 1987:109–111, 116; Guiart 1956b:11–14, 90–94, 107–115; Lindstrom 1981a:34–77). Two or more name-sets are commonly localized at each kava-drinking ground. Each name-set, or pair of name-sets, typically claims a side of the kava clearing as its own. A number of neighboring kava-drinking grounds, with associated hamlets, form a named territory or "tribe" (Guiart 1956b:11–12; Humphreys 1926:13). Many of these regional units are pie slices of the island, extending from shoreline to mountain crest. Valleys and ridgelines mark the boundaries between neighboring territories. People speak of these territories, and of the shared geographic affiliations of the neighboring kava-drinking grounds in a region, as "canoes" (*niteta*) or "places:" Imwai Nasipmine, for example, is the "place of" (*imwai*) "the people of" (*mine*) Nasip (an ancestral name). Nominalized, the term *imwa-* also means "house" (*nimwa*). People in each region who share a place are also all of the same house, or all in the same canoe. Guiart identifies around 85 such territories. More recently, Bonnemaison (1987:109) counts 116. Finally, the members of each name-set also belong to one or the other of the traditional island-wide moieties, Numrukwen and Koiameta, and their historical counterparts: Sipi (Trading Ship) and Manuaua (Man-of-War).

These wider structures of region and moiety today, however, do not often serve to organize everyday discursive interaction. They do not shape or constrain the dimensions of social conversation. The significant loci of conversation—the common action groups on the island—are families, village bodies, kava-drinking companies, and those congregations of believers who consume one or another body of politico-religious knowledge, such as that of the John Frum movement. In the Southeast, residential and kava-drinking groups tend to be doctrinally homogenous. Everyone in one hamlet accepts John Frum talk as true; or everyone accepts Presbyterian doctrine as true; or everyone accepts customary talk as true. People who live together and drink kava together, pledging the same truths, also vote and pray together.

Whereas enduring structures of personal name and associated rights to property, of kinship and parentage, and of place and landscape contrive and continually reproduce the island-wide conversational loci of family, village, and kava-drinking group, particular doctrinal organizations such as John Frum depend for their existence on the production and deployment of historically more ephemeral knowledge. Circulation and public consumption of doctrinal statements stitches the scattered, atomic kava-drinking groups into wider political networks.

Doctrinal knowledge is only worth something if it can be talked about and socially deployed. The Tannese, therefore, are proselytists. They missionize. Doctrinally-based groups, such as John Frum, attempt to extend a "hegemony"; to make universal their particular regime of truth. These attempts usually fail, as we will see in Chapter Six, for reasons that relate to the ultimate ineffectiveness of available discourse control procedures on the island. Doctrinally organized conversational loci such as John Frum, as opposed to durative local solidarities, have found it difficult to reproduce themselves over the long run. Existing regimes of truth and political networks come undone. Hegemony dissolves. Atomic local kava-drinking groups either go their own way for a time or, by consuming an alternative discourse, affiliate themselves with some other doctrinal organization. Tanna is thus a puzzle of contrary bodies of knowledge and rival doctrinal organizations. These organizations are political and religious groups that the wise found and lead by producing and exchanging knowledge statements. In this century, the two doctrinal organizations which most successfully regulated island talk such that their knowledge approached hegemony, were the Presbyterian "Tanna Law" and the John Frum movement. People occasionally refer to the latter, eurythmically, as "America Law."

Christian missionaries arrived on Tanna in the nineteenth century. They made scant headway, however, in convincing people to consume their knowledge statements for many years. They achieved no general success until the initial decade of this century. John Williams of the London Missionary Society first landed Polynesian Christian teachers on the island in 1839, the day before he sailed north to his martyrdom on the beach at Dillon's Bay, Erromango. After a futile conversion effort by George Turner and Henry Nisbet in 1842, the London Missionary Society gave way to the Presbyterians. The latter arrived on Aneityum, the island to the south of Tanna, in 1848. Following the initial failure of a missionization attempt between 1858 and 1862 by Scotsmen John Paton, Samuel Johnston, and John Matheson, the mission gained a more secure foothold at Port Resolution in 1868 and at Kwamera in 1869, the latter station occupied by William and Agnes Watt (see Adams 1984). By 1930, approximately two-thirds of the island's population accepted Presbyterian truth statements, although a substantial minority either resisted conversion or alternated between a Christian and a traditionalist (*kastom*) affiliation.

Presbyterian doctrinal success ensued when a number of young island men "colonized" and began to use in their conversations incoming Christian knowledge. These young apostles circulated Christian statements and organized new churches of Christian knowledge consumers. A discursive disjunction begins to cut here between traditional and imported doctrinal knowledge. Three emerging Christian conversational loci grew up around those mission stations that were active in 1900. Lomhai and Iavis led Christian converts at Lenakel in the West; Praun (Brown) managed Christian knowledge at Port Resolution; and Koukarei ruled at White Sands. In the rhetoric of missionary discourse, Thomson Macmillan at White Sands eulogized Koukarei:

Having himself come into the light, he was to the end of his life keenly interested in spreading the glad news of what he himself had found, and he never missed a chance of declaring his faith, even though, as often happened, he had to tramp many a mile to get to the place where he was to speak (1935:16).

Tramping many a mile, these young knowledge brokers served as Christian statement translators, mission adjuncts, and new Church elders, thus mediating between European missionaries and their fellow islanders. Many doctrinal converts abandoned traditional lands and migrated to the coast, joining the emerging Christian big-men in large new villages situated near the mission stations.

Koukarei, Praun, Lomhai, and the other leaders of Christian organizations declared new codes of personal conduct and bodily control that outlawed customary practices of kava drinking, dance, penis wrapping, work and amusement on Sundays, and also drinking, swearing, and adultery. Tuesday became a mandatory day of organized labor. Christians worked to clear and maintain a system of horse trails (to improve circulation of Christian truth statements), to clean and rebuild villages in the style of the new order, and at other set tasks. Christian leaders organized new police forces to arrest those yet unenlightened people who violated the hegemonicly established duties and truths of the new doctrine. In 1906, they also convened courts where they sat in judgment to try and punish sinners and falsifiers (Bonnemaison 1987:431–439; Guiart 1956b:130–138). These Christian knowledge statements and codes, supported by police and court, were the "Tanna Law."

Alternative Christian discourses infiltrated the island in the 1930s. Roman Catholic and Seventh-day Adventist missionaries, not respectful of the Presbyterian knowledge monopoly, imported their own doctrinal statements and succeeded after a time in circulating these. For those Tannese accepting the Adventist message, the holy day switched from Sunday to Saturday. More radically, pork (undoubtedly the most highly valued Melanesian food) became polluting. The incoming knowledge statement "pigs are unclean" encountered much resistance but also some support, perhaps due partly to its head-on subversion of traditional discourse. In Kwamera language, this statement could only have been phrased as "pigs are bad"; "pigs are forbidden"; or "pigs are different." At about this time, the goat made his appearance on Tanna, imported as a substitute, Adventist pig.

Presbyterian Tanna Law organizations, although losing a measure of support in the 1930s (a loss that forced a retrenchment in statement circulation networks), survived until the John Frum movement virtually silenced Christian talk in the 1940s. Subsequently, Pacific Islander and European missionaries have staged renewed proselytic campaigns. Five or six Christian denominations, in addition to the Baha'i faith, presently claim Tannese consumers.

Islanders, partially in response to imported Christian knowledge, produced a number of home-grown oppositional discourses (Gregory and Gregory 1984:75–76). The most successful of these alternatives has been the John Frum movement (Barrow 1952; Gregory and Gregory 1984; Guiart 1952, 1956a, 1956b; O'Reilly 1949; Rice 1974). The shadowy John Frum, appearing first at Iamwatakarik kava-drinking ground near Green Point, initially stated the necessity of reviving traditional knowledge that had been devalued in Christian discourse. He also talked of a coming cosmic inversion of relations between land and sea, mountain and valley, and black and white. His apparitions, in 1940, eventually attracted the attention of the British District Agent on the island who instigated a long series of arrests and deportations of John Frum leaders. The Condominium authorities attempted, unsuccessfully in the end, to repress the increasing dilation of John Frum knowledge.

This initial production of John Frum statements preceded by two years the arrival of American military forces in the archipelago. A large percentage of Tannese men subsequently joined native labor corps to work at the United States military Advanced Base established on Efate Island in 1942. America soon took first place in doctrinal statements as primary source of foreign wisdom and goods. It has since figured largely in movement tropology.

The Condominium government ceased its repression of the movement in 1956, and a number of men from Sulphur Bay, including Nampas, seized the opportunity presented by this freeing of their talk to found a John Frum organization *cum* church *cum* political party. This is an association of people who consume a particular interpretation of John Frum's message, a message that knowledgeable leaders continue to produce and circulate. Nampas and other organization big-men instituted a number of periodic rituals, and developed group policy in accordance with doctrinal tenets. Over the life of the movement, leaders have also recruited police forces and guards to further their control of doctrine and policy. They have also convened movement courts to try those people who offend. This is what people, in the late 1970s at least, calling to mind the events of the earlier Tanna Law period, named "America Law."

Although John Frum knowledge never achieved an un-challenged hegemony on the island, in the 1940s nearly everyone accepted its circulating statements as valuable wisdom. People abruptly abandoned their earlier Christian affiliations. The successful deployment of John Frum talk, which struck dumb the ruling Chris-tian discourse, effected a second discursive disjunction in the island's recent history. Presently, around half Tanna's population continues to consume John Frum statements, affiliated either with the organiza-tion headquartered at Sulphur Bay or alternately with other island groups that put forward competing interpretations of John Frum knowledge. One such conversational locus is the John Frum/*kastom* people of the Southwest (Gregory, Gregory, and Peck 1978).

Other island doctrinal organizations talk about knowledge that is neither Christian nor wholly within the bounds of John Frum dis-course. Some people, living in Middle Bush and above Lake Siui, claim to follow simple tradition. Others, in the north and at scattered kava-drinking grounds elsewhere, united in the mid 1970s under the "Four Corners" banner. A French *colon* promoted and circulated this knowledge in the terms of which he passed as King of the island (Calvert 1978; Guiart 1975). Another assembly of kava-drinking grounds in the Southwest affirms Prince Philip of Great Britain's kinship with Karpwapɨn, a prominent spirit residing atop Mt. Tuk-wosmera. The 1967 census reported 21.2% of the population over 15 years of age to be affiliated with Christian denominations of various sorts, and 78.8% to be "custom"—this latter category subsuming John Frum movement members (McArthur and Yaxley 1968:67). Current percentages are roughly the same.

The establishment of national political parties in the early 1970s added fuel to the flames of doctrinal competition (Tonkinson 1982). Novel political statements penetrated the island's conversational field. Nearly all Presbyterians joined the Vanuaaku Party (which took power as the first independent government in 1980). This party, that

British-educated religious and civic leaders founded as the National Party, demanded early independence and land reform. French *colons* and francophonic islanders, in response, founded a number of competing parties soon afterwards. These, supported by the French establishment in opposition to the anglophonic Vanuaaku Party, united several times under different names. In the elections of November, 1979, for example, they ran as *Le Parti Federal*. During the period leading to independence, French colonials and eventually nearly everyone referred to these collective francophonic parties as "the Moderates."

Moderate party leaders courted the John Frum organization on Tanna, in that John Frum people were already opposed to the Presbyterian faithful who had joined the Vanuaaku Party. John Frum leaders eventually agreed to take part in national politics and to found a John Frum party. A John Frum supported candidate won a seat in the national Parliament in the elections of 1975, 1977, 1979, 1982, 1985, and again in 1988 as part of the Moderate team.

After several years of maneuvering (Jupp and Sawer 1979; MacClancy 1981, 1984), all parties and the two colonial governments agreed to independence in 1980. The electoral success of the Vanuaaku Party in elections preceding independence precipitated a minor revolt, in 1980, by John Frum and other Moderate supporters on Tanna, and by Nagriamel people on Espiritu Santo. (Nagriamel is an organization Jimmy Moli Stevens established on that island in the 1960s [Hours 1974]). The rebels commanded a good deal of international attention. The world press absorbed some of their doctrinal statements. This journalistic textualization engendered an unusual *export* of Tanna's political statements. These circulated for a time within the world information system. The rebels also attracted monetary and other forms of assistance from French *colons* fearful of Vanuaaku Party rule, from elements in the French administration (Van Trease 1982), and from the Phoenix Foundation (Lindstrom 1981c). This latter is an ideological organization that a number of American capitalists founded in order to locate a new nation in which the beseiged principles of free enterprise and libertarian economics might be revitalized and put into full practice. The revolt on Tanna fizzled after the Member of Parliament who led a rebel noctural assault on the government station was shot down (Bonnemaison 1987:575–

581). The government, with the assistance of troops from Papua New Guinea, also put down the secessionist challenge on Espiritu Santo.

A decade after national independence, conversation on Tanna continues to be inflected by the outside world. The talk of this island world has for many years been coupled to both national and international information networks. Obviously, one can no longer know Tanna without taking account of these circumambient conversations. Local controls over discourse, nevertheless, regulate the importation and circulation of externally produced knowledge; island conversational practices absorb and often restate incoming knowledge statements (see Lindstrom 1981c). Although some of the communication technologies that transmit imported knowledge evade the control of local power regimes (such as the government radio and newspaper), those islanders who manage doctrinal discourses, whether Christian or John Frum, also manage something of the circulation, restatement, and local consumption of this adventitious knowledge. They restate imported knowledge in terms that conform to local practices of knowing.

KNOWING

Some of the shared knowledge that island discourses carry is epistemology. People produce statements that make comprehensible what knowing and knowledge are all about. Epistemological statements also express attendant local understandings of teaching and learning practices. On Tanna, epistemological theory is not a separate discipline; rather, it is integrated into island discourse as a whole, particularly in the tropology that people use to talk about knowing.

Knowledge, *nurukurinien*, like many vernacular stative nouns, is a nominalized form of a process, of the verbal *-rukurin*, "know." Like English "know" (which combines the French *savoir/connaitre* distinction) *-rukurin* conflates awareness, understanding, comprehension, ability, appreciation, and acquaintance. One knows what, knows how, and knows a person, place, or experience.

The local theory of knowing is more a theory of perception than of apperception. Knowledge exists externally. Knowledge is revealed, not individually created. It is passed down, not made up (see Lawrence and Meggitt 1965:215–218). A scholar does not learn by some inductive, introspective process of self-consciousness. Inspiration is expected, not creativity. People do not explain the production of knowledge in terms of a knower's individual talent, genius, or creativity. Local epistemology seeks authorities and not individual authors. Individual creativity, in fact, is devalued vis-a-vis external inspiration. One's own ideas are never as good as information externally revealed.

Knowing, therefore, is a matter of accurately sensing the world; a person learns through his eyes. Thus, one who really knows -ata asas "sees directly." The ignorant, on the other hand, -ati auapen "overlook" or -ata uau "see askew." This latter metaphor is drawn from the hunt: -erukw asas "shoot a bull's-eye"; -erukw uau "shoot but miss." A person who has failed to perceive the obvious rinifata ira mua riuan "attempted to see but perceived nothing." One also knows by one's ears: -regi asas "hears (senses) exactly." To learn, one listens. The word -atirig means both "to think" and "to listen." Men, drunk on kava, -atirig, "listen/think for an inspiring ancestral voice."

Island tropes also objectify what is perceived and therefore known. Knowledge is a thing. A wise man -rukurin nari "knows things." Knowledge is a possessed commodity. In this regard, as is common throughout Melanesia, people sell to others medical and magical recipes, spells, dance steps, artistic motifs, ritual practices, and new songs. A person can possess knowledge, exchange it, and consume it. In that knowledge is epistemologically an external object, teaching is pointing. The verb -ahatin means "point/teach"; iahatin is a teacher who points at knowledge. The other verbs people use to label the process of teaching also refer to its demonstrative characteristics. Verbs of teaching refer to the exhibition of either an external object or internal information: -osan(san) means "hold up" or "show" an object in one's hand; -avisau, "announce" and -avahag, "warn" both refer to the externalization of information.

Objective knowledge can be a slippery sort of thing. It is sometimes difficult to perceive, or hard to catch. Understanding may require pursuit: to know something one must -sui tarini, "chase it down." Perceived knowledge, on the other hand, may also be instantaneous; one hears what an ancestor whispers or looks where a teacher points. John Frum leaders prophesied several such practices of instant knowledge. When Americans arrived, they would make people wise with hypodermic injections; they would bathe the ignorant in streams; they would wrap them in lengths of calico cloth; or they would invest them with the "hat" of knowhow (-afafau pehe nurukurinien).

Since the importation of Christian discourse, perhaps, people also figure knowledge as light and ignorance as darkness. Christian hegemony portrayed itself as a renaissance of light. Those who refuse to consume the discourse's truths ramara ia nipituvien, "live in darkness" (Lindstrom 1982c).

The discourse procedures that regulate island conversational practice inform this metaphoric epistemology. Just as certain discourse procedures in the West, such as our belief in the existence and importance of truth and the author-principle, compel a particular epistemological perspective that attempts to grasp the foundation of knowledge, so too on Tanna does theory reflect practice. The oral nature of face-to-face discourse on the island informs an epistemological emphasis on sight and hearing. Whereas "thinking of" is listening (-atirig), "thinking that" or "believing" is stating for others to hear (-ua). Iakua means both "I state" and "I believe." One states what he believes; another knows what he hears. The practice of stating circulates knowledge; the practice of listening produces and consumes knowledge.

Similarly, the metaphorical externality of knowledge correlates with a diminuation of individual authors in knowledge production. The processes of learning and knowing require pursuit and inspiration rather than personal creativity. This pursuit demands external looking and listening so that one might see and hear. Theoretically, knowledge is no more social or interactive in its origins than it is creative. Learners watch and listen to teachers instead of actively questioning. Questioning, as a practice, is severely controlled so to protect the circulation of knowledge on the island (see Chapter Four). Students learn, instead, by unquestioningly and repetitively imitating others (see Borofsky 1987:78–92). Local theories about knowledge reflect this discursive silencing of the question. The grounds of external knowledge and the processes of knowing are sensual and passive, rather than reflective or interactive; epistemology, here, thus echoes discursive practice.

DISCIPLINE AND DOCTRINE

"Disciplines" sometimes appear to be an unhappy result of the disintegration and wizened specialization of Western scholarship. As a procedure for packaging knowledge statements, however, we find them also in non-Western modes of information, such as Tanna's: "The discipline is a principle of control over the production of discourse. The discipline fixes limits for discourse by the action of an identity which takes the form of a permanent re-actuation of the rules" (Foucault 1981:61; see also Bourdieu 1977:657). A discipline, thus, consists of a body of knowledge content (i.e., "statements"), and a set of rules and procedures for keeping that knowledge under control. Disciplinal organization of knowledge serves as a discursive control procedure that regulates both speakers and the statements they make. Disciplines confirm which statements are appropriately true, which are false, and which are inaudible: "In order to be part of a discipline, a proposition has to be able to be inscribed on a certain type of theoretical horizon . . . within its own limits, each discipline recognises true and false propositions; but it pushes back a whole teratology of knowledge beyond its margins" (Foucault 1981:60). On Tanna, for example, these theoretical horizons work to limit the truth and falsity of serious knowledge about illness, about prediction, and about personal identity and land ownership.

A discipline, secondly, disqualifies from conversation all but those people who know something of its knowledge content and its rules of propositional formation (see Bourdieu 1977:665, note 17). It sets conditions that determine who may speak about what. Those islanders who are qualified to talk about disciplinal knowledge are thereby conversationally empowered. Others, to learn something about regaining health, or about preventing rain from falling on their celebratory dance, or about establishing an authentic relationship with their place, must go talk with those savants who can produce the necessary kinds of knowledge a discipline makes regular and true.

I am taking two liberties with Foucault's notion of discipline that should be remarked. First, I sometimes speak of a discipline, such as that of island "medicine," as if this in itself composes a separate discourse. Self-defined disciplines, however, do not necessarily set the bounds of a discourse, particularly as this changes over time (Dreyfus and Rabinow 1982:59). Rather, a discourse is a group of statements that belong to a single "formation" (Foucault 1972:80, 107). A formation is not always isomorphic with one of the popularly recognized and labeled "disciplines" (Foucault 1972:135; 1977:200).

Second, and more seriously, I borrow and apply to Tanna disciplinal labels from a very different mode of information. I focus on three island "disciplines" that organize important knowledge that is common on the island: medicine, magic, and geography. The first organizes knowledge that speaks to people's interests in health; the second to their interests in prediction and control; the third to the relationship of people to place (and, nowadays given a growing cash economy, to land). My use of these three disciplinal labels that have no exact, translatable equivalents within island languages does not imply that these disciplines occupy on Tanna the same position they do in other cultures or other modes of information, such as our own. Nor does it imply that the relations between the three are the same as elsewhere. Although distinguished here, these separate "disciplines" may, in fact, be better subsumed within a single island discursive "formation." I find it useful, however, to separate the three in order to discuss knowledge statements, and the regimes of power this knowledge supports. These three island disciplines are a starting point for analysis of the making and deploying of locally serious knowledge (Foucault 1972:178–179).

Tanna's medical knowledge includes an etiology, a diagnostic, a pharmacology, and a therapy. Everyone shares local knowledge of disease etiology. This typically seeks imbalance in exchange relations within local groups, or between the living and the dead. Moreover, most men and quite a few women possess knowledge of pharmacology. They concoct medicines (*nimakwinari*, "effective thing," *nui* "water") that they prescribe for specific, diagnosed diseases. These preparations are typically infusions of plant leaves and bark. Pharmacologic preparation can be casual, or certain ritual prescriptions and prohibitions may be required. One man who knows how to make medicine for treatment of symptoms of tuberculosis, for example, only prepares this during what the Tannese call "the time of ancestors"—at dusk. People also know other medical therapies of massage and surgery. If a cure is particularly elusive, an invalid may take his case to a generalist with a reputation for diagnosis. These generalists, called *urumun*, are spirit mediums who contact ancestors to divine the cause of disease, which they then treat with a wide-ranging knowledge of medicine (cf. Tonkinson 1979). Western medicine is also available on Tanna. A European doctor ordinarily staffs the island's hospital, and other trained personnel run several local clinics.

Like medical disciplines elsewhere, Tanna's validates a limited range of acceptable diagnoses and therapies. It also qualifies its practitioners to talk in ways about illness and health that sound true. Medicine is for the most part a specialized practice. People restrict the circulation of their curative knowledge in order to maintain its private distribution. A curer inherits medicinal recipes either from his parents or namer. He might also buy a new medicine from someone else, or receive it in a dream, or in some other ancestrally inspired contemplation. The process of curing is thus one of a controlled information exchange. The sick, usually after some initial self-diagnosis, often initiate this exchange with an opening gift (*tinarip*, "basket") to a specialist they know commands a relevant medical therapy. This curer makes up his medicine in secret, stoppers it with green leaves in a bottle, and brings or sends it to the patient to drink. If the medicine works, the newly recovered patient gives the specialist a second small exchange token, perhaps a fowl or kava root.

The discipline of magic organizes talk about another kind of locally serious knowledge. Magical talking asserts control over the weather, plant and animal fertility and growth, rats and other garden plagues, eruption of Iasur volcano and the fall of its ash, tidal waves at sea and earthquakes on land, the success of hunting and fishing endeavors, illness, and death. The discipline thus fixes local truths about the prediction and control of chance and circumstance. It limits magical practice to a range of concerns it establishes. For example, it latterly has construed as false or unlikely a number of newfangled statements that claim magical efficacy over automobiles and exotic crops, such as coffee or tomatoes.

This discipline, too, has a specialized practice. Magical practitioners command requisite skills and technical accoutrements—stones in particular. Men (rarely women) inherit both their knowledge of magic and their sacred stones from fathers or namers. They restrict further access to this knowledge (except by their own namesakes or other heirs) in order to maintain its unequal distribution and continuing exchange value. A magical specialist, upon request, works his stones in private. A person organizing an upcoming feast often asks someone who possesses rain stones, for example, to "work' these in order to insure good weather. Restrictions on sharing magical knowledge permit a person to provide a magical service of this sort, but still maintain the privacy of his practice.

Missionaries and island Christian leaders, recognizing magic stones as one key to traditional culture, attempted to proscribe their use. Converts gave up stones to be shattered in fire or drowned at sea, as a token of their new commitment to Christian knowledge. Doctrinal leaders punished those sinners they caught working stones. Recently, even Christians have revalued positively traditional magical knowledge (Lindstrom 1982c). Many are troubled, however, by the fact that their grandfathers and fathers destroyed or lost the family's stones. A person might claim the disciplinally established right to work particular stones, and the knowledge of necessary technique, but be embarrassed by the loss of the stones themselves.

Magical discipline, however, has a response. Men who claim to have retained possession of other key stones, that work to locate misplaced objects, travel from kava-drinking ground to kava-drinking ground unearthing lost stones. Occasionally, magic stones come back by themselves. Kieri, for example, who inherited from the man who gave him his name the right to turtle magic, but not the requisite stones that disappeared during the period of Tanna Law, was astonished and delighted to find these as he walked one day through the forest. Local elders, upon his descriptions, validated the found stones and also helped him to reconstruct full knowledge of their practice.

Third, the island discipline of geography organizes local knowledge that relates people to place. The discipline sets the bounds of truthfulness of geographic talk especially pertinent to issues of personal identity and rights. It regulates and validates topological information, place names and boundaries, names of persons and namesets, kinship and genealogy, histories of land tenure—all the principles in terms of which a person must assert his or her local identity and personal rights to a particular place. This sort of knowledge most often comes to the fore in disputes over land. The disciplinal rules of geography qualify a line-up of appropriate people who may, with authority, talk about certain places.

For example, during one island debate, an accused wife-beater attempted to silence his critics by evoking his stronger local qualifications to talk, and to talk truthfully, in his own place:

Plis, iakni pehe ti kimiaha mua nieri me tapu tiapwah nagkiariien.	Please, I say to you that you brothers-in-law are forbidden to talk, you must not talk.
Saiou kastom iakamni, saiou kastom iakamni.	It's my custom I'm stating, my custom I'm stating.
Iou iema asori u, ua.	I'm the big-man here.
Iakni nipik u; nieri rini naha mata iakni nipik u.	I "speak the banyan tree" here (control the place); brother-in-
Iakni atukwatukw kamaspau matagi trerieri kwopin u.	law talks over there, but *I* speak the banyan tree here.
Kwasuahi Nikia, Mopse nah ramakure pesu!	I say correctly that one will see the cyclone shake this place (should illegitimate talk occur). An oath on my sisters Ni̇kia and Mopse living to the south!

The speaker here jockeyed to silence antagonistic talk, and to lend truth to what he said himself, by emphasizing his geographic subjectivity. All island disciplines work in this way to limit legitimate access to conversation, and to make some kinds of talk sound true and other talk sound false.

"Doctrines," like disciplines, also organize the social distribution of knowledge, as well as people's rights and qualifications to talk: a "doctrine binds individuals to certain types of enunciation and consequently forbids them all others; but it uses, in return, certain types of enunciation to bind individuals amongst themselves, and to differentiate them by that very fact from all others" (Foucault 1981:64). Doctrinal knowledge thus has greater potential than disciplinal knowledge to ground political organizations of believers (or, at least, of consumers of knowledge), whose subjectivity comes to be defined in terms of ruling doctrinal truths. If a person makes a statement that a discipline defines to be false or monstrous, he is a fool or a muddler. If, on the other hand, a person makes a John Frum statement outside the accepted confines of the doctrine, he is a heretic. He can be cast from the conversation, excluded, and silenced. John Frum leaders at Sulphur Bay, in this regard, have exiled a number of doctrinal heretics to distant villages in north Tanna.

Discipline v. Doctrine

Disciplinal knowledge, while exchanged within relations of conversational inequality, tends not to undergird politically organized groups of knowledge consumers. Doctrine, on the other hand, circulating within a politically organized conversational locus, circumscribes communities of believers who accept the same truths. "The doctrine always stands as the sign, manifestation and instrument of a prior adherence to a class, a social status, a race, a nationality, an interest, a revolt, a resistance or an acceptance" (Foucault 1981:64). On Tanna, the circulation of John Frum truths, of those of Presbyterianism and other forms of Christianity, of the national political parties, of *kastom*, of Prince Philip, or of Four Corners, unifies groups of believers from scattered hamlets across Tanna. These doctrinal adherences on the island are not *always* prior adherences. New doctrine about John Frum made a new political order. The circulation of novel doctrinal statements with exchange value, such as "the American is in his office," may bring into being new political associations. Those who control the production, deployment, and consumption of this kind of knowledge achieve power within emerging conversational relationships.

People's desires and interests give conversational exchange value to available disciplinal and doctrinal knowledge. We might roughly distinguish "operational" from "interpretive" human interests (see Keesing 1982:208–209). The disciplines of medicine, magic, and geography organize "knowing how," i.e., how things properly operate. Conversely, the various island doctrines manage "knowing what," or what things properly are. This distinction between operational and interpretive interests, and disciplinal and doctrinal knowledges, more-or-less correlates with that difference between leaders of local kava-drinking groups and those of island-wide doctrinal organizations, such as John Frum. Local leaders tend to specialize in the disciplinal knowledge of magic, of medical recipe, of the geographic details of place name and plot boundary, the history of land tenure, and so on. Leaders of John Frum and Christian organizations, on the other hand, deal in the production and exchange of interpretive or explanatory doctrine with which they attract companies of believers. These knowledge consumers form emergent, area-wide organizations that transcend, if only for a time, the durative discourses of local atomism.

Disciplines and doctrines, in sum, organize serious knowledge and serious talk on Tanna. Of the two, doctrines are an especially powerful procedure of knowledge regulation insofar as they can infect and regularize the disciplines, such that a specialist's qualifications to talk truthfully about medicine, magic, or geography may come to depend also on his doctrinal associations. This is serious knowledge with conversational exchange value. This is talk whose practice is unequal.

CONVERSATIONAL QUALIFICATION

Doctrines and disciplines work to limit access to conversation. They make talking about particular knowledge illegitimate for some. These people must profess public ignorance; at the least, they pretend not to know, as the Tannese often pretend not to know the details of one another's genealogies, given the disciplining of local geography. One's personal qualifications to produce and circulate serious knowledge in talk are, in part, fixed by the internal rules of the operative discipline or doctrine:

> Who, among the totality of speaking individuals, is accorded the right to use this sort of language (*langage*)? Who is qualified to do so? Who derives from it his own special quality, his prestige, and from whom, in return, does he receive if not the assurance, at least the presumption that what he says is true? What is the status of the individuals who—alone—have the right, sanctioned by law or tradition, juridically defined or spontaneously accepted, to proffer such a discourse? (Foucault 1972:50, see also 1980:93–96).

On Tanna, for example, an important internal condition common to all local disciplines and doctrines is the requirement that a speaker have a valid and acknowledged association with some authoritative source in order to talk legitimately, ordinarily, and truthfully (see Chapter Three). Those people without such inspirational associations are silenced. This source may be one's father or namer (who secretly bequeathed the knowledge of a cure or of a magical practice), or an inspiring ancestor. Only those who can demonstrate their association with such an authority can, "with authority," publicly produce knowledge statements that are associated with that source. Although other people, in fact, may have knowledge of a person's cure, or his magical practice, or his geographic histories, disciplinal rules prescribe that they may not publicly repeat this knowledge.

Unqualified talking or use of knowledge brings into play disciplinal policing procedures. Iati, for example, once happened to glance into Kiri's garden. He noticed a stalk of wild cane stuck into the roots of a young kava plant. Wild cane is part of a magical practice that promotes kava growth. Everyone knows that Kauke, a fellow kava-drinking group member, has best rights to this particular magical disciplinal knowledge and practice. Iati and his namer, Nɨkahi, see to the growth and fertility of area pigs; Kauke looks after the kava. At harvest, around April of every year, each side exchanges its product with the other. That wild cane stalk in Kiri's garden offended Iati. It suggested that Kauke had somehow violated disciplinal rules by revealing knowledge of his magical practice to Kiri. (This was the polite interpretation, the alternative being that Kiri had stolen Kauke's magical knowledge.)

Iati initiated disciplinal maintenance procedures. He called a kava-drinking group meeting at which he retrodicted that Nɨkahi's recent, lingering illness was due to the outrageous fact of Kiri's unqualified knowledge consumption, and his employment of the kava magic. After some talk, Iati and Kauke exchanged kava and small pigs. This reestablished correct disciplinal relations between the two and made Kiri, discursively at least, ignorant once again.

Beyond the limits fixed by the *internal* workings of a particular doctrine or discipline, such as the magical silencing of Kiri, a person's qualifications to talk seriously also depend critically on his or her subjectification within broader social discourses, particularly those of "sex" and "age." On Tanna, for example, common discourses about men and women, and about old and young, generally subject women and children so that they enjoy less conversational competence and opportunity to produce and circulate serious talk. Local knowledge about aging, on the other hand, does not disqualify elder Tannese men from participating in conversation to the same extent that the elderly are disqualified within our own orders of discourse. In fact, in a conversational mode of information, age is more easily equated with wisdom. Elders maintain powerful conversational qualifications as long as they retain their physical and mental capabilities.

Island discourses about being female, however, do disqualify women from talking seriously in public. Although a woman may, in a dream, produce some novel medical knowledge, the discursive facts about sex do not qualify her to talk about this knowledge in the same manner as could an adult man. And in the case of the battered wife, mentioned above, the injured woman had no public rights to speak during the meeting or to present her version of the beating, although she sat nearby throughout the debate.

Women, moreover, have certain interests that, in an altered discourse, might easily be opposed to those of men. Island men, however, produce knowledge statements about sex and gender that, insofar as women also consume these, serve to impede the appearance of alternative, perhaps more feminist kinds of talk about relations between men and women. All men, too, are not equal in their production of talk about the sexes. Even though local knowledge about men and women serves the interests of all males vis-a-vis females (at least if these interests are weighed in the terms of an alien, Western anthropological discourse), not all men partake equally in conversations that sustain it.

In a John Frum event of the 1940s, for example, leading men revealed knowledge that altered somewhat the contemporary ideas ruling conduct between the sexes; they led young men and women into the forest, bade them to practice animated dancing, and compelled them to bathe together in Lake Siui (Guiart 1956b:159, 170; O'Reilly 1949:199). The girls drilled with young men until they lost that womanly shame that existing gender discourse made natural. Schütz (1968:323) recorded one, probably exaggerated story about these years. One John Frum prophet "began by getting a young, goodlooking girl, the child of Nambas [sic], named Leispet [sic], and taking her to the bush to teach her nakedness for some days, so that she might not be afraid. Then he in turn took two other girls and showed them nakedness until they were not afraid." This spicey new John Frum talk, however, if anything elaborated and strengthened the basic truths about sex on the island. Importantly, the popularizers of these statements enjoyed conversational power not only over women, but also over those other men who willingly invested in a recharged sexual discourse that furthered their own manly interests.

In addition to sex and age, other kinds of personal disqualifications to take part in serious conversation exist in societies with complex divisions of labor, and inequality of access to the means of production. Like sex on Tanna, cross-cutting educational and socialization procedures qualify some people to speak about certain matters and disqualify others. To speak in the terms of educated discourses, a person must have learned an appropriate "voice:"

> We are obliged to recognise large cleavages in what might be called the social appropriation of discourses. Although education may well be, by right, the instrument thanks to which any individual in a society like ours can have access to any kind of discourse whatever, this does not prevent it from following, as is well known, in its distribution, in what it allows and what it prevents, the lines marked out by social distances, oppositions and struggles. Any system of education is a political way of maintaining or modifying the appropriation of discourses, along with the knowledges and powers which they carry (Foucault 1981:64).

Nowadays, islanders also realize the powerful and qualifying aspects of western-derived education, and attempt to purchase schooling for at least some of their children. Those children who are successfully educated, however, must leave the island for national conversational arenas where their educational qualifications have some exchange value. In the Tannese arena, educative knowledge is not yet able to realize all its potential worth.

A further qualifying discourse that commonly empowers people unevenly to know and to talk seriously is that of social entitlement or privilege. These broad discourses qualify people unequally as lords or liegemen, high caste or low, chiefs or commoners. On Tanna the durative cultural institution of personal names is an example of this sort of entitlement. Names differentially qualify and entitle people to rights and property, and to formulate and repeat knowledge about their inherited lands, local magical and medical practices, songs, and myths. Some personal names, moreover, privilege their holders to claim one of two sorts of "chiefly" titles on the island: *ierminu*, "ruler," and *iani niteta*, "spokesman of the canoe." One or more of each of these statuses is associated with most kava-drinking grounds. Presently, however, these titles do not much improve a man's personal qualification or opportunities to talk. Because of a multiplicity of claims to the titles, which have only occasional ritual importance, their exercise depends upon whose knowledge of genealogy is locally consumed. Those men whose claims to a chiefly title weigh heaviest tend to be already well-qualified conversationally on other grounds.

Finally, and more critically, economic resources may also qualify or disqualify people within a wide range of disciplinal, doctrinal, and everyday discourses. Money talks. Unequal economic resources and opportunities differentially qualify people to produce and consume culture. An economic qualification is especially familiar to those of us living within textualizing modes of information. This is the basis of Marx's discussion of elite control of the "means of mental production" that makes the talk of the ruling classes ring most loudly and clearly. In these kinds of modes of information, one can expect isomorphism between a person's economic and his knowledge powers.

In the textual world information system, discoursing itself, as well as many of the discourse control procedures, are expensive. A person only qualifies to talk seriously if he or she first possesses the wherewithal to do so. Access to necessary discursive resources depends on wealth and class position, as well as on sex, age, nominal entitlements, scholastic qualifications, and so on. People have to pay in order to produce or circulate knowledge within expensive media of knowledge transmission: writing, film, video, telecommunications, fax machines, etc. They also have to pay to consult knowledge archives. Those of us within textualizing modes of information who cannot afford (or have not learned how) to produce and circulate "audible" written, printed, or electronic statements have less opportunity to maintain or modify existing culture.

In Melanesia, where discourse occurs face-to-face and statements are stored in memory, conversation itself and the devices of its regulation are cheaper. Some Melanesian big-men, however, do acquire economic qualifications to talk seriously from their management of economic exchange and indebtedness. Based on their economic position, they possess greater personal competence and opportunity to produce and exchange knowledge statements in serious talk. By managing local conversations and repressing contrary knowledge, they can also safeguard and reproduce their economic position and political power. Because of their economic qualifications, ruling big-men are able to co-opt, silence, or trivialize alternative knowledge that appears on the scene, and to disqualify political rivals from producing or circulating threatening doctrine. Toaripi big-men in Papua New Guinea, for example, possessed the economic competence, based on a structure of interpersonal exchange debt, to cut the circulation of a new, dangerous doctrinal knowledge with sharp sarcasm (Ryan 1969). Potential converts were unwilling to offend the leading men they had to turn to in order to bankroll their marriages and other exchanges. Wealthy big-men sometimes can also afford to hire sorcerers in their service to further reinforce their conversationally dominant positions (see Hau'ofa 1981:250).

Technical information about how to produce and fix things is another kind of economic resource that sometimes qualifies people to talk seriously. The powers of knowledge of this sort become more and more obvious to us with the advent of an information economy. This is intellectual capital that the ignorant must tap for their economic reproduction. Widespread technical ignorance does not only characterize industrialized societies with involuted divisions of labor; people may be economically incompetent within other modes of production as well. Meillasoux, for example, partially explains the political power of doddering African elders over their vigorous young in terms of the relative complexity of agronomic and other productive technologies (1960:47). Because of a necessarily protracted schooling in technological detail, the technocratic old succeed in dominating their younger apprentices.

On Tanna, too, this kind of specialized economic knowledge has occasionally possessed exchange value, and qualified local technocrats to talk seriously. The introduction of coconut oil and subsequent copra technologies in the late nineteenth century boosted the few younger men who first gained access to this technical information from European residents or itinerant traders into a political prominence that, in some cases, lasted throughout their lifetimes.

There are serious limitations on this sort of personal qualification to talk, however, as Meillasoux notes. The difficulty with local economic knowledge is that it is learnable. Obviously, technology only retains productive value through time to the extent that it is transmitted fully from knower to knower. This total transmission potentially zeros out the ratio of inequality between a particular knower and his apprentice, and vitiates the further conversational exchange of those knowledge statements. Technology's value perishes in its transmission, assuming this is successful and entire. Relations of power based on an unequal control of technological information have been notably short-lived on Tanna. Unlike Western modes of information in which technological information is often private and unequally distributed, the knowledge that informs the economic production of material goods on Tanna is neither very complex nor privatizable. Simple economic information does not possess the richness and long-term conversational potential of the more esoteric disciplines of medicine, magic, and geography. Therefore, the doctrinal and disciplinal information that island technologies require overshadows practical economic knowledge, inasmuch as secrecy and restricted channels of information transmission secure the former's uneven distribution around the island.

The importance of the ritual aspects of Tanna's economic technologies far outweighs the practical within island conversations (cf. Granero 1986). This information is what people keep secret, not the technicalities of how to plant taro or dry copra. On Tanna, as elsewhere in Melanesia, "the requirements for both technical knowledge and the coordination of labour are slight" (Modjeska 1982:61). The island's mode of production does not much depend on the application of restricted technical knowledge. Technological information that supports productive activity is distributed evenly across the island, stored in multiple memories (Lindstrom 1984).

Everyone, for example, has enough knowledge to plant gardens, make copra, or work at locally available wage labor jobs. Many people, in addition, have enough knowledge to establish rudimentary trade stores, purchase trucks, or find their way to national centers of wage labor. If some exotic body of technical information penetrates the local market, it usually quickly diffuses about the island. This distribution occurs even though its primary consumers may attempt to prevent its wider distribution, asking agricultural and other development officers to restrict their efforts in order to keep the secret.

The relative importance of disciplinal versus practical knowledge is particularly notable in relation to land. Knowledge of land is markedly important across Melanesia in establishing economic rights to land. Land knowledge, however, does not involve nitty-gritty details of resource distribution, soil types, or the productive capacities of various garden sites. Rather, the information that men put forth to make claims to a plot of land concerns the history of its tenure, its name, and its boundaries. This sort of nontechnical, geographic disciplinal knowledge is distributed unequally among local people. For example, in the Trobriand Islands, "the recitation of the history of land is not only a 'mythical charter,' in Malinowski's terms, but is also a means of argumentation. Claims are awarded on evaluation of the accuracy of living memory" (Weiner 1976:42; cf. Hutchins 1980:32, 45, 109). Similarly, among the Tolai of New Britain, a local descent group head protects his group estate with "genealogical expertise as well as his knowledge of the boundaries of each parcel of land, how each came to be acquired and marked out, and the various transactions to which it has been subject" (Epstein 1969:127). This sort of knowledgeable man is the "official remembrancer" of his group whose "knowledge is a powerful weapon in conducting relations with other groups" (Epstein 1969:128).

On Tanna, control of unevenly distributed geographic disciplinal knowledge, rather than practical agronomic information, likewise supports land claims, and qualifies men to talk seriously. People assume that heirs, the namesakes of previous land holders, possess pertinent geographic knowledge of local personal names, place names and boundaries, past events, and neighborhood ancestors and culture heroes. Public repetition of disciplinal knowledge of this sort demonstrates one's authentic claim to the land in question. If two parties dispute the facts of land tenure (i.e., a plot's association with a name-set or personal name), they meet at a local kava-drinking ground to exchange publicly their geographic statements. Neighbors and fellow kava drinkers attend the debate, hear the revealed arguments, and come to a consensus. Ideally, this summary consensus is a decision in favor of one of the disputants taken on the basis of his greater and geographically more authentic command of pertinent land knowledge.

At one such meeting, which as usual lasted from morning to the evening kava hour, Uiuai with the support of Rapi disputed Iati's and Nɨkahi's claim to a plot of garden land. The meeting, which convened at a small kava-drinking ground where all the main disputants had traditional rights, was sparked when Iati stumbled upon and in a rage hacked down some banana suckers that Uiuai had just planted on the land. People deal informally with many social problems through simple avoidance, gossip, or quiet negotation between the parties concerned. Iati's precipitous and obvious destruction of the bananas, however, demanded a more formal, public response. Uiuai spread the word of his complaint against Iati, and with the agreement of leading local men scheduled a dispute-settlement meeting to try to resolve the issue of land ownership.

In the debate, various spokesmen from the neighborhood produced relevant geographic disciplinal statements to support the claims of Uiuai's or Iati's name-sets to the land in question. In one statement (selected from a recorded text of the debate), Rapi supports Uiuai's position by claiming that Iati's name-set possesses only usufruct over the land, not full rights of ownership:

Rosi Rasai, rosi Nisueiu a hamara mara ro mwi ianha i ua?

Perhaps Rasai and Nisueiu lived there, right?

Ikregi mua Iau ramini ianhu mua narimnari me pam i.

You heard Iau say everything about it.

Kimaha nakur Iakarui iahamrupwi kimiaha nakur Ipikarig ua.

We Iakarui people chased out you Ipikarig people.

Mata in nah narimnari me sakimaha.

All these things are ours exclusively.

Kimaha iahavahi raet tukwe.

We have the right to it.

Na kini nieri riti kwarana riti ua nimahan riti kwarana riti, paku Isaina ua Ikurupu ua paku?

Now about our brother-in-laws or exchange partners there, are they Isaina people or Ikurupu or what?

Hamerupwun kimiaha mata fulwan iema Iakarui.

They exchange with you but the real owners are Iakarui.

Na kini hamara mara, mara mara na kini nermama kitirimwai Iapwatu mine narifanah, nipunhi Neiporo, kitirimwai Iapwatu mine Nokout mine Kamti mine Neiporo kini havahi pen nahag mine Nisueiu.

Now they lived there because of our sisters, Iapwatu's sister and what's-her-name, Neiporo's namesake, Iapwatu's sister and Nokout and Kamti and Neiporo gave the names to Nisueiu [gave Nisueiu rights to use the land].

Havahi pen mi Nisueiu na kini

They gave it to Nisueiu who had a son Rasai.

rarahi Rasai.   Our fathers are his nephews, it

Na kanhkwanien tata me, na ro   is like that.

ianha i.   Nakweren took our sister Maui

Kitirimwamaha Maui na Nak-   and gave her to him [Rasai].

weren ruvahi raka muvahi pen   Everything belongs to Iakarui

min.   men, they rule over Ipikarig.

Narimnari me pam nema   Do you understand? All of

Iakarui, iraha hamerminu nema   them.

Ipikarig.   At the beginning, at the begin-

Ikata ro ianhu? Iraha pam.   ning was Tauru's namesake;

Ia sakupwin, ia sakupwin ia   afterwards, Manieua came and

nipunhi Tauru;   bore their nephew.

na kurira Manieua ruvehe mwi   Now Nouanou Kwenaiov, one

havahi nikwai nei savanraha.   injured Nouanaou Kwenaiov's

Na kini Nouanou Kwenaiov, kosi   arm [killed him]

rigi Nouanou Kwenaiov   and gave up Manieua in return

muvahi pen merupwun Manieua   for him in exchange with

i, merupwun savanraha nema   Iakarui men.

Iakarui.

Here, Rapi marshalls a number of geographic statements about
name-set personalities and historical events in which these ancestors
took part. These events included exchanges of women and men between three local name-set associations: Iakarui, Ipikarig, and Isaina.
Rapi's point is that Uiuai's Iakarui name-set possesses the nomenclatural rights to the land plot in question. He states that Iati's Ipikarig
people, who also claim the land, only possess use rights that they
obtained, partially, by exchanging sisters with Iakarui men.

By this statement, and by many others enunciated in the course
of the six-hour debate, Rapi and Uiuai succeeded in pushing Iakarui
claims to the land. Their success, in this case, was based on their
revealed knowledge's appearance of greater geographic authenticity
over that of Iati and Nikahi. Iati and his namer Nikahi, in fact, had
previously been placed into the Ipikarig name-set by Rapi's Iakarui
grandfather. At that time, Ipikarig had no living representatives.
Iakarui reactivated the set by assigning Ipikarig's empty names to

available individuals—to some of its own sons. Nɨkahi and Iati, who assumed their entitled rights as children, woefully realized that whatever pertinent geographic knowledge they possessed had originated within Iakarui. Rapi and Uiuai therefore would control this as well. As Nɨkahi several times observed:

Saiou nagkiariien ramo sampam ia kwopin u;

niamaha riuan.

Niamaha riuan tɨ nari nah mua saik paoa ikavahi pehe miou ua.

Krauo faet bak ia saim paoa.

Ripiko mha saiou iti paoa mata saik paoa ikamvahi pehe.

Ko iakɨnamirapw a ia nakwai rukwanu nari ik ikamini ua.

Nari ikamini nari ik ikɨnafafau pehe miou,

ikɨnafafau pehe miou.

Ikamavrani saik hat mama takwtakwnu.

Kɨnimrhi a iou mua takamen a kwara, ua.

Takaman raka kwara irenha.

Kɨna kapwah niniien mua takeuaiu.

Tukwo iakeuaiu, ihani nagkiariien tukwe na irouvni pam nieri mi.

Ko iakeuaiu pikata mha iermama iti mata?

Iakeuaiu mata kɨmirau fwe inherip.

My talk is over at this point;
I am not angry.
I am not angry because it is
your power [knowledge] that
you gave to me, right?
We two argue with your power.
It is not my power but your
power that you gave to me.
If I were to reveal it publicly, it
would be what you say.
That what you say, what you
have put on my head [taught
me]
what you have taught me.
You are wearing your hat
[knowledge] now.
One placed me that I proceed
on the surface [cannot go into
details].
I go on the surface.
One didn't tell me enough to
descend [into detail].
If I go into detail, you will
have already have revealed everything, my two brothers-in-law.
If I go into detail, who would I
see there?
I descend and meet you two
below.

Nɨkahi and Iati were left with a single effective debating point: in the past, Rapi and Uiuai had led them to believe that the land was Ipikarig's; but now they claimed that Iakarui had reserved "full rights" to the ground, thus contradicting the earlier understanding.

Other spokesmen present during the debate remarked the unequal distribution and revelation of pertinent geographic knowledge—that Nɨkahi was not able to "descend" into detail, his serious talk impoverished with only "surface" knowledge. A supporter of Ipikarig, in a final futile effort, attempted to call the debate a draw:

Ierghara Uiuai, ikineuaiu mo store,	Old Man Uiuai, you went into the story,
ikino store ia histore ikineiuaiu, ua?	you gave the history in detail, right?
Na marɨg pen naha ia kwopun naha mregi kwanamrɨg a.	Listening to the other side, one heard only silence.
Marɨg pen u iankaren mregi kwanamrɨg.	Listening to the other side, one heard nothing.
Na kurira ikɨn ikara muta pehe mwi muta pehe mwi kwopti.	But subsequently, you ascended somewhat [lost control
Na rouara rouregi irouahiai peri kɨmirau me nagkiariien me ia kurakwan kwopti.	of authentic geographic detail]. Afterwards, we heard the talk of both of you meet in the
Rouregi nɨkaren naha rɨskamter magkiari.	middle. We heard the other side stand and speak.

This last-ditch interpretation failed. Other speakers who were present gave the debate to Uiuai. The Ipikarig men acceded, temporarily at least, to Uiuai's knowledgeable talk about the disputed land plot. A debate participant observed:

Uiuai rɨmri rɨgin ianhu mɨni napwɨr mɨni suatuk muvehe men pen ianhu i iakua "po, Uiuai rɨno win."	Uiuai was conversant of the land boundaries and the roads such that I said "po, Uiuai has won."

Iakua nagkiariien iti sai Uiuai,	I say the talk is Uiuai's; there is
riuan nah iakimirahar.	nothing from you three.
Iakua "po, Uiuai rino win mvahi	I say "po, Uiuai has already
raka tina naha puta pare ua."	won the land up there."

The distribution of this sort of stored, disciplinal geographic information is far more restricted than that of more technical agricultural and economic knowledge. Specifics of the latter are probably shared by all area men and resident women, not to mention most small boys in the locality (cf. Howes 1980:340–341). As noted, technical knowledge that supports productive activity only retains economic value over time to the extent that it is completely transferable from one knower to another. Its common distribution around the island destroys much of its continuing conversational value. In land disputes, the technicalities of resource distribution are unimportant in establishing a claim to some land plot. Rather, technically peripheral knowledge, such as its tenure history, land names, and boundaries, is the conversationally powerful information.

If, by demographic change, or because of the niggardly personality of some elder, this disciplinal knowledge remains secret, never to be circulated, the essentials of the local mode of production are in no way altered. The technological knowledge that informs this mode of production is widely distributed. The basics of the island's economy are such that the ignorant (children, for example) may easily observe and successfully imitate those who know. This popularizes local technologies and perpetuates, here, a shared economic culture. Disciplinal and doctrinal knowledge, on the other hand, is not as ubiquitously distributed. As Elias observes, it is easier to monopolize knowledge that is learned only by revelation (and not observation as well); control of this sort of information is "a means of securing a high power ratio in relation to those who [need] this knowledge" (1984:259). Discursive control practices protect the unequal distribution of these statements—until, at last, a day of debate arrives for their public revelation in serious talk.

On Tanna, in sum, restrictions on exchange imbalance and widespread technical information inhibit the generation of much interpersonal economic inequality that people might use to establish a controlling position within conversation (see Lindstrom 1984). Purely economic qualifications to converse are illegitimate on the island.

Those few men who, because of the expanse of their coconut plantations or their government jobs, earn cash incomes much larger than
those of their fellows, are in a politically ambiguous position. They
consume much of their cash (e.g., by purchasing expensive trucks
that last only two or three years, or building European style houses
no one lives in) rather than exchanging it with others who would
inevitably fail in making a balanced return. People cannot use economic qualifications to finance the production or amplify the circulation of their knowledge statements. Nor can they use such qualifications to silence others. Economic inequalities do not handicap or
disqualify. The opportunity to produce and circulate disciplinal and
doctrinal statements, on the island, is in the main economically un-
encumbered.

Conversation on Tanna, if not entirely *degagé*, is to this extent
economically less inhibited than elsewhere. More important are the
internal requirements of each of the local disciplines and doctrines
that make competent a selection of speakers to produce and circulate
its knowledge. These doctrinal and disciplinal qualifications, in addition, draw upon the wider, cross-cutting qualifying island discourses
of nominal entitlement, of sex, and of age.

This lack of conversational handicap, due mostly to the absence
of legitimate economic inequality on the island, has important implications, particularly for the production and circulation of doctrinal
knowledge. In that fresh doctrinal knowledge may overturn a conversational order and bring into being new congregations and parties of
believers who challenge existing powers, the appearance of novel
doctrine on Tanna is always worrisome and unsettling to existing
power regimes. Because of the relative feebleness of economic, educative, and entitled qualifications to converse, the island's discursive
field is open, compared to that of other modes of information. The
powerful cannot always checkmate the production of a novel doctrinal knowledge or impede its circulation. New doctrinal knowledge
with exchange value may snap the fetters of discourse control procedures and overturn existing conversational regimes of truth and
power. This sort of disjunction happened once with Tanna Law; it
happened again with John Frum. Doctrinal discourse on Tanna is a
particularly dangerous kind of talk that sometimes gets out of hand.

Still, island discourse control procedures work most of the time.
All people do not operate equally within this mode of information.

Their sex and age qualify men, more than women and children, to discourse audibly. Among men, too, different conversational competences and qualifications exist. Some men are big; others are little. Some control valuable knowledge statements; others—even if they talk volubly—manage to enunciate only the commonplace.

Novel doctrinal statements only occasionally manage to pierce through Tanna's ruling conversational orders. John Matheson, one of the second, unsuccessful wave of Christian missionaries to hit the island, for example, described (in 1860) an initial failure of rudimentary doctrinal circulation:

> Some two or three profess to have renounced some of the worst and most disgusting abominations of heathenism—one of whom is the young chief of the district in which we reside. He has been living in the yard during the last six weeks and his conduct has been most exemplary. He says he is anxious to know the word of God, and embraces every opportunity of communicating to others what little knowledge he has himself acquired (Patterson 1864:459).

Camping close to an authoritative source, this young "chief" acquired and attempted to circulate a new field of statements. At that moment, however, the conversational procedures that regulate Tannese knowledge consumption managed for five additional decades to limit the deployment of Christian discourse.

What makes these silences? And what rends them? To know Tanna, her orders of knowledge and power and how they are reproduced to become shared culture, we must investigate the specific control procedures that regulate the production, the circulation, and the consumption of knowledge statements. Because people converse face-to-face, they often produce, deploy, and consume statements simultaneously. One control procedure ("questioning," for example) may concurrently regulate all these aspects of conversational discourse. In order to fix each in view, however, I disintegrate these three moments within serious talk. In following chapters, I discuss the regulatory discursive procedures that enfranchise a speaker to formulate or repeat knowledge (Chapter Three); those that permit a knowledge statement to circulate within the information market (Chapter Four); and those that make that statement audible, authentic, and attractive (Chapter Five).

3

Statement Production

Nagkiariien i takni asori:	I will announce this word:
Atirig ro ia kastom,	Listen to custom,
apwah navinavinien.	stop drifting about.
Iou, Mista Frum	I, Mister Frum
iakakwein iakimirau,	I call out to you two,
Aisak mini Henri, u.	Isaac and Henry, here.

—JOHN FRUM HYMN

Stating is a practice. Tannese spokesmen announce and call out knowledge in the terms of a mode of information that warrants and accounts for the production of statements: "To add a statement to a pre-existing series of statements is to perform a complicated and costly gesture, which involves conditions (and not only a situation, a context and motives) and rules (not the logical and linguistic rules of construction)" (Foucault 1972:209). Bourdieu, too, has noted the need "to analyse the conditions for the production of a discourse that is not only grammatically normal, not only adapted to the situation, but also, and especially, acceptable, credible, admissible, efficacious, or quite simply listened to" (1977:650–651). On Tanna, what are these conditions of discursive practice that make possible the formulation and repetition of credible knowledge? What procedures must a person obey in order to talk acceptably and seriously? What kinds of knowledge statements command an audience?

The foremost discursive condition for knowledge production is the requirement to have an authoritative source. A person should evoke some authority for his disciplinal and doctrinal statements. Authorization, as a discursive condition, determines the formal configurations that knowledge takes. Formally, a statement must appear to be revealed wisdom from some external source. The style of island statements is not one that deliberately attempts to manifest a creative, individual voice. Islanders, for example, appreciate a good songsmith for his communicative connections, not his inventive craft. Demand for authority also conditions a knowledge statement's public enunciation. Knowledge is possible, and sayable, to the extent that it can pass itself either as a newly formulated revelation, or as the repetition of some past revelation. A non-authoritative knowledge statement is practicably more difficult to add to a series of preexisting statements. Creative knowledge has less discursively established authenticity and less exchange value.

Two additional discursive conditions supplement authorization. To repeat in public conversation a serious knowledge statement, a person must possess its "copyright"—or, more accurately, its "restatement" right. Copyrights depend on one's geographic and other associations with a source. Following from this, to formulate new or augmentative knowledge statements, a person must appear to control one of the known means of access to recognized knowledge sources. On Tanna, these means are inspirational, rather than creative. Only those islanders who can legitimately claim a recognized means of access to an authoritative source are qualified to formulate or repeat its revealed knowledge.

Conversational control procedures delimit a number of speaking "positions and functions" that islanders must occupy in order to talk seriously (Foucault 1972:200). In particular, island doctrines and disciplines qualify people differentially to speak. Those best able to talk seriously, in order to maintain their discursive competence, have an interest to safeguard their personal qualifications. They protect their sources; they attempt to enforce copyright; and they guard their access to the recognized procedures of knowledge production. Personal qualifications and opportunities to converse, however, are not inviolate. Those people who find themselves silenced within an existing discursive order may appropriate a speaking function if they can acquire a copyrighted source. Tain, at Isina, qualified himself to talk seriously because he had located a novel authority—his official American.

The importance of Tanna's three discursive conditions of authorization, copyright, and demonstrated access to a means of inspiration appear, to begin with a small example, in a short narrative about two small uninhabited islets located far south of the island. In 1983, the Republic of Vanuatu decided to challenge in international judicial venues long-standing French claims to Matthew and Hunter islands. It disputed the assertion that these are part of French New Caledonia with geographic, geologic, historical, and cultural evidence. The latter built on traditional accounts and legends of ni-Vanuatu contact with the two islets that government researchers collected throughout the southern district. These narratives tell of transmarine associations between people of southern Vanuatu and the two disputed islets.

This unexpected governmental interest in minor Tannese legends inflated the conversational value of the knowledge in question. The few Tannese who claimed to hold the copyright of pertinent southern voyage stories suddenly found themselves with a new opportunity to talk seriously. They also found themselves in the typical knowledge exchange dilemma on Tanna. Government researchers demanded they repeat their knowledge so that it could be tape-recorded for possible courtroom use in The Hague. A public recording would clearly demonstrate their claims to actually know the stories. This revelation could also, however, popularize the myths. The requirements of courtroom dispositions violate local conversational norms in which serious knowledge is typically kept secret and only revealed in the last instance. Worse, rivals might seize the opportunity to accuse those men telling stories about Matthew and Hunter of ignorance, of misrepresentation, or of perfidy.

At one attempted interview, Reia, who claimed knowledge of a copyrighted story about a mysterious southern isle, agreed to talk to a government researcher. Given the dangers of complete revelation, however, he avoided telling many of the details of his story itself, but rather focused on his rights to tell it (thus disappointing the researcher who knew that World Court justices would look for a richer mythology). Still, in this strategic discourse, we can overhear Reia evoke the local rules and conditions of Tannese knowledge production that make his story authoritative and that highlight his own personal rights to tell it (even if he does not). Holding the microphone, this is what Reia said:

Iou, iou Jif Reia, Ianarauia nim-
warim saiou Ianarauia.

Iou iakni ianha ira mini mua
kaha saiou Mwatiktiki.

In nini tukw iou ira mini minua
iakavin mata in fwe Imwai Nei.

Iakara fwe ikin kimrau min rouara rouara fwe ikin iakrerig
mavehe.

In nini tukw iou ianha ira mini
mua in, Mwatiktiki,

in ramani naveginien fwe
Ianarauia.

E, iakamo naveginien sanani
Ianarauia.

Ruvehe mani mata in ramara
fwe Imwai Nei.

Iakamata fwe Imwai Nei, kimrau
min iarouara fwe ikin.

Iarouara rouara, in ruvehe mwi,
iou iakino muvehe.

Muvehe msegi pare iou fwe Iakweiau, iarmara fwe ikin.

Kipiko mha iou atukw iakni,
mata Mwatiktiki,

kaha Mwatiktiki in mini.

In mini tukw iou, ia laen saiou
mesite iou takwtakwni.

Iakamara takwtakwni.

Iahavahi store tukwe mesite pehe

I, I am Chief Reia, Ianarauia is
my kava-drinking ground.

I say about this that Mwatiktiki is my grandfather.

He spoke to me, telling me to
go see him at Imwai Nei (an
invisible islet somewhere to the
south of Tanna).

I live there with him, we live
there until I return.

He spoke to me saying that he,
Mwatiktiki,

he will eat at Ianarauia.

Eh, I prepare him food at
Ianarauia.

He comes and eats but he lives
at Imwai Nei.

I see him at Imwai Nei, I stay
with him there.

The two of us stay, he comes
again, I return.

He comes and places me
(names me) at Iakweiau; we
stay there.

It isn't I alone who speaks, but
Mwatiktiki,

grandfather Mwatiktiki speaks.

He speaks to me, to my line
until myself presently.

I am living now.

iou takwtakwni. No sam pam.   We've received stories from
him up through myself at pres-
ent. That's all.

In this statement made to the government researcher, Reia
stresses his personal qualifications to tell the story of the island of
Imwai Nei, most of the details of which he nonetheless avoids revealing. Mwatiktiki (Mauitikitiki in Polynesia) is an island culture hero.
Stories chronicle his historic, creative feats while present-day ritual
practices, such as sacrifice to him of the first-fruits of the yam, sustain
the appearance of an ongoing communicative relationship. In addition to Reia's claim of an identity between Mwatiktiki's island home
(Imwai Nei) and either Matthew or Hunter, one of the disputed
southern islets, his statement also exhibits the effects of local discursive conditions on serious talk.

Reia firsts asserts his geographic qualifications that give him a
personal right to tell the story of Imwai Nei, as opposed to any rival
savants that the government might also wish to interview. Reia
evokes his own name and Ianarauia, his place: "I am Chief Reia,
Ianarauia is my kava-drinking ground. I say about this that Mwatiktiki is my grandfather." These geographic facts, according to the discipline, make him competent to talk of the historical events linking his
ancestral namesakes and local spirits at this place—a series of Reias
who all lived at Ianaruaia. The qualifying geographic truth, here, is
Mwatiktiki's long-term ritual and festive associations with Reia (and
his previous namesakes), as well as with important local places—the
kava-drinking grounds Ianarauia and Iakweiau.

Second, Reia next identifies his authoritative *source.* He himself is
not the author of the story; rather, he is merely the spokesman for his
grandfather Mwatiktiki. "It isn't I alone who speaks, but Mwatiktiki,
grandfather Mwatiktiki speaks." Mwatiktiki is the knowledge source.
Reia denies that he himself produces or invents the story. Instead,
grandfather Mwatiktiki speaks through him as the present, geographically entitled representative of his line.

Third, Reia is concerned to demonstrate his control of a recognized means of inspiration. He is Mwatiktiki's messenger; he therefore knows how to receive the message. Reia stresses his travels to
visit Mwatiktiki at Imwai Nei. He also alludes to the fact that he

continues annually to offer the first-fruits of the yam to Mwatiktiki. Every year, the culture hero comes to Ianarauia for a harvest feast. "He comes and eats but he lives at Imwai Nei. I see him at Imwai Nei, I stay with him there." Reia thus remains in position to receive, face-to-face, continuing transmissions of knowledge from the authoritative voice. These ongoing transmissions authorize him to add new knowledge statements to existing series, such as his novel equation of the southerly islets with Imwai Nei.

The discursively required authorization of disciplinal and doctrinal knowledge, in sum, establishes conditions that people must meet in order to qualify themselves to formulate or repeat knowledge. When talking seriously, a speaker must assert and demonstrate (1) his association with some authoritative source, be this his namer and other geographic forebears, or some supernatural prolocutor; (2) his copyright to repeat the corpus of *extant*, previously revealed knowledge statements, including stories like that of Imwai Nei, John Frum dogma, Christian prayers, medical recipes, magical techniques, and so on; and (3) his access to a least one of the means of inspiration that sustain the revelation of *new* knowledge statements in public conversation.

The Tannese, in these discursive requirements, establish the likelihood and account for the appearance of serious knowledge on the island. Also established here is a structure of domination within public conversation. Some people formulate and repeat more serious statements than others. Those who are personally qualified, or who more competently operate within the various discursive conditions that regulate the production of knowledge, make their voices heard the loudest within the island's conversational field.

AUTHORIZATION

Serious knowledge is revealed. This does not imply that people never learn by trial-and-error experimentation or are unable to plan and execute creatively in order to validate or falsify some idea. Nor does it suggest an exotic or undeveloped island cognitive psychology. This revelatory emphasis is, rather, a discursive condition. To produce a disciplinal or doctrinal knowledge statement, a person must be able to cite some implicit or explicit authority. He does not account for his production of knowledge in terms of some flash of mental creativity, his fertile imagination, genius, individual talent, brilliance, ability, gift, brains, mind, reason, intellect, intuition, insight, perceptivity, or any of the other creative tropic figures used to talk about knowledge production within other modes of information, such as our own. Creative self-citation of one's own nature or intellect is, on Tanna, discursively improbable.

Tannese emphasis on inspiration challenges our own beliefs in creativity, and also in the intellectual. Terdiman (1985:50) points out that the notion of the intellectual within Western orders of discourse dates to the nineteenth century. Saint-Simon "invented" (if I can use this word) the term to label a conversational position combining "the skills of the man of letters and imagination of the artist with the knowledge and prestige of the scientist" (Terdiman 1985:50). Gramsci further elaborated the functions of intellectuals as "originators" and propagators of cultural hegemony in his *Prison Notebooks* (1971). Intellectuals, of course, can only exist where creativity is an admitted discursive condition. On Tanna, the position and propagating functions of intellectuals are instead filled by "mediums"—men and women who transmit knowledge from external authorities.

Not surprisingly, in Western modes of information that stress creativity, people also believe in individual intelligence. In inspirational systems, on the other hand, intelligence in its Western sense does not exist. Carrier, for example, has noted that Melanesian islanders on Manus, New Guinea "do not invoke notions like 'intelligence' or 'a capacity to learn.' They have no word for intelligence" (1984:61). This is also the case on Tanna. Where knowledge is, discursively, inspirationally produced, the important thing is to *have* "intelligence"—in the other sense of that word: to know where to find the right sources; to have good contacts; to struggle to hear. An overpowering belief in the reality of personal intelligence, and its educational and economic consequence, are artifacts of our own orders of discourse.

In inspirational systems, on the other hand, people explain successful learning in terms of hard work and struggle, not in terms of intelligence or how smart one is. Young notes of Melanesians in Papua New Guinea:

> The way in which educated Papua New Guineans talk about the process of getting an education is revealing. Images of struggle, climbing up, and escape are dominant. . . . Almost all references to the *process* of acquiring knowledge stressed hard work or struggle of some kind (1977:32).

Islanders' autobiographical comments about their education in the collection *The Story of My Education* (Weeks 1977) are also revealing:

> I couldn't really bear the fact that my fellow students saw me as a different person (I wasn't, really) because they thought I possessed "brains"—something they didn't possess. After all everybody was equal (as far as personal rights are concerned) and the sources from which we got our knowledge were the same (1977:35, see also 44, 49).

Within our own discourses about creative knowledge production, control of the "means of creativity" is a focus for struggle, implicated in the maintenance of social inequality as Bourdieu and others have noted (e.g., Bourdieu and Passeron 1977). In revelatory modes of information, on the other hand, the "means of inspiration"—how a person contacts external knowledge sources—are equally charged. All means of inspiration are socially regulated to protect existing knowledge and power structures.

In that the Tannese presume inspiration, not creativity, to govern the production of serious knowledge, they are not concerned to pursue a knowledge statement's moment of origin and explain this by some act of individual intellect. In island discourses, as noted, no author-principle exists that might limit chance appearance of alternative knowledge "by the play of an identity which has the form of individuality and the self" (Foucault 1981:59). Islanders, discursively, do not privilege a creative, transcendental subject as "the cause, origin, or starting point of the phenomenon of the written or spoken articulation of a sentence" (Foucault 1972:95). No island authors police the dangers of discourse. Here, the operative condition that accounts for the origin of statements and, to some extent, regulates their subsequent conversational circulation is, rather, an "authority-principle."

A songsmith, for example, does not make up, think up, devise, or compose a new song. Instead, he overhears it (and in this is mislabeled by our discourse a songsmith, writer, or composer). He operates one of the known ritualized or informal procedures for contacting ancestral authority. He may, for example, retire to a tract of the forest he knows ancestors and spirits to inhabit. Here, he prepares and eats a white rooster and drinks a special variety of kava (see Crowe 1986; Bonnemaison 1987:123). This ritual "tuning" opens a channel of knowledge transmission across which he receives phrases of song. He thus produces his newly formulated song as a revealed statement, one he passes down rather than makes up.

A knowledge producer cannot originate or authorize his own statements. Instead, supernatural prolocutors and other authorities perform this function. If the latter are somewhat removed from the immediacy of everyday life (e.g., deceased forefathers, namesake testators, off-island knowledge brokers, etc.), this externality and distance generally enhance their authority. A person in this manner authorizes his disciplinal statements about medicine, or magic stones and their practice, or geographic nomenclature by citing his recent ancestors—his fathers and namers. He claims merely to repeat the knowledge that they privately taught him. This knowledge might be the truth about a land plot boundary, an available personal name, a cure for scabies, or pig fertility magic.

More distant sources commonly authorize doctrinal knowledge statements. John Frum, for example, shares his podium with a number of lesser authoritative voices including Mister Mataru (cited in the song that heads Chapter One) and Mister (or Captain) World (Guiart 1956b:221; Rice 1974:9). Culture heroes such as Mwatiktiki, more remote ancestors, or exotic knowledge missionaries stand behind a speaker's talk about doctrinal truths. On the Christian side, of course, important authorities include God, Jesus, and the Holy Ghost. Back in Papua New Guinea, Eyre quotes one Melanesian preacher: "I do not speak these words. This man [Jesus] speaks truly to me, this man. It is not me" (1987:3). Identical statements circulate on Tanna (and also in the West, in that religion remains for us, at least in part, an inspirationist discourse).

Discursively, island knowledge production is subsumed, therefore, under knowledge circulation. A person produces knowledge by serving as its messenger, advocate, mouthpiece, or prophet rather than as its maker. This condition obliges people, in order to talk seriously, to acquire and manage knowledge sources they publicize by citation. Only those speakers who can claim and demonstrate a communicative relationship with an authoritative voice are competent to produce serious knowledge statements about America, about *kastom*, about national elections, about medicine, and so on (see Schwartz 1962:401). To this extent, this discursive condition is more restrictive than an author-principle that permits people, in other modes of information, to authorize their own statements by citing their personal creativity, nature, or intellect (see Harrison 1986:283–287). Even so, most Tannese men have some competence to produce disciplinal statements. If a man's father or namer neglected to transmit valuable knowledge of medicine, magic, or geography in life, he may yet contact his heir in a dream to rectify this failing. An authority-principle cannot, moreover, disqualify people from contacting *new* sources in order to produce alternative, possibly heretical doctrine. The docket of island knowledge authorities is potentially unlimited.

Nevertheless, an authority-principle does bring into being and maintain conversational inequalities in the type, number, length, and audibility of the knowledge statements different people produce. Men are subjectively qualified and are presented greater opportunities to manage more authoritative sources than women, and adults more than children. Among men, some receive from their authorities knowledge statements that others currently desire. "The American is in his office" was a particularly desirable statement. The wise often succeed in exchanging their knowledge with large audiences. Other people, conversely, overhear only cant or trivia that listeners reject.

REPETITION

If a statement, properly authorized, appears in the island's knowledge market, it may or may not be subsequently repeated: it may or may not be absorbed into shared culture, as this is presently constituted. Repetition of knowledge depends on its continuing storage in individual memory. A statement is repeatable only if people can call it to mind. A particular knowledge statement, therefore, may be widely or spottily distributed throughout the island's information market, depending on the number and location of people who remember.

Not just anyone, however, can repeat publicly shared and memorized knowledge. A second discursive condition regulates the repetition of previously formulated statements. This procedural "copyright" disqualifies some people from repeating or talking further about certain statements, such as local stories, genealogies, spells, or John Frum prophesies. Copyrights and patents over valued knowledge are common throughout Melanesia (see, for examples, Barth 1987:25; Campbell 1978:4; Carrier 1984:14, 79; Eyre 1987:2; Harrison 1986:281; Young 1983:195). The traditional pursuit of knowledge, in this part of the Pacific, is not organized in terms of what we like to call free intellectual inquiry; rather, it is rigidly territorialized so that, unless one possesses requisite copyrights, entire domains of knowledge remain off-limits within public, serious talk.

It is important to note that although a person may, in actuality, know everything known by copyright holders, he may not use, augment, reveal, or discuss this publicly without encountering reaction and opposition. Even though a large number of people may, in fact, be able to recall a statement to mind (having heard this in the past), they are discursively disqualified from repeating that statement during serious talk. Only the spokesmen who possess its copyright can restate its authorized version (see Bonnemaison 1987:68; Vansina 1985:96–98).

Island copyright also protects a person's exclusive claims to an authoritative source. It gives him the right to repeat knowledge that the source authorized in the past; it also gives him the right to reveal any additional statements the source may provide. In his statement, Reia asserted this kind of copyright to repeat stories about Mwatik-tiki. Only he could narrate the story of Imwai Nei into a tape-recorder. The geographic facts of a speaker's personal name and place, in particular, give him the right to repeat local disciplinal knowledge. The source of most of these statements is a man's line of ancestral namesakes who lived where he now lives. Only those with an appropriate local name thus possess the copyright to repeat publicly local knowledge of magic or medicine, concocting with this knowledge cures and spells they exchange with others.

A man with an appropriate personal name, associated with a particular place, is also qualified to repeat statements about local genealogy and ancestral names, and about neighborhood culture heroes and those stones and stelae that today mark their historical doings. In fact, when reciting a myth or giving an account of a historic namesake, a person often uses the first person singular pronoun "I" (*iou*): for example, "I did that." Old Iaukarupwi, for example, talking with me about a nineteenth-century namesake who had dealings with various European explorers, missionaries, whalers, and traders who anchored at Port Resolution, slipped into the first person singular pronoun. This "heroic I," as Sahlins has called it (1983:523), occurs in a range of Pacific societies (see, for examples, Harrison 1986:279–280; Lindstrom 1985; Sahlins 1981:14). It clearly marks one's geographic copyright, based in personal name, over a set of myths, stories, and songs. The "I" of today does more than repeat his ancestors' stories; he enacts them by making himself the hero of the narrative. A related conversational practice, which shifts from the side of "I" to that of "you," is the application of kin terms according to a person's name, rather than actual family relationships. Thus, a man may call his son "grandfather" (*kaha*) or "father" (*tata*), and not "son" (*niruk*), if the boy carries the name of one of these ancestors. This, too, marks a person's copyright—his nomenclatural and geographic qualifications—to talk publicly about the knowledge associated with his name.

Men invoke their copyrights to silence anyone who illegitimately talks about or uses their knowledge, as Iati stilled Kiri's use of Kauke's kava fertility magic. If one man hears another talk about names and places that he claims, copyright can be cited in order to counter this conversational piracy.

In the land dispute introduced above between Iati and Uiuai, Iati warned Uiuai in this fashion to stop talking about other people's namesakes:

Tinua iarouen ti nagkiariien,	If we two debate, please,
iako a plis,	I say we two don't talk;
iakua tarouapwah niniien rouni;	he doesn't repeat mine,
in trapwah niniien saiou,	and I don't talk about his line
iakapwah niniien laen savani.	(ancestors).
Rini atukwatukw savani, rosi	Let him speak honestly of his,
sanaha savani atukwatukw,	of what is correctly his,
mapwah niniien saiou rosi	and not speak of mine, such as
Iakarui.	Iakarui (name-set).
Iou naha ikin.	I am there.
Trini atukwatukw savani—mata	He should state correctly what

sanaha kamavahi in,	is his—that which one be-
mua kinifavahi in ira, ran atuk-	queathed him,
watukw.	or whatever one gave him, let
Ran men naha ikin in rini atuk-	him go on correctly.
watukw.	There, he speaks justly.
Mata trapwah nuvahiien saiou	But let him not take mine and
mosisumun pen ira.	mix them with his.

In the course of debate, no matter the warning, Iati several times accused Uiuai of breaching copyright and talking illicitly:

Ik ikagkiari ianha i iakregi iakua	You speak thusly and I hear
ikamo a tokbaot.	you talk wantonly.
Na mata tikini nagkiariien nah	But one must only repeat the
iermama rini savani.	statements [speech] a person
	calls his own.

These island copyrights to talk about geographic disciplinal knowledge, that depend on people's names and places, delineate sets of what might be called "geographic oeuvres" on Tanna. Only the members of a localized name-set may repeat publicly its serious knowledge. Sets of stories, songs, medical recipes, and magical technologies become associated with various kava-drinking grounds on the island. Each kava-drinking group, for example, has a repertoire of memorized songs that tell of local personal names and places. Dance groups from other areas can sing these songs, performing them during a night of dancing, but only with the explicit permission of local copyright holders.

Although one man may have best rights to talk about and use some body of extant knowledge statements, other members of his name-set also have vested rights of repetition. When a person dies, or if no individual currently carries an appropriately entitled personal name, rights of repetition may be generalized throughout the neighborhood. And everyone throughout a region may claim best rights to talk seriously about more widely distributed local knowledge, including local language. For example, one possibly apocryphal story has it that after an Australian linguist visited patients at a regional hospital to collect terms from several of Tanna's languages, leading men from one region demanded that he return the words he had taken away. The linguist repaired his copyright violation by mailing back a copy of the word list.

Geographic restrictions on the identity of those who can talk publicly about particular disciplinal knowledge statements correspond to the relative formalization of these statements. A geographic oeuvre generally comprises more text-like, formulaic statements such as genealogical lists, stories, legends, songs, sets of local names for men, women, and pigs, maps of land plot boundaries, medical recipes, spells, and magical technologies. A geographic oeuvre of this sort functions in somewhat the same fashion as a literary oeuvre. It enforces unity and coherence on discourse by arranging and distributing extant knowledge (Foucault 1972:149). Moreover, it regulates the proliferation of statement versions insofar as most of the island's population is disqualified from publicly repeating serious knowledge except for that within their own local geographic oeuvre (see Foucault 1979:159). In conversational modes of information, knowledge content that is stored in memory and reproduced in talk unavoidably mutates. Discursive limits on the number of people qualified to talk about something legitimately work to reduce the number of competing versions in the field, and to retard transformations within genealogical lists and other local knowledge.

To this extent, geographic oeuvres limit the operation of knowledge restatement and commentary. They maintain the formalization of disciplinal truths. Although, in private, people may repeat at will, gossiping about some extant knowledge statement, only a discursively qualified person has the right to produce this statement in public conversation. He alone controls the public version, thus sustaining an authorized statement morphology, and limiting the conversational propagation of alternative formulations of the knowledge. These alternative formulations always exist, of course, but they lack the conversational exchange value of the discursively legitimate version.

It is more difficult to copyright the statements of authorities who are not local ancestral namesakes, statements that fall outside of geographic oeuvres. A person is not qualified by his name or place to claim an exclusive access to a source such as John Frum, or to exotic knowledge missionaries. People might occasionally scheme to localize an external authority, such as by warning missionaries or anthropologists of the dangers of visiting neighboring villages, but they have less discursive right to silence others from also claiming access to the same nonlocal authority and body of knowledge.

Geographic subjectivity (or personhood), therefore, does not disqualify people from repeating *doctrinal* statements in the same manner it does *disciplinal* knowledge. Copyright procedures do not regulate with the same force the repetition of knowledge about John Frum, America, God, *kastom*, and on so. Doctrinal knowledge statements are not apportioned into geographic oeuvres, as are statements about neighborhood ancestors, regional magics, and medicines. Even though speakers may attempt to assert their exclusive access to some authoritative source, such as John Frum, those who first produce a doctrinal statement may or may not succeed in controlling its further repetition. Original John Frum spokesmen from Green Point have yet to forgive Nampas, Tain, and other leaders from east Tanna for capturing John Frum, their authoritative source. A geographically unlimited number of spokesmen is potentially qualified, subjectively, to repeat and expand doctrine. Additionally, the more a spokesman's doctrinal statements are repeated and circulated, and the more his authoritative source is cited, the more audible his voice becomes in the information market. Doctrinal spokesmen have contradictory interests in both privatizing and popularizing their authoritative source.

Correspondingly, aside from those exotic religious and political corpora of knowledge that arrive on Tanna partially as literary text, doctrinal knowledge statements are less formalized than most disciplinal stories, recipes, or practices. A choir of voices around the island may repeat such statements and, in repeating them, restate them. John Frum's message, for example, taken up by various spokesmen, has drifted and been transformed. It began as exhortations to good, cooperative behavior; it then stressed cultural revitalization and a return to customary truths; then predicted eschatological change and an exodus of the European colonials; then the arrival of American soldiers and shiploads of cargo; and it has latterly absorbed Western discourses of "modernization" and economic development (see Lindstrom 1981c:107).

Islanders today continue to cite John Frum's authority for a wide range of statements. These, occasionally, are written down by journalists and travel writers visiting the island. Two recent examples are: "The promised land is still coming. . . . America will bring it. John

Frum said so" (Ashbrook 1986:2); and "'We must live by our customs,' Naiva, a local chief said. . . . John Frum, who appears in dreams or visions to comment periodically on contentious issues, is now cited as authority against a thatched grass disco erected in a clearing in the jungle" (Kristof 1987:1). Beyond disco dancing, the contentious issues on which John Frum's authority can be evoked are unlimited. Compared with the disciplines, many more people can qualify themselves to talk about doctrinal knowledge. A plurality of spokesmen, restating as they repeat, disturbs the formalization and stability of doctrinal statements.

Doctrinal spokesmen are less concerned than disciplinal with managing the repetition of already produced, circulated, and memorized knowledge. Insofar as others consume their statements and repeat them in conversation elsewhere, they extend the circulation and political consequence of that doctrine. Doctrinal spokesmen, rather, are much more concerned to manage the several means of inspiration that sustain the revelation of new statements. Knowledge power here depends more on control of the means of knowledge formulation than on a priestly copyright over some repetitive liturgy or recited text. Powerful conversationalists control various recognized means of access to authoritative sources. Without personal geographic or other nominal entitlements to monopolize the repetition of doctrine, leaders must continue talking. Island doctrinal leaders, therefore, manage the means of talking seriously, more than an extant copyrighted text. The powerful maintain their elocutionary dominance and also silence others by a continual formulation rather than a simple repetition of knowledge.

FORMULATION

If, discursively, statement formulation demands that people contact some authoritative source, access to authority becomes the critical issue. In conversation, speakers must demonstrate control of the locally recognized means of knowledge production. If, in textualizing modes of information, the conditions of discourse require people to be creative, on Tanna discourse requires people to be inspired. The island's formulatory means of knowing, unlike those that privilege an author, are not devices that advance individual creative intellect (e.g., education or various cognitive, research, or linguistic skills). Rather, they are practices that promote the transmission of a knowledge statement from authority to spokesman. By these means, a person discursively formulates (or, on Tanna, receives) knowledge that he subsequently can talk about seriously. A person maintains his ability to contribute statements to serious island conversations as long as he controls access to the acknowledged means of their production.

Island discourses thus bring into being the conversational position of the inspired subject. Individuals who successfully occupy this position secure the conversational right to talk seriously. Reia, who controls a recognized means of access to Mwatiktiki—his grandfatherly source—in this manner asserts his right to talk about that information the Government of Vanuatu proposed to exhibit in world judicial forums. Conversely, people who fail to present themselves as inspired, like the subjects of other modes of information who fail to appear original or creative, have less subjective competence to formulate knowledge statements and to talk seriously. The mediocre, the boring, and the commonplace of the West is, on Tanna, the uninspired.

There are several means of inspiration on Tanna. Different authoritative sources necessitate different methodologies of access. The common denominator of these is some practice that serves as a channel of information transmission leading to an authority. From this source, a person learns (i.e., perceives, sees, hears) knowledge. John Frum's means of acquiring instant wisdom, such as bathing in a stream or putting on a hat, have parallels across Melanesia. Apprentice wood carvers of the Trobriand Islands, for example, absorb woodworking knowledge by drinking a magical solution prepared by an expert carver (Campbell 1978:7). Some of these means of inspiration, in a sense, work automatically. In dreams, for example, people may receive spontaneous communications from an ancestral voice. Other procedures consist of ritualized practices by which islanders purposely set out to learn new knowledge by inviting inspiration.

Ritual Keys

Formalized learning practices include a number of ritual techniques by which people can initiate communication with external, typically supernatural authorities. Islanders who command these procedures use them to signal an authority that they desire knowledge. This cue serves as a key or password that opens a channel of information transmission. A person may be geographically entitled to the knowledge of a procedure of this sort, having inherited this from his namer, or he may acquire a ritual key itself through inspiration.

Songsmiths, who know how to prepare a white kava and white fowl, how to consume these properly, as well as the location of those forest glades infested with helpful spirits or ancestral mentors, often acquire their ritual keys from their namer or father. Control of a means of inspiration is thus sometimes part of a person's nominal, geographic subjectivity. If requested to produce a song, a songsmith using his key signals his desire to learn and settles back to await inspiration (see Crowe 1986:7). Songsmith Kahi, for example, after keying his ancestors for a message, explains that he sometimes receives a complete new song, and sometimes only smaller bits and verses. His knowledge thus authorized, he convenes dance practice sessions in which he teaches the received songs to people of the local kava-drinking group that commissioned his formulation of new song. After teaching the songs, Kahi receives some payment (kava and, occasionally, a small pig) for his inspired efforts.

Islanders may also learn, inspirationally, how to be inspired. An authoritative source itself provides the key by which a person might contact it again. This Aladdin's lamp principle ("rub me and I'll appear") underlies the knowledge production of many of the island's spirit mediums. These *urumun* build a reputation based on their knack for receiving ancestral communications. Various inspirational practices support their knowledge of how to know. Some of these "clevers" (Bislama: *kleva*), for example, demand small change that they then manipulate in order to initiate communicative relations with an authoritative source. Nampas's daughter, herself a *kleva*, manipulates flowers in order to spark knowledge transmission. She is in contact with several spiritual figures by whose authority she formulates knowledge statements. These statements include diagnoses of illness, explanations of familial conflict, and divinations of lost objects.

Flowers and brightly colored leaves, in general, adumbrate a supernatural presence on the island. According to local doctrines, flowers (like John Frum's more high-tech wires) mediate between natural and supernatural, living and dead. A month or so after burial, for example, people clean the grave and plant flowers and shrubs to mark it. Decorative plants also mark the boundaries of kava-drinking grounds and land plots—visible reflections of ancestrally established places. Men wear, as arm bands, leaves with a powerful fragrance when they dance through the dead of a night. Flowers decorate both Christian and John Frum altars. During John Frum ceremony, after praying and singing, celebrants leave flowers at the foot of the squat red crosses on the Sulphur Bay football ground. Worshipers also leave flowers at the base of the poles flying American flags.

Nampas's daughter, in her ritual key, alludes to this common doctrinal truth about flower power. When a person comes to her requesting that she produce knowledge, she takes his flower offering and retires to the privacy of her house. Here, she may be heard mumbling until she receives an information transmission that she then publicly reveals. Other knowledge formulators also use flowers as an inspirational mechanism. John Frum leaders, to contact the spiritual Mister World for example, once employed flower telephones. A spokesman talked into one trumpet-shaped white flower (*Datura* sp.) and listened through another. This bellflower telephone technology recalls the telegraph poles and antennae erected by supporters of various cargo movements around Melanesia to send and receive knowledge (e.g., Worsley 1968:55, 200).

Island means of inspiration support the production of a number of different kinds of knowledge statements, both instrumental and explanatory in scope. People, in addition to receiving novel ancestral songs, can also augment or reconstruct their disciplinal knowledge of magic, medicine, or geography if they can contact dead namesakes or other authorities. (Convincing others of this authority is a subsequent problem.) People receive knowledge statements that address all sorts of interests and questions, ranging from simple informational queries about a wayward pig to dark enigma. Some spiritual knowledge exchange partners, although perhaps invisible to the rest of us, appear to teach a desired medical cure, the location of a lost knife, the identity of a thief, and so on. Others, such as John Frum, furnish answers to more pressing questions.

Missionary wife Agnes Watt provides a text that records Tannese statements about a woman spirit medium who was inspired to produce knowledge in 1882–1883. These events prefigure themes of importance within more recent island conversations:

There was an old woman to the west of us who professed to have communication with the unseen world. Many who had lost relatives sought unto her; and she brought beads, turkey-red, tobacco, pipes, and knives, from the departed. One man, a very sensible fellow in many respects, brought a knife he had got from a deceased son-in-law; I forget the maker's name, but it was a Sheffield-made knife. In vain we showed him the maker's name, and told him it was all a hoax, that the old witch was befooling him. He declared that he heard his deceased son-in-law speak to him, and tell him to stretch forth his hand in the direction of the voice and he would receive the knife. He did so, and there was the knife:—now was not that proof positive? Day by day new messages came from the dead; some sending for goods and others giving back return presents. As one piece of turkey-red is much the same as another; why, the poor deluded creatures actually believed that that very piece of turkey-red or that pipe which had been buried with their relative, was now sent back from Ipai (Hades)! Of course, we were branded as deceiving the people. We challenged the old witch and her believers to come and take something out of our house. If she did so, with closed doors, as she professed she was able to do, we would reward her liberally. "Oh, she was coming, she was coming; Missi, you will see that you are wrong. She can get things out of a house without opening the door; her deceased husband is the medium." I fancy she was more rogue than fool; she did not come, and as a reason, she told the people that her husband refused to go to premises where there was so much worship. He could not work where the gospel was. Lately, she has given up her trade, and is now a poor decrepit body, unable to walk (Watt 1896:214–215).

All the familiar elements are here: a means of inspiration; knowledge and goods from the dead; ancestral knowledge authorities; dislodging cargo from missionary storehouses; and conflict between competing wisdoms.

Aside from evincing these two nineteenth-century doctrinal regimes of truth on Tanna, the subjects of which accuse one another of bewitchment, tomfoolery, and mendacity, Watt's account records something of the procedures by which islanders formulate knowledge statements and the authoritative means of that production: conjured Sheffield knives, hands stretched forth, the speaking dead. It also records the exchange value of this talk, a value that sustained conversational inequalities. By the authority of her deceased husband, the woman clever produced knowledge statements that attracted an audience.

By controlling a ritual key with which one contacts an authorizing source to initiate learning, a spokesman thereby manages the production of serious knowledge. If current interests and desires accord his statements conversational value, he attracts knowledge consumers. By virtue of emergent relations of information exchange, he more than his auditors dominates serious talking within island conversations.

Dreaming

Textualizing disciplines that account for the practice of dreaming, in general, sap the reality of dreamed knowledge. Dreams are fantasy, delusion, or conceit. Those few Western discourses that allow dreams to retain some validity suppose dreamed statements can be genuine only as a plan for a desired future, or as the disguised sign of some internal psychological state. In Melanesia, however, dreaming is a widespread means of inspiration that regulates the formulation of authentic knowledge (see Bonnemaison 1987:198–199; Stephen 1979, 1982). As people sleep, they pass over to the other side (the "side away"), and enter into conversation with the dead. Dreaming authorizes the production of truth. In dreams, people receive (that is, overhear or observe) knowledge from authoritative sources. Those who dream well thereby qualify themselves to talk seriously.

Although several ritual procedures exist to induce dreaming on Tanna (sleeping on an appropriate species of leaf, for example), dreams often effect unwitting inspirational messages. Dreamers sometimes envision objects (e.g., pigs, species of trees) or events that, on waking, they interpret as omens of the future or as ancestral commentary on current affairs (see Weiner 1986). Kauke, for example, dreamed of a fight within his kava-drinking group in which his wife, who was currently visiting an aged father having one of his bad spells, suffered a cut hand. When he talked about this, two of his auditors drew the same conclusion: the cut hand signaled the old man's death. A third person accepted this interpretation as reasonable, but suggested that it might be only a "side" of the dream—one of several possible readings. Dreamed knowledge statements, and interpretations thereof, are not always accurate; events and secondary readings must prove them correct (see Chapter Five).

People, in their dreams, encounter ancestors and spirit beings who catch them up and lead them to the side away. A person, in dreamed interaction, here engages in face-to-face conversation with an authoritative source. Dreamed statements may restate or formulate new disciplinal knowledge of medicine, magic, or song. Songsmith Kahi, for example, accounted for and made authentic his production of a couple of his songs by this device. In one dream he perceived a singing ancestor shadowing behind him. He managed to overhear two verses of an ordinary dance song, and two verses of a song in the style of those performed at regional *nakwiari* festivals. He remarked that he hoped to overhear, in further dreaming, additional song verses to round them out.

Dreamed authorities may also inspire more serious truths. John Frum's initial instructions to return to dancing, kava drinking, and home lands are similar to prescriptions and explanations a man might receive in his dreams. Reia, who is also a clever who communes with Mwatiktiki and other ancestors in his dreams, by this device accounts for the knowledge of lost objects and disease diagnoses he produces. He explains that, upon awakening, he contemplates the meaning of dreamed messages, and occasionally textualizes these by writing them down on scraps of paper.

Drunkenness

Before going to sleep, island men partake in another event that also inspires the formulation of knowledge. Every evening, men gather at local kava-drinking grounds to prepare, drink, and get drunk on the root of *Piper methysticum* (Brunton 1979; Gregory, Gregory, and Peck 1981; Lindstrom 1980, 1981d, 1982b, 1987). This daily happy hour is a major venue for serious talk. It also furnishes a discursive procedure for statement production. Drunkeness, like dreaming, is a useful channel of authoritative knowledge transmission.

To prepare kava, men bring the root to the local clearing where they clean and divide it into pieces. With the assistance of their sons, they chew the kava, breaking its fibers and mixing it well with saliva. After they have readied and set aside three or four mouthfuls of masticated root, they infuse these in cold water, straining the murky liquid through a piece of burlap-like coconut frond sheathing into a coconut shell cup. While preparing the drug, men talk about the events of the day, plan those of the morrow, and gossip. After drinking, each retires to the periphery of the kava-drinking ground and sits in silence to listen (*-atirig*), or think, to his kava.

This silent drunkenness accounts for subsequent serious talk. Men demonstrate their qualifications to know and account for what they say in terms of this formulary device. While under the influence of kava, a drinker communes with authoritative sources (Gregory, Gregory, and Peck 1981:130). Drunk, he relaxes near the graves of his ancestors and namesakes who are buried along the clearing's circumference. Speech ceases as drinkers listen, instead, for messages. The circulation of knowledge during kava preparation gives way to a practice for its production.

In addition to inspiring talk, kava drinking also provides a channel along which men send information back to ancestors. Approaching the bottom of a coconut shell cup of kava, a drinker tosses away the dregs and violently spits out his last mouthful. After this spitting, he utters one or more short prayers—or, more exactly, short sets of instructions—that the invisible, surrounding ancestors receive (Lindstrom 1980). Drinkers advise ancestors what they are currently about, and expect their cooperation. Communicative ritual spitting is also an integral part of medical and magical practice. When a man works his pig fertility stones, for example, he spits kava in order to inform his ancestral namesakes.

Men typically spit messages at important and ticklish points in life. Most send off some small communication nightly after kava. Message content ranges from announcements of an individual's assumption of a new social identity after his naming, circumcision, marriage, death, or involvement in other rites of passage, to simple demands that ancestors stop the annoying rain. Men spit to ensure a good harvest; to assist herbal cures; to change the direction of ash fall from the volcano; to request that a dispute-settlement meeting render a favorable consensus; to ask that America at last come (or not come) to Sulphur Bay; or to insist that a particular political party win an election. Spitting works as a mechanism of communication with the "other side" away from the kava-drinking ground as well. Curers spit medicine into the faces of their patients. Men spit if they pass an ancestral spot, a place where the other side draws near. They spit if they hear the call of the white-collared kingfisher, or if someone mentions the name of a man who once controlled magic stones of death. These are occasions when the world of ancestors closes with that of the living.

In their daily consumption of kava, men thus both send and receive knowledge statements. Kava drunkenness offers the Tannese a means of inspiration and permits them to claim authoritative sources for the knowledge they talk about. They thereby satisfy the local inspirational condition that regulates formulation of knowledge. Their serious talk appears inspired, as the authority-principle demands, and thus escapes the ignominy of seeming to be the product of some illegitimate personal creativity.

Travel

Given the necessary face-to-face contiguity of speakers within a conversational mode of information, personal travel serves as an important mechanism of knowledge circulation. It also, insofar as a person might travel to learn from an authoritative source, supports statement formulation. Movement is thus "dangerous," in Foucault's sense of the word. Like all other means of inspiration, the powerful attempt to control journeys so to forestall the production of alternative knowledge. Controls on travel are perhaps apparent in the commonplace Melanesian greeting. Instead of our own "how are you?", which focuses attention on the individual, the creative Western "author," islanders ask each other *ikamfai?* or *ikuvaku?*—"where are you going?"

By the time Cook called at Port Resolution in 1774, the Tannese appear to have abandoned the production of canoes large enough for extensive ocean voyaging. As Cook, however, encountered a number of people from neighboring islands when he refreshed in the harbor, islanders continued, at least, to navigate about the southern end of the archipelago. The range of their travel expanded during the first half of the nineteenth century. Various exploiters of whale, trepang, and sandalwood at the edge of an expanding capitalist frontier sailed local waters, and recruited islanders as boatsmen and casual laborers (Shineberg 1967:190–191).

Overseas labor recruitment developed further with the establishment of sugarcane and copra plantations in neighboring regions of the southwest Pacific. Plantation agricultural production required large reserves of inexpensive labor that was unavailable locally. Planters thus looked to the islands to fill their labor needs. Those Tannese who were recruited, willingly or not, to work on Benjamin Boyd's New South Wales ranch in 1847 were the first of many men and women who boarded labor recruiting vessels sailing out of Queensland, Fiji, and New Caledonia. An estimated 4,244 Tannese, from 1863 through 1904, recruited for Queensland plantations alone (Price 1976:114). Many more traveled to New Caledonia and Fiji. By the end of the nineteenth century, most men had probably spent some time abroad. Missionaries, in 1872, estimated that 1,200 of the 2,000 males above the age of seventeen had gone overseas at least once (Campbell 1873:212).

Foreign travel accords people access to exotic knowledge sources and statements. One kind of knowledge that men learned abroad was Pidgin English. People at Port Resolution spoke a linguistic ancestor of contemporary Vanuatu Bislama as early as the 1850s (Inglis 1854:67; J. Paton 1890:189). Returnees from the Labor Trade also brought back knowledge of the darker sides of European society, much of which hapless missionaries working back on Tanna had hoped to "edit" or keep secret.

Missionaries living on the island tended to dislike labor returnees because of their command of this knowledge. Homecomers circulated information that all Europeans were not Christian nor kept the Sabbath holy; that whites drank, smoked, danced, and fornicated often excessively in the coastal and sugar towns of Queensland (J. Paton 1890:190). Watt complained that only one returnee attended church in 1871 (Kay 1872:63). Thomas Neilson's succinct reply to the query "what has been the general effect of these emigrations upon the native population at Port Resolution?" was "absolutely ruinous" (Kay 1872:60). Beatrice Grimshaw, a woman journalist who visited Tanna the year the White Australia policy was actualized by the deportation of most of the Pacific Islands' work force back to home islands, wrote of the trouble these returnees were fomenting. She overheard disturbing anticolonialist statements of "Tanna for the Tannese" (1907:318).

Europeans were most often disappointed that the power of certain of their own discourses (e.g., the Christian, political and economic morality, treatment of the body and of material objects) did not immediately remake the island and its inhabitants. A popular argument supporting the Labor Trade held that three years' work in Queensland cane fields were a civilizing experience that would uplift the islanders. Travelers abroad, however, consumed European goods and skills according to their own interests. Homecomers occasionally, however, did carry back to Tanna knowledge that both they and missionaries found acceptable. Some of this achieved a measure of exchange value within island conversations. Mrs. Watt, for example, met a self-made island missionary named Johnny Pata at Black Beach. Pata had returned from Fiji with some amount of Christian knowledge and a number of books (Watt 1896:128). He was attempting to attract followers (a congregation) by circulating exotic doctrinal statements that his travel had discursively authorized him to reveal.

Today, whether by airplane or traditional canoe, travel continues to provide a means of access to authoritative sources of exotic knowledge (Bonnemaison 1984b:140–141). Presently, most men and many women have been abroad. Young men go to work on nearby southern islands or to Port Vila, Vanuatu's capital. Some go as far as neighboring New Caledonia (Bedford 1973; Bonnemaison 1979, 1985). Women travel to accompany brothers or husbands, and sometimes also undertake off-island wage labor. People go abroad for various reasons, including nowadays their increasing need for money (Bastin 1985).

Islanders employ their travel experiences and perceptions abroad to justify subsequent serious talking. The verb *-isua,* which means "paddle" or "travel at sea," if used metaphorically, also means to be wise. Travelers often purposely call public attention to their journeys (that authorize them to speak) by renaming a piece of their land after some experienced overseas location or event. Uiuai named his village Iakanata (Canada) in the 1940s in honor of the Canadians he worked with in Port Vila during World War Two. A plot of ground near Port Resolution appears on topographic maps as "Ombus" (a name that geologists have also given to nearby volcanic formations). This is actually "Homebush," the namesake of a Colonial Sugar Refinery plantation near Mackay, Queensland. A traveling homecomer renamed the area early in this century.

In that travel is a means of access to knowledge sources, the powerful must regulate this formulary device in order to ensure reproduction of their own qualifications to speak, and in order to maintain existing relations of conversational inequality. Leaders attempt to control followers' travel to abort the appearance of alternative truths. Traditionally, women and children were subjectively less competent to travel. This is changing, although the existing mode of information continues to depend in part on travel regulations. In the nineteenth century, labor recruiters described a contention for the right to travel. Wawn (1893:70), for example, recruited young men and women who were delighted to have escaped their elders attempting to prevent them from going abroad: "From Aneityum I proceeded to Port Resolution where the first recruits were engaged. One of these ran away from his friends, shouting and jeering at them when he arrived on board and found I was getting underway to leave the place" (see also 1893:259, 296).

Older men, today, still attempt to manage travel. Speakers at several decision-making meetings proposed that young people might only depart for Port Vila if they first obtained a "passport." Local elders would only issue and sign these papers for those travelers with good reason to leave the island (e.g., a job or school appointment). They proposed that police stand at the airstrip and at sea passages in order to regulate journeys. Conversely, at a local primary school celebration, fathers rented a number of taxi trucks to transport groups of their children to various parts of the island. The geographic range of children, in southeast Tanna, is very narrow. Many have not traveled the 25 kilometers across the island. Their parents' gift to them was the experience of motion, and the prospect of unaccustomed landscapes.

The danger of travel is also apparent in a small dispute between an Australian overseas volunteer and John Frum doctrinal leaders. The volunteer let it be known he had applied for overseas funds with which he proposed to fly a number of men, including two from Sulphur Bay, to America. He perhaps hoped that a personal encounter with the reality of the United States, magnificent and sordid, would perhaps disabuse movement talk of its common Americophilia. Older leaders at Sulphur Bay, however, alarmed at this challenge to their own control of the American voice, refused to sanction this tour and, in fact, had doctrinal police irregulars threaten the volunteer to induce him to mind his own business. "Come Independence, one said, they were going to tie him to a tree" (MacClancy 1983:388). The volunteer "was offering cultists access to his road to

America" but Sulphur Bay leaders insisted that "they already had
their own small road to America—through the volcano" (MacClancy
1983:388). Control of formulation of doctrinal truth statements was
at stake here. Unsanctioned travel to the authoritative American
source could have short-circuited ruling leaders' asserted management of the Tanna-America connection. Schwartz (1962:289) describes similar travel controls during the Paliau movement on Manus.)

Reading

Those exotic bodies of knowledge that have penetrated island conversations during the past two hundred years have often arrived in the
form of literary texts. To facilitate access to this knowledge and improve its circulation, knowledge brokers faced the problem of teaching islanders to read. The discourse of both the London Missionary
Society and the Presbyterian Mission that succeeded it emphasized
the function of the Bible as the primary means of access to knowledge
of God's will and plan. In some ways parallel to island epistemology,
this Christian discourse asserted a kind of perceptual theory of learning: people read, therefore they know. The Bible itself could convert a
chance reader; the word, internalized by reading, reconstructs and
seizes the soul for Christ.

In southeast Tanna, George Turner and Henry Nisbet in 1841,
John Paton in 1858, and William Watt in 1869 all set themselves the
tasks of learning the local language, producing orthographies, and
beginning the work of Bible translation and textualization. The Tannese managed to roust Turner, Nisbet, and later Paton off their island
in quick fashion before they had much of a chance to produce significant literary output. Turner and Nisbet, with the assistance of Samoan
Christian teachers previously landed at Port Resolution, did manage a
couple of short texts (Turner 1845). Paton, also, translated several
hymns before escaping his post in 1862. But it was Watt, accom-
panied by a linguistically competent wife, who managed to last out
Tannese hostilities to produce numerous texts. His *chef d'oeuvre* was a
translation of the New Testament in 1890, produced with the assistance of Tannese pundits such as Nasuai (Watt 1896:323).

Alongside translations, Christian knowledge brokers also established schools to teach reading so that people would have access to
the texts they produced and deployed. Reading, like travel, serves as a

means of access to an exotic authoritative source of knowledge, although, in this case, the writing stands between the message's authority and an individual receiver. Ancestors speak directly in dreams or drunkenness; God most of the time speaks indirectly in codified text. To gain access to His knowledge, one obviously must read.

Missionaries Turner and Nisbet consciously attempted to increase the exchange value of their textualized doctrinal statements by limiting access to reading skills. They proposed to attract to their first school only the sons of "chiefs" (Nisbet, diary entry 7/11/1841). Christian knowledge brokers hoped, in effect, to challenge traditional power structures with books and reading—with an exotic knowledge authority and a novel discursive procedure of knowledge access.

Existing island leaders, however, soon recognized that danger in reading. They succeeded, for several decades, in restricting access to Christian knowledge, in part by associating books and reading with the alien diseases that were then raging on the island. Paton, in 1860, noted "the Tannese had a superstitious dread of books, and especially of God's Book" (1890:202). He also reports the burial of Christian texts (1890:283). Agnes Watt wrote of one village:

> Although they wished the Aneityumese teacher to remain, very few attend church; and still fewer can be constrained to try to learn to read. Let me give an instance of how much they dread the gospel and books, and how disheartening it is. I lately accompanied Mr. Watt on the Sabbath, and was disappointed to find only a few old women labouring away at the alphabet (1896:130).

A literary change of heart occurred in 1888. Mrs. Watt pinpoints this year as the one in which "the dread of books, so common on Tanna, seems to have broken down. It was pleasant to see so many anxious to get a book" (1896:287). This collapse of the traditional conversational order and its regimes of truth that had, to this point, repressed both desire for and access to literary sources adumbrated a discursive disjunction. Alternative Christian Tanna Law doctrinal statements began to circulate with increasing velocity in island talk. Whereas people once had shunned books, the new doctrine transvalued book ownership and reading skills. These literary means of access to new Christian authoritative sources now came to underpin a person's qualifications to formulate knowledge statements in the new conversational order. To talk seriously, one now must read.

Paton's son Frank, who established a mission on the west coast in the 1880s, noted that "the people were eager for books, and as soon as it became known that I had hymn-books with me, a rush was made for the tent, and they were all sold out in a few seconds" (1903:165). Mrs. Watt reports that whereas in 1879 there were only 30 books and 1 school in southeast Tanna, 10 years later there were 300 books in circulation and 8 mission school outstations (1896:318, see 324). She noted "the thing that above all other has given an impetus to our reading classes has been the distribution of the New Testament" (1896:322–323). With the appearance of Christian texts on the island, and the achievement of this literate knowledge of conversational exchange value, reading joined the other, inspirational means of access to authoritative sources (see Meggitt 1968).

Older men today, leaders of Christian villages, nearly all possess reading skills that they learned in mission schools. They exercise their skill at local Sunday services during which they read aloud portions of Watt's New Testament to fellow worshipers. Generally, they also control the few remaining copies of this book. On the other hand, younger men who learned to read more recently in an expanded government school system are able to read Bislama and French or English. Elders, frequently, cannot read well in the colonial languages or Bislama; the young, today, are unschooled in reading their own language. Their French or English reading skills, however, provide them access to various information sources, including newspapers and political party platforms. Reading thus authorizes their talking about these different sorts of serious knowledge statements.

Reading aloud to others demonstrates one's connection with an authoritative source. Conversely, learning to read for oneself allows a person to do without literate middlemen, and to find the source on one's own. Those islanders who can read have access to textualized messages. They are thereby able, according to local conditions of discourse, to talk authentically and seriously about scripture and other textual knowledge within island conversation.

PRODUCTION CONTROL

These several means of inspiration that authorize the formulation and repetition of knowledge within Tanna's mode of information admit danger at two levels. With the available procedures of discourse control on the island, those people who are best qualified to produce knowledge can not always succeed in silencing competing voices. Rivals may overcome those presently in control of conversation, appropriating their discursive function within this as "spokesmen." More seriously, the appearance of alternative knowledge may provoke a discursive disjunction (see Chapter Six). More than upsetting current structures of conversational domination, this may transform those of personal subjectification as well.

Island discourses establish possible speaking positions, and variously qualify people to fill these, repeating extant knowledge statements or producing new ones. In the disciplines of magic, medicine, and geography, for example, subjective qualifications of sex, age, and name determine one's access to known ancestral and namesake sources, both dead and alive. Islanders are thereby authorized to repeat existing disciplinal knowledge, organized by geographic oeuvre, and to operate the means of inspiration that account for the appearance of new knowledge in these fields. Although doctrinal leaders need no geographic qualification, these spokesmen, too, must still establish some claim to an authoritative voice, and assert control of an inspirational means to contact this source.

The discursive control procedures that regulate island knowledge production make some people less competent to talk seriously. Women and children are often speechless because of their subjective incompetence to get drunk on kava, their lack of nomenclatural entitlements to ritual keys, and their ignorance of travel and reading. Even today, more boys than girls get sent to school. More men than women go abroad. To this extent, there is a sexual division of intellectual labor. This is maintained, in part, by the discursive facts of sex that disqualify women from using some of the available means of knowledge production.

Nevertheless, there remain other discursively acknowledged avenues to inspiration. Women and other of the conversationally powerless occasionally find a voice in these mechanisms. In this regard, those in control of serious talk sometimes fail to prevent others, even women, from gaining access to a means of knowledge production. Recently, gender-based prohibitions on learning to read and on travel have weakened. Local discourse is now unable to preserve all of its gender liabilities. Moreover, the island is less isolated from the world information order that nourishes a growing desire and necessity for cash. Both women and men may earn money by traveling abroad; women are no longer stationary. Local gender discourse is also unable to prevent off-island knowledge agents, such as government educators, from teaching both sexes to read, or from talking about women's rights. This contemporary failure recalls the previous impotence of traditional discourses to prevent nineteenth-century Christian knowledge brokers from attracting, in the end, a young male audience and indoctrinating these men with dangerous reading skills.

Moreover, anyone may dream. Stephen (1979; 1982), who describes dreaming's importance for knowledge production throughout Melanesia, suggests that this continuously renews local knowledge. Dreams may, more than this, generate novel explanatory statements that challenge the conversationally dominant and what they know (1982:117; see also Herr 1981; Meggitt 1962; Schwartz 1962:392–393; Wagner 1972:68–78). Openness of access to this means of inspiration sometimes destabilizes relations of inequality: "Important visionary dreams may thus come to anyone, not merely ritual experts" (Stephen 1982:119).

It is significant, here, to note that one of the few claims to knowledge power that island women legitimately can assert rests on their reception of dreamed messages from ancestors and other spirits. Similarly, among the Baruya, as Godelier notes, the exercise of shamanistic curing is "the only domain of social practice in which the powers of the two sexes can to a certain degree confront each other" (1982:16). Mrs. Watt's old woman clever, who trafficked in Sheffield knives and statements from the dead, for a time at least controlled a significant mechanism of knowledge formulation, justifying her serious talk (see also Schwartz 1962:395).

The discursive control procedures of authority-principle, repetitive copyright, and geographic oeuvre, as well as the various means of inspiration by which people account for their production of knowledge (ritual keys, dreaming, drunkenness, travel, and reading), only imperfectly regulate statement production. Those spokesmen in control of knowledge formulation and repetition occasionally fail to maintain their conversational domination because they fail to restrict others' access to powerful means of inspiration and to important authoritative sources. Existing "silences" and established personal qual ifications to talk seriously may collapse with the production of some alternate set of doctrinal statements that invades island conversation.

External authorities, for example, are popularized insofar as the devices of knowledge (or, in general, cultural) production are not amenable to monopolistic control. Those Green Point spokesmen who first reported John Frum's message had difficulty in protecting the exclusivity of their source. Nampas and other spokesmen in east Tanna seized a discursively available speaking position by appropriating and citing John Frum's authority for themselves. Green Point rivals continue to deny the authority of that knowledge. John Frum, in this regard, is the object of what might be called an auspicious competition. Spokesmen in different corners of the island's information market produce sometimes contradictory knowledge statements they assign to his authority (see Gregory and Gregory 1984:84).

Furthermore, although only properly entitled individuals are qualified to repeat publicly the more formalized knowledge statements organized into geographic oeuvres, this copyright is also often breached. People, in private, freely rehearse this knowledge. They also, while careful to avoid a public repetition of a genealogy, story, myth, or spell itself, may comment on its content and on the correctness and circumstances of its repetition.

Before Reia iterated his copyright to repeat Mwatiktiki's story, his kinsman, Kafua, tape-recorded this sort of critical commentary (outside of Reia's hearing):

Ouah, iakrukurin store sai Reia,	Yes, I know Reia's story,
store sai Reia ramasan, ramasan	Reia's story is good, exceed-
puk anan.	ingly good.
Mata in nah nah kwatia, kwatia.	But there is one thing, just
Iakua ramwhen mua, ramwhen	one.
mua in rati irapw aotsaed anan,	I say it's as if he looks too far
mini aelan, mini aelan.	outside,
Iou iakreirei mua aelan savai	telling of the island, the island.
Mwatikitiki	I don't know whether this is
ua aelan savai ramak aotsaed.	Mwatiktiki's island
Na mata tina naha, naghun nah	or another that is further off.

Imwai Nei, Imwai Nei nah ipaka.	However, that land called Imwai Nei, Imwai Nei is nearby.
Ipaka. Ipaka ti sa Ianatom mine Futuna,	Nearby. Close to Aneityum and Futuna,
ua Ianatom mine Futuna isupwin anan, Imwai Nei ipaka mwi kwopti. Na mata store sai Reia ramasan, mua ramasan.	or Aneityum and Futuna are further away, Imwei Nei is even closer.
Na mata kwati a naha, aelan aotsaed anan.	However, Reia's story is good, good.
Na iakreirei mua niparhien ua nekuaien.	Just this one thing, that island is too far away.
	I don't know if [his story] is truth or lies.

Kafua, who is careful to remark Reia's copyright over the story itself, and who states twice its excellence, nevertheless questions its truth: "I don't know if his story is truth or lies." Kafua challenges Reia's equation of Imwai Nei with the distant Matthew and Hunter islands. He suggests that Mwatiktiki's home is hidden just off Tanna's coast and not, as Reia is claiming, much further to the south. Reia's geographic copyright here fails to prevent Kafua's commentary on the oeuvre.

In addition to highjacking someone's authority or breaching his geographic copyright, the powerless can also escape their incompetence to talk seriously by running away to sea, by seizing ingressive opportunities to learn to read, by getting drunk, or by dreaming. They thereby are able to assume a discursively situated position to talk knowledgeably. From this position, they are sometimes able to challenge existing structures of conversational domination.

More seriously, when those who once were silent find their voice, the existing conversational order is potentially vulnerable to disjunction. This is more than the seizure by one subject from another of an available speaking position. It also may critically alter the details of subjectivity itself. In Melanesia,

leaders are constantly threatened by the possibility that their cultural definitions of reality, their criteria of excellence and achievement,

> may lose popularity and hence legitimacy in favour of the growing
> possibility of either an entirely new definition or a definition that
> had previously been of a purely marginal kind (Allen 1981:106).

Tanna's procedures of discourse control have not always forestalled the threat posed by the appearance of alternative knowledge in people's conversations.

First, the island's authority-principle, unlike the West's author-principle, cannot regulate knowledge by the individualistic facts of its origin or formulation. An authority-principle fails to classify and assign known or chance statements according to some transcendental individual source. Island authorities, unlike authors, do not necessarily die and fall silent. The dead keep on talking, and their authority can be used over and over again for new purposes. The ancestors continue to reveal dreamed knowledge that can contradict previously revealed doctrinal statements and challenge ruling discourse. Rediscovery of some "lost" work that negates a lifetime's oeuvre cannot embarrass an ancestral authority in the way it might embarrass an author. Moreover, there always exists the possibility of a wild source. Some new inspiring voice, like John Frum's in 1941, establishes an authority for novel revelations.

Although discursive control procedures that require inspirational knowing prevent people from authorizing their own statements, inspiration may be a less effective device than is creativity for maintaining knowledge continuities. The emplacement of mediating spokesmen who receive revealed knowledge weakens the bond between knowledge and its source. This is not a direct creative relation between author and statement; it is a complex, indirect association of an authority, a spokesman, and a message. Numerous spokesmen, making contradictory doctrinal statements, may claim the same authority. Or, rival advocates may assign similar doctrinal statements to different sources. People, moreover, may revise their communicative relations with their sources, alloting existing knowledge to newly contacted or rehabilitated authorities. Alteration in these details of authority citations—the acknowledged bibliography behind island conversation—may thus emend existing connections between a knowledge statement and its inspiring source.

An ample corpus of statements, for example, that describe Noah, an ark, a hill, abandoned carpentry tools, and a flood circulate about

Tanna's information market (for an example story, see Bonnemaison 1987:586–590). People who repeat these statements today assign them to diverse authoritative sources: to exotic Christian knowledge brokers and Biblical authority, to local ancestors, or to John Frum. In a conversational mode of information, people have a lot more opportunity to tamper with authorities than others elsewhere have to tamper with authors.

Second, as noted, in a conversational mode of information, commentary often prompts *restatement* rather than a stereotypic repetition of knowledge. It allows discursive slippage. The greater the number of people qualified to talk seriously, the increasing dangers of restatement. Constant restatement, through repetition of knowledge from one conversation to the next, leaves cultural discourses open to alteration and drift. No text serves here as a drag anchor. Furthermore, restatement permits existing discourses to absorb whatever object, wherever constituted, they encounter. In a conversational mode of information, people can deny any object's novelty and claim that this was *always* their own. Here, new truths are discursively allowed to pass as a repetition of old knowledge. By these means, Noah has become a Tannese ancestor.

This sort of discursive absorption and restatement enabled Reia to appropriate Matthew and Hunter islands within his own geographic oeuvre. He restated these islets to always have been Mwatiktiki's Valhalla. Similarly, newly formulated statements, whether they are contradictory or supportive of present knowledge, can succeed in passing themselves off as customary wisdom. They come, after all, from ancestral sources, even if the channel of transmission is yesterday's dream rather than some centuries-long, memorized oral tradition.

To maintain their competences to talk seriously, powerful spokesmen attempt to silence others by claiming an exclusive connection with an authoritative source, by citing a repetitive geographic copyright, and by controlling the means of inspiration. The local discursive control procedures that regulate knowledge production, and thus reproduce shared culture, however, sometimes fall short of stilling other voices and aborting alternative doctrine. Reia fails to silence Kafua; men fail to silence women; traditionalists fail to silence Christians; Christians fail to silence John Frum talk. There are obvious dangers in this relative openness of knowledge production. If a regime of power and truth is to reproduce itself, it must overcome and defuse elsewhere the alternative dangerous knowledge that people produce: a statement that fails to circulate very far within conversation, or a statement that no one hears, loses much of its potential danger. The powerful, therefore, must fix their attention as well on other, complementary discursive control procedures that regulate the circulation of knowledge and also its conversational consumption.

4

Statement Circulation

Aue Nariga Tommy	Oh Naringa Tommy
iakamara ia wok u,	I abide in this work,
imwak ia Pot Aelan.	my home at Port Island.
Kitaha samata nimrhi Tomi,	We see Tommy's face,
niteta ramurkurau takwtakwnu.	the canoe circulates now.
Rahatin suatuk amasan,	He teaches the good road,
rahatin pen ikin,	he points to the place,
Iamerika, Iamerika.	to America, to America.

—John Frum Hymn

Tannese knowledge statements, whether prosaic or formulaic like this doctrinal hymn, pass from one islander to another within the island's informational field or "market." Collins has noted that "conversation is an exchange. . . . We may thus conceive of a larger conversational market in which relationships of all sorts are bargained" (1975:133–134). Tanna's conversational marketplace is not an unstructured, neutral field of talk. Rather, it is regulated by a set of discursive conditions and procedures. These circulatory procedures are more than the locally available material channels of information transmission (talk, gesture, literacy) and information storage (memory, writing). They are a discursive practice that establishes a patterned deployment of knowledge among people, and that regulates the exchange of statements in conversation. Circulatory procedures also function to store knowledge, and to maintain its uneven distribution around the island. They work to make culture both shared and un-shared.

Given the island's conditions of discourse, some people are better able to circulate knowledge than others. Bourdieu also has suggested that "the objective relation between speaker and receiver operates as a market which applies a censorship by conferring very unequal values on different linguistic products" (1977:658). As the John Frum hymn proclaims, "We see Tommy's [Nampas] face, the canoe circulates now." Nampas' John Frum talk once flooded the market. His linguistic product—his serious talk—was a way of bargaining new relations of conversational exchange on the island.

All people come to the market endowed with different kinds of conversational resources. There is an unequal personal access to both the means and places of knowledge exchange. Those islanders who are best able to talk seriously may sometimes restrict the public range of some of the knowledge they produce; or they may use available circulatory procedures in order to disseminate their statements widely around the island. They broadcast common knowledge, and they restrict, or "narrowcast" secret information. Their talk resounds within the island's conversational market. They teach the good road. They command an audience.

STORAGE

For a knowledge statement to remain part of a nonliterate mode of information, beyond the deaths of those who know, it must be communicated in some way to survivors within a conversational field. It must somehow be stored to remain part of shared culture. On Tanna, individual memory is the principal knowledge store. Cultural knowledge may also accumulate in material objects such as paintings, carvings, architectual structures, manufactured goods, and so on, all of which encode information. Objects, unlike rapidly fading speech, can preserve knowledge of a sort through time; exosomatically stored, a knowledge statement sometimes outlives its producer.

On Tanna, however, material storage time is rather shorter than it is elsewhere. Except for those of stone, island objects are not remarkably long-lived. Moreover, aside from women's face painting during dances, and the symbolic arrangement of living and gardening spaces, the Tannese (compared with other Vanuatu societies) produce only the simplest of objects and designs in which knowledge might inhere. Typically, island artifacts are plain and straightforward. Whether plain or complex, the meaning of "objectified" knowledge statements is often opaque. Few codes that build upon concrete symbols match the efficiency of the linguistic. Reading objective codes requires considerable interpretive effort. Of course, this is also true of verbalized knowledge, though given the richness and definitiveness of linguistic codes, interpretation of these latter is generally less of a problem.

Knowledge that is made concrete in writing or print might also be called objectified. This textualization of knowledge frees discourse from the tyranny of individual memory. When stored in print, knowledge also escapes other limitations of conversational modes of information, including the necessity of propinquity and face-to-face exchange. On Tanna, although people today recognize literacy's utility for acquiring, storing, and exchanging knowledge, they still continue to circulate most of what they know vocally. Only the exotic knowledge brokers, such as missionaries and government representatives, store and circulate much knowledge in books or newspapers. And these written and printed materials on the island have a short life expectancy. Only a few specimens of Watt's translated Biblical publications, for example, are extant, having barely survived the passing of wet, tropical seasons.

Apart from scrawled accountings of goods exchanged, occasional letters to family members and friends abroad, and minutes of local governmental meetings, islanders neither store nor circulate much knowledge in written form. Men who are presented goods at a life cycle exchange ceremony may write down as marginalia in their children's school notebooks the numbers of mats, lengths of cloth, kava, and pigs received. By storing these sums literately, they have a written record of how many of each good they must return in future to restore exchange balance. Islanders also occasionally circulate family information in letters they mail to kin working in Port Vila or elsewhere overseas. A new national telephone system, however, now permits the exchange of this sort of information conversationally as well. The dozen or so telephones on Tanna, that neatly reconstitute the face-to-face conversational practice of the island's mode of information, are in part supplanting the letter.

Given the absence of efficient material means of knowledge storage, and the rapid fading of verbalized statements, individual memory remains the principal means of storing most disciplinal and local doctrinal knowledge on Tanna (cf. Brandt 1980:134). Some of these knowledge statements, such as songs, are formalized according to the stylistic requirements of local narrative and choral genres. Because of its formulaic shape, this sort of stored knowledge is perhaps easier to learn and to remember. The rules of form serve as a mnemonics to recall the statement. Island "formulary devices" (Ong 1971:285) of this sort also include an archive of common metaphors and maxims.

Songs, in particular, formalize stored knowledge throughout Melanesia. In an August dawn of 1774, James Cook noticed singing emanating from the eastern point of Port Resolution. Singing (*-ni nupu*) remains an important aspect of island ritual. People dance (*-orupu*) to a large repertoire of *nupu* 'dance/song' each time they celebrate some rite of passage, or an area-wide exchange festival such as *nakwiari* or *nieri*. Groups of dancers execute the same *nupu* dance figures over and over during a night's performance. Children join in with the adults dancing at a kava-drinking ground. Although they may not yet know a song's words, they soon learn its tune and also dance steps by imitating their parents and older siblings. By actively participating in hundreds of festive dances, a person learns and gradually builds up a large repertoire of memorized songs.

Nupu dances comprise handclapping, footstomping, and counterclockwise circling. Men dance in the center of the kava-drinking ground surrounded by a circle of women, all circling counterclockwise. Each *nupu* dance segment lasts several minutes, depending on the length of song verse. A song generally has several of these component segments (*napei nupu*); the dance is resumed again following a short pause between verses. People may perform scores of different songs during a night's festival. In dance, men and women from the several kava-drinking groups involved in an exchange each present their local geographic choral oeuvres.

Singing is also an important part of doctrinal ritual. Last century's missionaries quickly perceived the importance of song for the storage and circulation of knowledge in the local information market and attempted to bend this towards Christian ends. Turner (1845) produced a book with three Kwamera hymns. The Watts also busied themselves with hymn translation. Converts assisted them in this and some, such as Sasairo, Praun, Poita, Iouikou, Seroki, and Nirua, composed hymns themselves. Watt published a number of Kwamera hymnals during his years on the island. The last, which appeared in 1919 containing 145 songs, still serves in today's Christian services. Hymn melodies, for the most part, are adapted from those of nineteenth century European and American revival movements (e.g., Sankey, McGranahan, and Stebbins 1896).

Following World War Two, a new musical style was heard on Tanna (Nabanga 1979:5). "String bands" composed of guitars, ukuleles, and home-made gut-buckets, strumming a few simple chords for rhythm, perform songs in today's widespread pan-Pacific musical styles. Hymn and string band song are both different stylistically from traditional *nupu*, which has a distinctive tonal quality and meter.

The style and the knowledge content of songs signify the doctrinal affiliations of those who are singing. Anyone who hears a fragment of ritual song can identify the singers as adherents of Christian or John Frum doctrine. Although all islanders perform string band songs during nontraditional celebrations and feasts, supporters of the John Frum movement specifically appropriated this form to phrase a new doctrinal hymnody (Bonnemaison 1987:493–494). John Frum string bands perform their hymns at Friday night ceremonial dances at Sulphur Bay. Teams of supporters from kava-drinking grounds across East Tanna meet weekly at doctrinal headquarters to perform their song repertoires.

As is true elsewhere in Melanesia, Tannese songs are "serious." Traditional *nupu*, John Frum songs, and Christian hymns, all store important knowledge. *Nupu* songs, in particular, chronicle geographic information about places and personal names. They also record events in which the ancestors took part. Songs are thus a register of historical and geographic information (Bonnemaison 1987:67, 356; Waiko 1986:28). Every time people perform a song at a dance attended by members of neighboring local groups, they publicly rehearse an archive of knowledge statements. This performance refreshes stored statements in memory, and also speeds the circulation of those statements within the island's information market.

In that geographic knowledge of personal and place names,

along with the copyright to discuss seriously such names, legitimizes a person's claim to local lands, this sort of song-stored knowledge has significant exchange value during land disputes. It is not uncommon for disputants, in the course of debate, to burst into song in support of some claim they are making to a name or place. *Nupu* songs that are performed and circulated at festive dances, therefore, subsequently may be cited during dispute-settlement meetings. People describe these small, strategic revelations of song-stored knowledge as to *-avsini nikukua* "count the mark" or, nowadays, "read the book."

Songsmiths continue to produce new *nupu* that archive geographic names and local)events, such as does the following:

Kariuakw revi nuai reia	Kariuakw yanked a tail feather
navahi pen Marireg.	sent it to Marireg.
Iauha ramavahi raka,	Iauha took it,
muvsini pehe ti nupu Ikurupu.	changed it into Ikurupu's song.
Iramanien ramisua apwiri iou.	The spirit wakes me
Ihanekwehi niteta	You break up the group
sakimiaha Naraimene.	of yours, Naraimene.
Kamata nimigi nep.	One sees the club handle.
Nasipmene hata minisua,	Nasipmene sees and realizes,
mata tafaga.	sees that action.
Rukuarkuar pukah manasanas	It overflows, pigs are every-
Ia takurei nakogar	where.
mosatukw minu ia naiuaiu,	at the top of the *nakogar* tree
ravahi uta rous misansan i.	stretches the bird in the storm,
	lifts up the women's skirts and
	reveals it.

Setting aside its sexual metaphors and other symbolic content, we can note that this *nupu* records the names of several men (Kariuakw, who commissioned the song by sending a "tail feather" (i.e., a fowl) to Iauha via Marireg); a place name (Ikurupu); two local group names (Naraimene and Nasipmene); and a number of events, including the production of the song itself.

Songs in this way archive geographic information about the participation of named individuals in specific historical events. Subsequent namesakes may assert personal rights to a place, or to a copy-right to repeat geographic statements and other knowledge, by citing stored choral information. One man, for example, who presently lives in another district of the island, claims rights to a kava clearing near Port Resolution. As evidence for his claim, he performed a song that stores knowledge statements about the participation of men with personal names from his name-set in a number of nineteenth century events that occurred at the harbor:

Nipitoga huvare Ivea	The whites landed at Ivea
mhuvsini irapw us	tossing out the anchor
mhamarer namevi namak.	standing to pull and moor.
Riskamter minamapwah	He rises up, no longer wanting
mai nirfwerig	the dry banana leaf [things of
mamaiu mata irapw Ivea.	the past] and runs to Ivea.
Mares Kipkini savani	They ask Kipkini
pikamaraki nikipisi ikin.	to go pile up his sandalwood
Iaken nimtameta,	there.
ramasan mevi misi,	Newborn child,
ramakahak mata irapw Ivea.	it is good to invite the missionary,
Nies mine Iueai, prisini me	it is dawning at Ivea.
Tuitui, Iahunuvo, Kwanfwaga.	Nies and Iueai, brothers
Paoa sakimiaha,	Tuitui, Iahunuvo, Kwanfwaga.
nema ia tinatina me,	The power of you people,
na tihapirhi	men of all lands,
takwarau nipwia.	you sweep
Ti nipin riti	the southeast wind.
kamuvin imwanraha.	One day
Nipran mha hamatui	someone is going to their place.
mamiu muvin iankunei tisi.	The wives left behind scan
Misi ruvehe mavahi mane,	the horizon of the sea.
mavahi nimrhinraha i	The missionary came bringing
miri iraha men Isamoa.	money,
	purchased them with it
	and led them off to Samoa.

This song rehearses a set of personal names (Kɨpkɨni, Nies, Iueai, etc.) the holders of which dealt with sandalwooders, missionaries, and other early visitors to Port Resolution. As a statement archive, the song warrants its owner's nominal claims to a large ridge of now depopulated land west of Port Resolution.

In debate, disputants may also repeat *nupu* statements that inform other topics of concern. Documenting his claims about correct gender relations and the masculinity of supernatural power, for example, Rapi broke, in this manner, into song:

Tata rosi iou	Father strikes me
mama rosi iou	mother strikes me
aue, takasak makwein si in u	alas, who can I cry to
aue, tata kwumwesin.	alas, father God.

Rapi offered this song as an archive of stored, valuable ancestral information about proper relations between authoritative men and submissive women.

The other genres of island song also serve as registers of personal names and events. Hymns record and circulate names of important Christian personalities such as Iesu (Jesus). John Frum songs, in addition to Tommy Nampas, also mention Maxim, Peter, Isaac One, Henry, Captain World, and John Frum himself. These hymns, celebrating movement leaders and authorities, enhance the circulation of doctrinal messages and serve to spread leading names more thoroughly throughout the conversational marketplace. They also remark copyright claims over particular authoritative sources.

More secular string band songs likewise serve as registers of names and events. Many of these songs, for example, circulate statements about contemporary incidents, including Vanuatu's achievement of independence and the problems of a new nation:

Long 1981 mi stap	In 1981, I was
hom blong mi.	at my home.
Mi harem nyus i kam	I heard the news which came
long ples blong mi.	to my place.
Nyus ia i talem se	The news said
yumi mas pem takis	we must pay tax

be ol man blong yumi	but all our men
ol i no wantem pem takis.	they don't want to pay tax.

Other songs circulate statements about more local events:

Takevin maru	I go to bathe
ia nui sakrau Ivapusan,	in our stream Ivapusan,
takrerig muvehe.	I turn and come back.
Tiki tirhum, tiki traoses.	Skin of your mouth, skin of
Krouakure apa,	your trousers,
ikares mo jik ianirak.	We two sit apart,
Takrerig mamevin fwe im-	You ask and insult me.
wamrau,	I return going to our place,
stupid trasak.	stupid cries.

and,

O brata, yu wan bigfala man	Oh brother, you're a big-man
yu rao long mi	you row with me
yu wantem faetem mi.	you want to fight with me.
Mi sem long fes	I am shamed before
blong plenti man.	many people.
Yu wan man blong Hakui gav-	You are a Hakui government
man,	man [local leader],
talem long mi se	tell me that
yu mekem wan aksen.	you will get me.
Mi ansa bak long yu	I answer back to your threat,
long aksen blong yu,	your jealousy
jelas blong yu	causes you to fight with me.
yu mekem blong mi.	

These last two string band songs circulate information and commentary about local disputes—the first a quarrel between a married couple, the second an argument between two neighbors. In the latter song, the songsmith suggests rather maliciously that his opponent's anger is based on jealousy about his wife's affair with a third party.

People purposely produce or commission *nupu*, hymns, and string band songs to record events, and to facilitate the deployment of this knowledge in the island's conversational marketplace. Formalized information of this sort, frozen into song, remains stored and available for conversational exchange as long as people continue to rehearse songs during regular traditional and contemporary dance performances. These songs, and other Tannese formulary devices, including name lists, metaphors and maxims, spells, and narrative genres, function to formalize and store knowledge within the island's conversational mode of information.

DISTRIBUTION

Tanna's discursive practices maintain an unequal distribution of songs and other memorized knowledge within the island's conversational marketplace. These procedures ensure that much of local culture remains unshared; that available information is distributed unevenly. Unevenly distributed knowledge is the basis of serious conversational exchange. If cultural knowledge at some point came to be universalized within the marketplace, then statement circulation, revelatory exchange, and contingent relations of conversational inequality would all terminate. Circulation of knowledge differs from that of material goods in that, with the latter, the giver relinquishes his personal possession of the exchange token, although he gains a debtor. With exchange of information, the giver merely increases the number of those who know, continuing to know himself.

Even through an uncontrolled exchange of knowledge statements promotes distributive equality of knowing (as opposed to the exchange of material goods that often promotes inequality of possession), knowledge still can be a valuable exchange token. Obviously, establishment of long-term relationships of conversational inequality demands controlled knowledge circulation to maintain its uneven distribution; to maintain some unshared culture. Discursive procedures must address this principal contradiction of information exchange: conversational power depends simultaneously on a person's ability both to keep and to tell his secrets. A person is empowered by his public revelation of knowledge. In the act of deploying his statements, however, he must reveal what he knows. Commonality of knowing may threaten existing relations of conversational inequality. A spokesman can thus undermine his own discursive position. Although his auditors may, for their common knowledge, be in his debt, if they are satisfied with the knowledge they have consumed, they may also withdraw from further conversational exchange.

Several of the island's discursive procedures work to circulate knowledge yet maintain the privacy of the statement. They allow a person's secrets to become conversationally "conspicuous" (Schwartz 1962:390), but still remain a little hidden. These practices sustain inequalities in island knowledge distribution so that serious conversation may continue. Important circulatory procedures on Tanna include a regulated practice of questioning and answering, secrecy, budgeted revelations, and the conversational importance of nonsense.

Because most knowledge is memorized, the principal device of gaining access to stored information is the "question." Questions are essential within any conversational mode of information and, because of this, they are also politically charged and discursively regulated (see Borofsky 1987:83–88). Uncontrolled questioning may threaten the existing distribution of knowledge; uncontrolled answering can equalize knowing throughout the informational marketplace. Questions particularly illuminate power ratios among those engaged in conversational exchange. A questioner, by asking, risks calling attention to his ignorance. An answerer, conversely, should he reveal knowledge, thereby invites the possibility of criticism from others who do not like what he has said.

As noted, islanders talk about learning in perceptual terms (observing, listening) more than in those of apperceptual or interactive learning by means of the question. In fact, the subjectively powerless, including children, confirm and reproduce their conversational impotence by asking more questions than others. Most adults, contrarily, avoid asking straightforward questions in serious talk that request someone else to reveal his memorized knowledge. Similarly, if a person is asked for knowledge he really ought to command but does not (say, about his genealogy or lands), he may hide his ignorance behind a pretense of knowing stares and wise nods, or evoke the protective demands of secrecy. Only small children, or others in clear-cut relationships of inequality who do not mind confirming their conversational impotence, risk revealing ignorance by asking many direct questions about serious knowledge. To avoid undermining one's position, the safer course is to listen and look for oneself, until knowledge is eventually won.

The kind of knowledge thus affects questioning practice. If this information is something a person really ought to know, he usually avoids asking obvious questions about it. Instead, he may maneuver to obtain memorized information cautiously and indirectly (Borofsky 1987:86). People ask questions in a way that implies they probably already know the answer. They ask roundabout, or "pretended rhetorical" questions of one another.

In kava clearing debates, for example, when a person asks questions, he risks admitting ignorance and undermining his position. When he answers questions, on the other hand, he risks revealing information that might be used against him. Revealed knowledge lays itself open to criticism and restatement, as Kafua condemned Reia's story about Mwatiktiki's island home. During debate, men must pursue a difficult rhetorical strategy. They attempt to convince their audience that they know, but also attempt to avoid revealing many of the details of that knowledge. Conversely, they hope to trap their opponents into making impolitic revelations. During the land debate we have been following, Uiuai quizzed Iati in this roundabout way:

Tata mi krinifini ia tuprena naha ua nah i?	What did our two fathers state about that land?
Krina roupwah niniien tukw ik i?	Didn't they tell you anything about it?
Nua tuprena paku tuprena naha puta pare Souarim nakwai.	I'm talking about the land up there that Souarim cleared.
Iakua kraumini tukw iou i.	I say they told me about it.
Rerik ragien tikni nagkiariien tukwe.	I'd be pleased if you make a statement about it.
Taem nah tikni nagkiariien tukwe.	It's time for you to give your talk about it.

In that Iakarui men had named Nikahi and Iati with available Ipikarig names, the latter's command of this requested geographic knowledge was weak. Uiuai also played on this point, asking Iati about his name-set and its wider traditional affiliations:

Na mata iakni ianha i mua
ikavahi traeb sai si?
Takwtakwnu ikavahi traeb sai
tata naha,
mata takares ik niteta krouiva
pen naha, krouiva pen ira tak-
wtakwnu.
Na ikamarer ia nife niteta?
Niteta mi na krouamak Iank-
wanemi.
Ikamarer ia nife niteta, Numruk-
wen ua Koiameta?
Na ikni nagkiariien tukwe ratuk-
watukw kroueva pen ira.

Now this is what I ask, what
tribe [name-set] are you? Now
you belong to father's tribe,
but I also ask you about the
canoes [moiety groups] that
we are now talking about.
Which canoe are you in?
Iankwanemi [kava ground] has
two canoes.
Which is your canoe, Numrukwen or Koiameta?
You make a correct statement
about this and we will discuss
it.

Iati, whose knowledge was shaky here, attempted to throw these
questions back to Uiuai and draw out *his* knowledge. Iati noted that
Uiuai had many supporters present and he expressed his hope that
they would judge the veracity of Uiuai's talk. Iati, meanwhile, attempted to entice Uiuai's hidden knowledge out into the open:

Iakata, mata ikapwah hi noien
klia ira,
mua tikni ianha i ikua nah ikni
kimaha nema Iakarui nah.
Iakamares ianhu i mua ruvehe
men naha Iakarui ua ruvehe
men naha Ipikarig?

I see, but you haven't yet ex-
plained it clearly,
you say that we are Iakarui.
I ask whether he came from
Iakarui or from Ipikarig?

This sort of strategic questioning during the debate perhaps in-
duced both sides to reveal more geographic knowledge than planned.
Revelation of knowledge can reduce its future conversational value as
Kieri, one of the witnesses present, observed. He suggested that once
a knowledge statement is revealed, it loses power:

Iahakure mata amwhen
nagkiariien sakimirau,
na mata iahata mata
nanumumirau in ia kwopun u.
Mata fwe Iamanuapen pwah iou
iakni saiou ianha i.
Iarauan Misiuaren ripikrukurin
mha nari ia rerik.
Saiou naha iakni.
Iakamo lo saiou fwe rerik,
iakamakw tamiri.
Mata niteta u, irouo u ia
kwopun u,
irouo kout kasua u ia niteta u ia
kwopun u.
Saiou fwe Misiuaren
ripikrukurin mha nari ia rerik.
Ti nipin ipwet iakakwi eri irapw
nari ianha i maghiri in.
Mata sakimirau!—sairapw
mhini apenapen a ia kitaha me.

We've sat here and judged the statements of you two, we have seen your souls [private knowledge] here. But at Iamanuapen [his own kava ground], let me explain my practice. If Misiuaren and I debate, he does not know what's in my heart [private knowledge]. This is my way I'm explaining. I rule my heart, I hold it tightly. But this group, you two here, you two are informers [people who cross group boundaries] between the canoes [groups]. As for me, Misiuaren doesn't know what's in my heart. Until one day I will let it out [the knowledge] and flatten him with it. But you two!—we are revealing wantonly among ourselves.

In his statement, Kieri identifies the discursive contradiction of knowledge exchange. A spokesman's revelation of statements deploys these within the conversational marketplace and, insofar as they are publicly consumed, helps establish common knowledge—including that of legitimate entitled rights to land. It also, however, equalizes knowledge distribution. To prevent wanton revelations, conversational practices of roundabout questions, and other ploys such as hinting and indirect knowledge claims, allow people to hide both their ignorance and their knowledge.

Something of the political dangers of the question, and local discursive strategies to avoid its presumption of ignorance, appear in a letter that a John Frum spokesman dictated to his English-educated daughter and mailed to an American anthropologist (phrasing and spelling are preserved here):

> Could you please help us. The 26 Team would now asked [sic] you if you could see the Americans to send what they asked you for. These words were agreed by John Frum Nampas & the Americans. It was agreed before & when the Politics came, wiped it all out but now we really need it. We begged for your help please. We are now waiting to see what will happen. Could you please contact Noah's family for help & write to us soon. The 26 Team are now still playing at Sulphur Bay & waiting to see what will happen. The American's flag has not come up yet. We've been hearing secret news that it will soon come up but we are not sure where.

This request is graciously posed in such a way that presumes knowledge all around. The statement rhetorically invests the American correspondent with knowledge that he, as an American, really ought to know, including the following: what the 26 teams asked for; what was agreed; and where to find Noah's family.

Like questions, answers are also a discursively contentious practice, maintaining uneven knowledge distribution within conversational modes of information. As the inverse of roundabout questioning, answering the unasked question likewise confirms relations of conversational inequality. If a person undermines his position by admitting ignorance with a question, he can build this by answering the questions of others—even if unasked. In this sort of exchange, the wise "teach" (-ahatin), "warn" (-avahag), "advise," (-avisau) or otherwise attempt to force auditors to hear what they say. The conversationally powerful, in debate and in the other forums of knowledge circulation, frequently produce advisory and didactic statements for the benefit of their audience. They preach about proper custom, historical facts, and other knowledge they uphold as common and true. This instructive speaking confirms their conversational position, and their greater qualifications to talk seriously.

On the other hand, people openly question those spokesmen who control valuable disciplinal and doctrinal information in order to gain access to their secrets. Here, questions and answers function as the exchange of knowledge between the wise and the ignorant. This is the basis of the prototypic conversational relation of inequality on the island. Although questions may equalize, to some extent, the distribution of memorized knowledge in an information market, they at the same time enact and confirm structures of conversational domination between those who ask and those who reveal. Island discursive practices of questioning and answering, thus, sustain both an unequal distribution and an unequal exchange of serious knowledge around Tanna.

Conversational controls on questions and answers, of course, imply that the Tannese like to keep secrets. An island secret, *nari afafa*, is something "unlit, shady, concealed, or hidden." Knowers "hide, conceal, or bury" (*-arukwafa*) their knowledge, emotions, plans, and so on. Given the memorization of knowledge, local practices of secrecy and revelation regulate the market's distribution of stored cultural information (see Barth 1987:25). On Tanna, there are no encyclopedias and no dictionaries to go to for answers—just people with secrets.

Secrets turn knowledge into property that can be exchanged (Luhrman 1989:136). People throughout Melanesia swap or sell their secrets and/or their knowledge copyrights for pigs, money, and other goods. Marketable information of this sort includes spells, medicines, songs, dance steps, metaphorical words with new meaning, artistic motifs, and so on. Hidden knowledge in general, aside from its occasional economic value, empowers a person to answer questions in serious talk. In revelatory conversations, islanders assume available discursive positions of "spokesmen" and "auditors," or "answerers" and "questioners." By preserving a pattern of ignorance within the information market, secrecy fuels serious talk between people who do not know and those who do. It ensures continuity of conversational exchange. Knowledge that remains under discursive copyright is often, in fact, known by many people who merely lack the right to use this in serious talk. Secrecy, on the other hand, brings into being and maintains conversational patterns of ignorance. Here, people cannot repeat and use serious knowledge because they have not been able to learn it. Secrets protect unshared areas of culture.

As implied in the local construction *-ni afafa*, "tell secretly," secrets have no conversational weight unless people ultimately tell them. Apart from empty secrets, the mystery of which is that there is no hidden knowledge, a stored statement does not long survive in an information market unless it is revealed to others. In a mode of information where stored knowledge is memorized, knowledge survives only in conversation. Untold secrets are subtracted, in the end, from shared culture. For social patterns of knowledge distribution to be reproduced through time, however, secret telling, like questions and answers, must be ordered.

A common discursive practice that protects secrets as they are told is budgeted revelation. Incremental revelation of knowledge serves to extend conversational exchange through time (cf. Meleisea 1980:26). As Salmond notes, for example, if a Maori elder "teaches all he knows to a younger man, his sacred powers may soon dwindle away" (1982:83). Knowers, rather than destroying all their secrets in some impressive flow of information, carefully time their revelations so that these last from conversation to conversation. Here, secret tellers may indicate to auditors that they are holding back the real truths of their knowledge, although they communicate enough to convince people of the existence of their secrets to make these conversationally conspicuous. They may also claim that they continue to receive additional knowledge from an authoritative source, as did Reia with Mwatiktiki. The book of secrets, in this case, is a never ending story.

Elsewhere in Melanesia, the importance of the timing of revelation is institutionalized in sequential rites of passage wherein initiates through their lives, gradually receive from older knowers more and more of a revealed truth. A number of grades, degrees, or levels of secret knowledge exist to which men only progressively achieve access (e.g., Barth 1975). Throughout Melanesia, there is also a pervasive suspicion that the wise take care never to exchange what they know in its entirety. The translated Bible, perhaps, is missing its first, most powerful page (Schwartz 1962:257). Or, the spell one has just purchased is sure to lack several key words (see Campbell 1978:3). Because of this, children frequently complain that their parents never got around to telling them everything important before they died (see Barth 1987:26, 48). Parents who hold back secrets to sustain some influence over their heirs are surprised by sudden death. Valuable knowledge, or so people believe, in this way goes missing: the last, most powerful line of the spell; the hidden magic stones; the bag of gold sovereigns all are lost. (Still, future dreamed rediscoveries always remain a possibility.)

In addition to budgeting revelations and the roundabout question, other ways of revealing but still keeping secrets include the public, but *silent*, performance of spells and songs. Crowe (1986:226) describes "mute" songs of northern Vanuatu. People observe a man singing to himself powerful songs that they are unable to overhear. Or they observe a magician working garden magic, but cannot hear his muttered spells.

Finally, we can note the conversational functions of nonsense. Valuable Melanesian knowlege, such as formulaic songs and spells and dreamed revelations, typically includes a lot of nonsense words. Much serious talk is semantically opaque (cf. Barth 1975:17; Lawrence 1964:90, 271; Schwartz 1962:251, 316, 389–390; Weiner 1986:114). Two of the words of the John Frum hymn that heads the following chapter, for example, are nonsense—*mhen parori*. The songsmith here also purposely included several English words ("okay," "paradise") that singers may or may not understand. People often refer to this nonsense, that sometimes consists of borrowed forms from neighboring languages, as the "speech of their ancestors." Many doctrinal songs include senseless words of this sort. If John Frum supporters yodel nonsense in their weekly Friday night meetings, so do Christians who are content to sing hymns in an alien English or French.

This opaque nonsense is an important discursive procedure that permits people to seem to be revealing their knowledge while maintaining its secrecy, privacy, and thus its continuing exchange value. Furthermore, nonsense takes on the symbolic function of signaling valuable knowledge. People suspect that nonsense, were it to be plumbed successfully, might actually reveal itself to be powerful information. As a corollary, they expect powerful knowledge to be difficult to comprehend. Bourdieu has noted the authoritative functions of nonsense elsewhere that can induce listeners to grant "the discourse (a lecture, sermon, political speech, etc.) sufficient legitimacy to listen even if they do not understand" (1977:649). Doctrinal spokesmen on Tanna often practice nonsense to this end. Nikiau, a 1940s John Frum leader, taught young people nonsense songs he claimed were in John Frum's language. This is mumbo-jumbo with exchange value. Discursive nonsense, like mute songs, roundabout questions, and budgeted revelation, permits a spokesman to circulate knowledge—in this case meaningless words—and at the same time maintain the secrecy of the revealed statement.

EXCHANGE

Two general sorts of discursive procedures regulate the revelation of secrets and the circulation of knowledge. These are practices that influence the times and places of knowledge exchange. Procedures of the first type protect the privacy of the statement, reproducing uneven patterns of knowledge distribution, by restricting the number of people who know. This sort of *narrowcasting* exchange ensures that a knowledge statement remains partially hidden. Procedures of the second type, conversely, *broadcast* the statement to a large number of auditors. By mechanisms of this latter sort, spokesmen deploy information widely about the island's information market.

Given Tanna's conversational mode of information, both broadcasting and narrowcasting procedures rely, in part, upon personal travel. Knowledge exchange requires that people come within at least bellowing or yodeling range of one another. More propinquitous interaction is required for the exchange of more detailed information (see Collins 1975:131–132). Tanna's geophysical landforms and the existing networks of traditional communicative "roads" shape the flow of information around the island, but so do discursive regulations on personal mobility. Those people endowed with greater rights to travel have more opportunities to spread serious talk, and to hear serious talk revealed.

In general, adult men have greater rights in personal mobility than do women and children. Ranges of travel for females are significantly narrower than those of males. Although women may produce valuable knowledge, deployment of that knowledge remains a problem for them. If a woman produces an important statement, some man often steps in to circulate this. Female dreamers or mediums provide the talk that empowers their more mobile husbands, brothers, or fathers. Nampas's original knowledge about John Frum's sons, for example, was produced by his daughter and niece who held hidden conversations with these spirit-boys under a banyan tree (Guiart 1956b:158–161). Thus men who enjoy greater rights to travel can appropriate and circulate female-produced messages for their own ends.

Narrowcasting

Exchange procedures that circulate knowledge privately restrict the range of statement transmission. Such exchanges prototypically involve a knower who communicates a statement to another person in private so that third parties are prevented from overhearing that information. Tannese use a lineal tropology, common throughout Melanesia, to represent metaphorically their narrowcast exchanges of knowledge (see also Yamamoto and Yamamoto 1985:177–182). Disciplinal knowledge passes from one namesake to another, from father to son, in a communicative exchange relationship islanders describe figuratively as a "vine" or "rope" (*kwanakwus*). A similar lineal metaphor represents narrowcast knowledge transmission through space. Spatial conversational exchanges follow "roads" (*suatuk*). Some of these roads actually exist—paths and trails through the forest that connect kava-drinking ground to kava-drinking ground; others are metaphorical only, describing some established knowledge exchange relationship between two men or two local groups.

The "road" is the basic, underlying blueprint for the restricted circulation of knowledge statements. Spatially, a road is a thin, sometimes hidden track through the forest. This narrow structure controls information exchange by lineally restricting its deployment. Those men who occupy the endpoints of an exchange road maintain the privacy of whatever information travels the line. A man's communicative contact or exchange partner at the far end of his road is, idiomatically, his "pupil" (*nipigi nenimen*, "eye hole") or his "bed" (*nimahan*). Roads that extend for any distance have a series of nodes. They are made up of successive pairs of communicative exchange partners. A man situated at some mediating point along the way has the power to facilitate or block the further transmission of passing messages. This man, as people sometimes have it, is a "gate"; a portal through which knowledge flows on its journey down one-dimensional structures of exchange that link two men or two places. As men look down their roads, their prospect along the way is one of lines of men: some have friendly eyes, others are obstructive gates (see Bonnemaison 1987:165). The John Frum hymn that sings of "teaching from the gate in the East" exploits this local understanding of narrowcast knowledge exchange, as have cargo movements elsewhere in Melanesia (e.g., Schwartz 1962:293).

A complex network of reticulated exchange roads criss-crosses Tanna (Bonnemaison 1984b, 1987:75, 171; Brunton 1979). A system of major, named information highways connects nodal kava-drinking ground to kava-drinking ground from one end of the island to the other. In the Southeast, a road named Kwaterhen follows the coast, Nimwatakeiv and Maininhupwi traverse the crests and upland ridges, and Takwarau leads north to White Sands. The first three of these are extensive. Running over much of the island, they link numerous kava-drinking grounds. Guiart traces Kwaterhen, for example, from Ituga on the northwest coast, round south to Kwamera, and up the east coast as far as Weasisi (Guiart 1956b:104–105).

Exchange roads regulate the flow of goods, people, and knowledge. People send along roads information about upcoming debates, marriages and other ceremonies, messages about group ventures, requests for labor assistance with copra making, invitations to string bands to come and play at dances, and reports to doctrinal leaders. Kava roots often accompany a transmitted message. Recipients prepare and drink this as they listen to the person who has arrived along a road to communicate a message.

At each locality, particular men inherit nomenclatural entitlements to positions of control along sections of those roads that link their kava-drinking ground to its neighbors. If one group desires to send a message to another, one of its members may possess the right to carry the statement along the linking road. He acts as group spokesman. If the two communicating groups are not adjacent, those men with the right to activate each portion of the intervening stretch of road must transmit the message, carrying it from point to point. If a mountain village wants a turtle from the sea, for example, the men at intermediate kava-drinking grounds, who control the flow of knowledge and information along the road, must convey the message in the middle reaches from the mountain to the shoreline.

An analogous circulatory device once regulated information transmission between the traditional island moieties. In those regions where people of both moieties were present, certain men possessed the nominal entitlement safely to pass war-related knowledge between the two sides, to transduce information between two segregated conversational loci. These were the *kout kasua*—men who controlled the right to "maintain a flow of information so that each side knew what the other was doing" (Brunton n.d.:8; see Guiart 1956b:94–95).

In the past, occupancy of nodal circulatory positions along the roads undoubtedly presented knowledge middlemen with considerable opportunities to control information deployment. Traditionally, warfare and local hostilities impeded individual mobility. People, today, state that ancestral namesakes did not travel a stretch of road controlled by others without their permission. The more travel was impeded by fear and hostilities, the greater the control of middlemen along the roads over circulation of information.

Today, road middlemen continue to protect their geographic qualifications to circulate messages (e.g., requests for a string band, or information about upcoming marriages). Those who control spatial narrowcasting take care to assert their rights to oversee the passage of goods or information down their roads. Men with rights to transmit information lineally from place to place are angered if some message sent between two points travels directly, circumventing the middle, or detours off the roads. If men of two distant villages exchange sisters in marriage, for example, middlemen along the way may demonstrate ritually their nomenclatural rights to sanction this transaction. At an exchange in which people transfer the woman from one group to another, her guardians lead her to the center of the kava-drinking ground. There, men in charge of middle stretches of road take her by hand and deliver her to her future husband's people, seated on the opposite side of the clearing. Those who control the roads also rest their hands on the heap of goods that accompanies the woman. This symbolizes their management of her passage along their roads.

In that the "road" is both metaphor for restricted circulatory practice and a description of the physical structure along which goods, people, and information flow, islanders often signify a disruption of satisfactory communicative relations by blocking linking roads. Tree-felling is a common political strategy that symbolically cuts the flow of goods and knowledge between groups. During electoral campaigns it is common to see a lot of trees felled across local roads. Fast-growing forest may quickly transform the symbolic closing of a road into a real one. Roads remain open only as long as people, carrying goods and information, continue to traverse them. As they pass, travelers constantly hack back vines and branches that threaten to overgrow the path.

Similar lineal structures govern the temporal narrowcasting of knowledge statements as well as the spatial. Here, exchange partners (father and son, or namer and named) are linked together through time as a family "rope" or "vine"—a temporal metaphor analogous to the topographic roads. The lineally restricted transmission of disciplinal knowledge of medicine, magic, and geography protects its secrecy. This reproduces the general pattern of disciplinal knowledge distribution in the conversational market as a whole.

In this manner, specialists protect the privacy of their knowledge as they transmit it to heirs, maintaining its cultural currency. Nɨkahi, for instance, who owns stones that guarantee pig fertility, works these stones periodically for the benefit of his neighbors. He is careful, though, not to reveal the stones' hidden location or associated magical techniques and accoutrements to anyone but his heir. In the same manner, a medical specialist provides medicines but maintains the privacy of his knowledge by keeping secret his recipes. Islanders exchange with others the products and services their knowledge contrives, but not the details of that technology itself. These they teach only to a "rope" of heirs.

In circulating secret knowledge, people thus encounter a discursive practice of roads and vines. This consists of an existing system of named, narrowcasting exchange routes in place, and an uneven distribution of personal rights to operate along stretches of these roads:

> while in other parts of [Vanuatu] physical roads may be used as an idiom for certain types of social relations . . . the Tannese have reified them into an inescapable system which largely predetermines all significant interaction. . . . There is an inflexible network of relations which prevents individuals or groups from creating or abandoning links as changing circumstances might otherwise dictate (Brunton 1979:101–102).

Even so, people can acquire additional opportunities to circulate information by cutting new roads. Cutting a conversational exchange road involves the discovery of some new knowledge exchange partner. Men can sometimes make new roads with an initial exchange of women or goods. Consumers of Prince Philip doctrinal knowledge several times have offered the Prince his choice of wife, hoping to widen their roads to him (Frater 1980:57).

Occasionally, islanders also write letters to tourists and other overseas sources, hoping to broaden a chance acquaintanceship, or to develop a new one (Bonnemaison [1987:447–448] provides one example). The letter, like a spatial road or a temporal vine, also serves to narrowcast information in order to keep this secret. It allows private access to the knowledge of external, authoritative sources. Like the John Frum letter cited above that was posted to a visiting anthropologist, Nampas's daughter also has attempted to get letters through to then President Ronald Reagan by passing these to an American priest.

I, too, relied on the letter in order to qualify myself fully to speak. My own road to Tanna was partly established by the meeting, at an academic conference in Sydney, of my thesis advisor and a Presbyterian missionary working on Tanna, both originally from New Zealand. Ultimately, I followed Christian roads into Tanna and was invited to live in Samaria, a Presbyterian hamlet. My hosts and new friends were closely related to people living in Iapiro, a neighboring village 500 yards away. A father in Samaria might have a son in Iapiro; and brothers in one village had sisters and brothers in the other. Although living in Samaria, I wanted also to talk with the people in Iapiro who I met daily along garden trails and at village kava-drinking grounds. Iapiro, however, was one of Sulphur Bay's 26 John Frum teams. For three months, although willing to engage in endless small talk, no one in Iapiro would tell me anything "serious" —including the information I needed for an economic survey I thought I was working on at the time.

John Frum leaders at Sulphur Bay had sent me to Coventry, or the Tannese version of such. They ordered the team not to talk with me. I was dangerous. If I were really an American, why was I living in Presbyterian Samaria and not in Sulphur Bay? That February, John Frum leaders had raised an American flag. This was the first time Sulphur Bay had shown its colors since 1957 when Nampas, home from exile, displayed his red U.S. Army danger flag to celebrate the end of government repression of the movement (see Bonnemaison 1987:485). The talk was of big things happening soon because of that new flag. Obviously, I was lying. I could not be a real American. No doubt, I was a useless Australian or perfidious New Zealander. This denial of my nationality solved the problem of my anomalous residence. Without an American geographic identity, I also forfeited valuable conversational qualifications.

I sent word to Sulphur Bay that I wanted to come down and explain my research and prove my nationality. The message came back: No, I could not come. And Samaria's Christian big-man ought to look out for himself, too. But my roads, in fact, did reach to America. I wrote my mother in California a letter asking for Stars and Stripes. When five of these of different sizes arrived, I pulled them out of the package, with a studied innocence, in front of my John Frum neighbors who were preparing our kava at the local drinking ground. A second message soon arrived from Sulphur Bay inviting me to visit. There, I managed to blame my anthropological teachers for my presence in a Christian village. If I had my choice, of course I would live at Sulphur Bay, but my chiefly professors demanded that I live out in the Nife language area which had yet to be studied. My real roads, therefore, were those of American academia, and not those of the Presbyterian Church. My apologies and my distortions of the exigencies of research, along with a display of my California State Driver's Licence, worked. My John Frum neighbors in Iapiro received permission from movement leaders to talk seriously with me. They also signed onto my yearlong economic survey.

No doubt, my clumsy excuses had less effect in unknotting my conversational problems than the increasing intensity of political competition during the two years that preceded national independence. This struggle focused Sulphur Bay's attentions on more important issues than myself. Still, demonstration of the efficacy of my personal roads to America, via the letter, proved my geographic identity and requalified me to converse seriously as an American. Flags appeared, and I could now talk.

In general, letters are an important means of acquiring information and other goods from distant sources. Like roads and vines, they are restrictive devices that transmit knowledge yet keep it secret, thereby sustaining a person's conversational resources for serious talk.

Broadcasting

Restriction of information circulation, from kava-drinking ground to kava-drinking ground, or from knower to heir, sustains the viability and privacy of a statement within Tanna's information market. A complementary set of local exchange procedures regulates the broadcasting of knowledge, working instead to deploy this extensively in island conversations. As opposed to secret disciplinal information, the conversational consequence of doctrinal knowledge depends on the extent to which it is diffused about the island. The successful deployment of this sort of information, in which people aim to publicize what they know and not keep it secret, makes cultural knowledge common.

Although it may be "only with the later phases of capitalism, with the development of a system of mass education, that the techniques of transmission of the dominant ideology become at all effective" (Abercrombie 1980:24), Tanna's mode of information at least approximates the broadcasting proficiency of mature capitalism. In this small island marketplace, gossip and other practices of information deployment match the effectiveness of the mass media within much larger, textualizing modes of information in spreading knowledge. A small example of local circulatory efficiency is the rapidity with which minor toy-making and game-playing innovations sweep through the island's information market. Children from all corners of Tanna, almost in concert, will all begin making toy trucks out of sticks and tin cans. Suddenly, these disappear as traditional panpipes are remembered and reappear in every child's hand. And these panpipes, in their turn, also vanish as some new form of toy floods the market.

Several institutionalized conversational forums supplement the constant background noise of gossip in spreading knowledge. These discursive events include traditional dispute settlement meetings that convene at kava grounds, the periodic masses and rituals of the doctrinal organizations, and also occasional "schools" and "courts" that leading spokesmen have organized. In these contexts for serious talk, islanders exchange and popularize knowledge face-to-face. Here, spokesmen take the floor to broadcast what they know.

The main forum to broadcast and debate traditional, disciplinal knowledge is the dispute-settlement, or decision-making meeting that takes place on kava clearings. In addition to dance, song, kava drinking, and ritual exchange, islanders come to kava clearings for serious talk. If in informal conversation, people begin to touch on hidden knowledge statements, they often move to continue their debate at the local kava ground. When a debate is convened, anyone interested comes to the clearing in order to hear what people say. This is often an audience drawn from several neighboring groups. During meetings, leading spokesmen have the opportunity to deploy and publicize their disciplinal and other knowledge widely and, if they wish, make this common.

Tanna's discursive structures of open kava-drinking clearing and narrow linking road together make up a topography of knowledge circulation. Some knowledge circulates secretly, narrowcast along lineal roads that snake through the forest, or in the private conversations between a knower and his heir. Other knowledge circulates publicly, broadcast from open clearings to a surrounding audience. Some of the circulating statements that people initially send along restricted lineal routes of information exchange are ultimately broadcast from the center of a kava clearing. In their land dispute with Iati and Nikahi, Uiuai and Rapi took the floor to reveal restricted secrets of this sort. Kava-drinking grounds are discursive loci for the public exchange of this kind of serious talk. Roads begin and end at kava-drinking grounds. It is here that the people, goods, and knowledge that follow restricted exchange routes arrive ultimately to be revealed.

The debates that people convene to contest what they know are themselves simply called "speech" or "talking" (nagkiariien). People in any locality may organize several of these a month, and they also attend other discussions convened by their neighbors. Talk begins mid-morning when participants arrive, and frequently continues until dusk when men disperse to prepare and drink kava. Debators seat themselves along those arcs of the kava clearing to which they have best rights—that part of the periphery where their own roads debouche. Women sit behind and to the side of male spokesmen, just inside the surrounding bush. As a man makes a statement, he stands and enters the center of the circle, delivers an opinion or makes a statement, and then returns to his seat on the periphery.

In debate, leading men speak for themselves. They may also speak for another person where clear relations of conversational inequality exist between the two. Typically, men represent women in that the latter have no discursive qualifications for public speaking at debate forums. Thus, for example, if a women desires or is asked to contribute a statement to a debate, her father or husband usually talks for her. Even if someone requests that a woman herself make a statement, some male spokesman may step in to represent what she knows to the audience. One debate participant, for example, suggested that a newly married woman, Tonga, herself explain her problems with in-laws:

Kua Toga in trini pam ro nuk-	Tonga should state her
wanen ua	thoughts [head]
mata in nah ko kimiaha nakur	but you big-men have gone
asori ihani mhuvin mhikurigi	and turned off the discussion.
tarini nagkiariien tukwe.	We don't know if that is her
Sareirei mua in naha iankwanen	opinion or not.
ua riuan.	Why not let her say all that is
Mata in trini pam rerin ua.	in her heart.
Sarakure mamo tingting me ira	The one sitting thinking there
mua manumamun mavahi ma	[Tonga] was agitated and came
maiu ti tauien.	running to brother-in-law.
Trini pam rerin ua, pwah saregi	Why not let her tell her feel-
pam.	ings, let us hear all.

A male proxy, however, responded instead to represent Tonga's head and heart for her:

Nari u niamaha u sarukurin	This thing, this anger, we all
pam niamaha u ua.	know this anger.

Further into debate, other male spokesmen also represented Tonga by broadcasting for her a statement of her desires:

Toga rokeikei savani iermama,	Tonga loves her husband,
nagkiariien kwana iakuvni raka.	as I have already said.
Rokeikei puk savani iermama.	She really loves her husband.
Ripikokeikei mha trata mwi blem	She doesn't want to see blame
riti naha ia nenimen.	in his eyes.

In ihi kwana i ro nakwai iema fwe:	It is according to the wisdom of the ancestors:
[SINGS] "Rerin rahua ira re-rinrau riti a."	"Wherever his heart is, there their hearts are one."
Nari kitaha nakur asori sano pam.	We big-men are through with this thing.
Iemanmirahar namwhen raka kwarana.	Three men, it is enough (debate).

This sort of conversational representation—in which one person broadcasts the statements of another—exhibits and maintains existing relations of communicative domination. In situations where lines of conversational inequality are less clear, spokesmen are more circumspect in representing in their statements another person's position (cf. Myers 1986). During debate, they may take note of the right of fellow participants to broadcast knowledge on their own and participate in serious talk:

Irau tripikrouagkiari, mata saiou me naha tipikni pam.	They two will make a statement later, but as for my [thoughts], I will explain.

Here, restrictions on representing a conversational equal's statements in debate parallel copyrights on the repetition or use of another person's disciplinal knowledge of geography, medicine, or magic.

In debate, broadcasting the statements of others demonstrates existing relations of conversational domination. In these relationships, speech and self-representation give way to silence and other-representation. By circulating other people's knowledge, local leaders represent their neighbors, fathers represent their households, and doctrinal leaders represent their congregations. These others, conceding their lack of qualifications to talk seriously, permit the powerful to represent and broadcast publicly what they know. In a discussion attended solely by co-residents of a kava ground, most men and perhaps even some women will speak. At larger debates, on the other hand, only those people who have acquired or entitled personal rights to broadcast knowledge dare to speak. Spokesmen represent the conversationally silent here.

In debate forums men may contend their personal qualifications to broadcast knowledge in serious talk. Some of the once silent, younger men particularly, here maneuver to improve their personal qualifications to claim the discursive function of "spokesman." The not-yet-qualified may venture to add a few words to a discussion, aspiring to the broadcasting competences enjoyed by older, experienced spokesmen. If a young man's audience accepts his first tentative words, through further statements he gradually enters into conversational exchange. In this regard, many qualified speakers will be sure to broadcast at a debate forum, even if their knowledge adds little of substance to the run of the argument. This gratuitous speaking asserts and maintains their acquired right to broadcast information. Thus, at any meeting, those men who have most successfully appropriated the conversational position of spokesman do most of the talking (Lindstrom 1981d:386).

An immature conversationalist employs a number of rhetorical strategies to induce others to listen to what he says, and to consider it serious. One of these strategies is to attempt a self-aggrandizing association with already known spokesmen. At the debate between Iati and Uiuai, for example, a younger man continuing his long effort to qualify himself fully to talk seriously so associated himself as he instructed Uiuai:

Na takwtakwnu naha irouarari	Now you two turn again to the
mwi ia store,	story,
na oke, sanaha namreirei naha,	but okay, no one knows what
namreirei.	you are talking about.
Iakani iakua kitaha nema asori	I say, with all we [inclusive]
ik tikvahi eraha niteta.	big-men, that you lead the
Na mregi niteta rikit na sairapw,	canoe [group] poorly.
ik atukw mwi a tikamisa ira.	Hearing the canoe creak we
Mata tukwo ikvahi amasan mo	take care of it,
amasan skelem i, mvahi pen	you too should help with this.
amasan narimnari me tukwe,	If you lead well, judge well, do

ko ikregi mregi ramarinu a	the right things,
mame.	then you find the waves are
	calm [good relations].

Those spokesmen currently in charge of broadcasting serious talk, in response, may attempt to maintain existing relations of conversational domination and representation by making the young silent again—by denying, in this case, the claim to be included with "all we big-men." The young speaker, here, was a Iakarui man who supported Iati because they recently had come to share a Christian doctrinal affiliation. After suffering through several such statements that contended his position, spokesman Rapi asserted himself to shut down further remarks by his classificatory son:

Na neruk nimikmiki nei ramara	Now my son, we all have
ia nimrhitaha pam.	motes in our eyes.
Mata flas nagkiariien ikni.	But your words are insolent.
Ikni nagkiariien naha, nagkiari-	You make statements, state-
ien naha reraha.	ments that are bad.
Mata ikrukurin ro ianhu i ka-	You know that this brings dis-
vahi kamumu mi niteta.	cord to the group.
Ikatirig tukwe, ko ikni	Consider this, if you speak
nagkiariien nah	thusly
nipin riti iou iakreirei mwi ik.	I may someday no longer
	know you.

Debaters may also dispute the qualifications of others to broadcast serious talk by challenging their copyright to the knowledge in question. During debate, Rapi and Uiuai were faced with a second potential challenge to their position. Kauke, although another Iakarui member, nevertheless was sympathetic with Iati's and Nikahi's claims to the garden plot. Rapi, however, managed to silence Kauke's talk by asserting his own closer relation to the ancestral source that had authorized the relevant geographic knowledge:

Kauke nah ramakure si, nari sai	Who is Kauke sitting there,
si nah?	whose is he?

Rakw paku naha mvehe mama-	Where did he come from to sit
kure?	here?
Kua iakni Souarim ro pam	I say Souarim [Rapi's grand-
narimnari.	father] accomplished every-
Ruvahi muvahi pen tata,	thing.
rarahi Napau, Napau rarahi in,	He told everything to father,
a.	father bore Napau, Napau bore
Nari saiou, iou bos Kauke	him [Kauke].
kurira.	This is my concern, I am the
Kauke trini nife nari savani?	boss, Kauke follows behind.
In rino nife nari?	What can Kauke state that he
No, no nari riuan, nari riuan ia	alone knows?
Kauke.	What can he do?
Kauke bihaen mi.	No, no there is nothing, noth-
	ing of Kauke's.
	Kauke is behind me.

Uiuai supported this silencing and Rapi's copyright over his grand-father Sourim's knowledge:

Kauke ko ripikni mha	Kauke cannot make a state-
nagkiariien riti.	ment.
Kauke ko ragkiari ia voes sai si?	Whose voice [knowledge]
Sai Souarim.	would he produce?
Rivi akeser ragkiari ia voes sai	Souarim's.
Souarim.	He slips if he speaks with
	Souarim's knowledge.

The opportunity to talk seriously within broadcasting forums allows the conversationally powerful to appropriate and represent the words of others. In so doing, they manage the organized circulation of common knowledge—or shared culture. Furthermore, they store debate consensuses in their memories and may, in the future, recall these to public mind. Given personal inequalities in access both to the discursive means and forums of statement circulation, and in qualifi-cations to take part in the making of public consensuses, those who dominate debate conversation also direct much of everyday discourse as well. Their serious talking during debate works to confirm and extend common knowledge. Although considerable numbers of people may attend a debate in order to take public decisions, the spokesmen who broadcast knowledge during kava clearing debates enunciate these joint decisions with the silent and de facto agreement of women, children, and ordinary men.

If disciplinal knowledge tends to circulate publicly during serious talk at kava clearings, spokesmen deploy doctrinal knowledge statements during the periodic assemblies of Christian, John Frum, and other island organizations. Both the Christian and John Frum regimes have established regular masses and ritual holy days. Christian villagers, on Sundays, and John Frum villagers, on Fridays, gather at their doctrinal headquarters to participate in weekly forums of knowledge circulation. Supporters come from scattered villages across the eastern part of the island. Some walk, to and fro, more than 20 miles for these observances. Regular events of this sort, at which the attendence of the faithful is required, are important contexts for serious talk in which spokesmen broadcast doctrine and other serious information. Knowledge exchange takes place during ritual itself, in the form of hymn, sermon, or prayer. It also takes place, more informally, both before and after the service. Sulphur Bay leaders, for example, often instruct their John Frum congregations the morning after all night Friday dances, before these people leave to return to their home villages (Bonnemaison 1987:495).

Another circulatory island forum at which spokesmen publicize and deploy doctrinal knowledge is the "school." This broadcasting forum differs from traditional debates in its establishment of even severer restrictions on who may speak. Although debates have a restricted participation, multiple and contrary voices are still heard there. In a school, on the other hand, the ruling conversational position is that of the teacher. Teaching—as a kind of answering—is thus a more powerful function than that of the traditional "debater" for the control of serious talk (see Borofsky 1987:97–100).

In contemporary island classrooms, a teacher's tutorial "questions," in fact, are usually a kind of rhetorical answer; they are attempts to elicit from students knowledge the tutor already has in mind. Where students accept the power relations implicit in classroom social relations, they may agreeably listen and respond to what a teacher has to say. Where classroom relations are more of an issue, however, students may attempt to escape the political implications of conversational exchange. Here is advice from one Melanesian student to his fellows regarding (in this case) European teachers:

> The European behaves as if he knows everything. . . . In class, do not answer the questions the teachers ask. There is no point in it; it would be a waste of time (Meek 1982:173).

Many Europeans came specifically to Tanna to circulate some body of exotic knowledge. Early traders, concerned with profit, depended on deploying knowledge of copra making and the significance of money after a supply of silver coins became available in the late nineteenth century. Similarly, missionaries arrived to teach Biblical knowledge. These overseas knowledge brokers also imported foreign statement circulation mechanisms from European modes of information. They established schools as a new forum to broadcast their knowledge. The Bislama word *skul* soon became synonymous with the church, and *man skul* with Christian. E. Macmillan, wife of the missionary at White Sands, wrote: "Indeed, the natives use the word 'school' where we would say 'church.' Those who attend church are spoken of as 'school people,' in contrast to the heathen" (1924:22). Government schools today continue the deployment of mostly Western knowledge, including Christianity.

Spokesmen of local doctrines have adopted this alien, circulatory forum that permits a new kind of discursive function—that of "teacher." Neloiag, leader of a 1940s John Frum organization in the north of the island, pretending to literary wisdom, established a school in which he instructed his followers (O'Reilly 1949:202). Given its powerful discursive utility, it is no accident that leaders of other Melanesian cargo cults have also borrowed the European "school" to broadcast their knowledge (cf. Lawrence 1964:89). More recently, a daughter of Nampas at Sulphur Bay has also convened a school. She teaches students to read and write a language she claims is John Frum's true tongue. Some of her students, at least, name this language *Tumorumo*. Her scholars write down in copybooks the statements she broadcasts during morning school sessions. The interpretation of this powerful nonsense is entirely hers alone, and not open to debate. Many of these statements take the form of song.

Although virtually everyone has access to at least some of the apparati of statement broadcasting—to gossip, particularly—access to others is subjectively more restricted. The practice of meetings and schools is such that many people lack circulatory competence to talk seriously in public. Only those who have acquired such personal qualifications are able, first, to organize a school or call a debate and, second, to broadcast much knowledge in these conversational forums. Island discourses of gender and age regulate who can broadcast meeting statements. Furthermore, only those people who are competent to travel to attend a debate or school have the physical opportunity to publicize what they know in serious talk.

In addition, discursive structures of debates and schools establish limits on the sorts of knowledge people may circulate. Local interests circumscribe the objects of dispute, and people bring only certain of these arguments to public debates. Similarly, only some kinds of knowledge fit into school curricula. Even so, if some new body of knowledge achieves conversational exchange value, its spokesmen can use the powerful circulatory practices of gossip, and perhaps the debate, the ritual mass, and the school as well, in order to deploy their message. At these institutionalized forums they broadcast to large audiences.

These discursive circulatory procedures, which regulate a knowledge statement's storage, distribution, and its broadcast or narrowcast conversational exchange, reproduce a pattern of both unshared and shared cultural knowledge around Tanna. They also establish personal inequalities in islanders' qualifications and opportunities to talk seriously. Tanna's conversational marketplace is rich with circulating knowledge. Not all of this, however, enjoys the same exchange value. A third set of island discursive practices make some knowledge easier to hear, some easier to "consume." They make some knowledge statements ring true, and others sound like lies.

5

Statement Consumption

Aue iou me nepwun	Alas my people
kamoraha kimaha	we are spoiled
ti nari imwamiaha ikin.	by things of your place.
Aue, aue **mhen parori**	Alas, alas **[opaque language]**
Maksim oke Pita oke oke	Maxim okay Peter okay okay
nagienien paradaes.	happiness paradise.

—John Frum Hymn

Times have been both good and bad for the John Frum doctrinal organization, and for its dogmatic competitors as well. Although its asserted knowledge has never completely cornered the island's information market, this has enjoyed high conversational exchange value, attracting large audiences. Not everyone buys the message, however. Some people reject this in favor of available alternatives. For them, gnawed pig bones carried out of an office become the stated sign of lies and foolishness, and not that of a hidden and wise American presence.

The reproduction of a particular mode of information depends critically on controlling the conversational value of available circulating knowledge. This management nourishes and sometimes engenders people's desires to "consume" certain serious knowledge statements, and organizes that consumption conversationally. Some islanders have access to and consume more knowledge than do others; and some interfere with or otherwise condition the knowledge that others consume.

Practices of knowledge consumption are both material and interpretive. Materially, people first must be in a position to receive a circulating knowledge statement in order to consume this. They must have access to the media of information flow and reception. They must, on Tanna, be able to hear. Second, conversational statements are not only heard; they are interpreted as well. They are "read," to use a metaphor from textual modes of information. A statement has no immanent meaning that listeners must discover; rather, people interpret a knowledge statement, and give this meaning and value, by situating it within wider cultural discourses (cf. Hall 1979:344–345). This is a sort of interpretive "cooking" that prepares raw circulating knowledge for consumption. Reproduction of Tanna's mode of information necessitates that adventitious or sinister knowledge be defused. Dangerous statements must be trivialized or edited. Discourse control procedures of selection, editing, and validation work to convert circulating knowledge into a form that islanders might comfortably, and harmlessly, consume.

Listening consumers, of course, interpret for themselves the knowledge statements they hear, but much knowledge is, in a sense, precooked. Unequal conversational opportunities and qualifications permit some people to manage a good deal of the selection and editing of shared island culture for public consumption. Those who are favorably situated by the discourse control procedures that regulate knowledge production and circulation also have more conversational opportunities to interpret and validate the statements that islanders consume.

Where discourse control procedures of editing and silencing operate most successfully, one set of knowledge statements that comes to dominate the information marketplace may achieve hegemony. Its producers and circulators, capturing and cooking the truth, manage to silence or edit all rival knowledge. A discourse hegemony is born within a mode of information in which conversational control procedures operate so efficiently that only dominant knowledge statements are audible. Here, there is a "'spontaneous' consent given by the great masses of the population to the general direction imposed on social life by the dominant fundamental group" (Gramsci

1971:12). A conversational hegemony "holds together a specific social group, it influences moral conduct and the direction of will"
(1971:333). Moreover, beyond the shaping of individual conduct and
will, hegemonically deployed knowledge feeds back to influence subjective desire. People's questions, in part, come to depend on ruling
answers.

During the past century on Tanna, several doctrinal discourses
have achieved a near-hegemonic monopoly of the island's information marketplace. These orthodoxies include the Christian Tanna Law
of the early colonial period, and John Frum's America Law of the
more recent past. Within regimes of truth of this sort, the powerful
maintain and reproduce their conversational positions and functions
by managing the material and the interpretive requirements of cultural consumption.

HEARING

In a conversational mode of information, communication retains its
original double meaning: a circulation of both messages and mes-
sengers. Island vocal/aural technologies of information transmission
require consumer presence. Because of this, one can censor conversational exchange by constraining personal mobility. In the island's
mode of information, statement consumption is hearing and, to hear,
a person must move physically into a materially determined range of
audibility. Local travel restrictions thus control individual opportunities for knowledge consumption, as they do also opportunities for
knowledge circulation and production.

Consumer presence signals the reception of a message in a second, more symbolic sense. Physical presence signifies people's conversational and political alliances, their support and engagement
with a social group. People mark the fact of their membership in a
group, and their ascription to that group's knowledge and points of
view, by attending events at which group knowledge is revealed,
discussed, and circulated. At the neighborhood level, daily presence
at a kava clearing, or in a residence group, testifies to a man's ac-
knowledgement of village leaders and the local wisdom.

Presence symbolizes a person's willingness to hear—to take part
in communicative relations of inequality, consuming the statements

produced and circulated in local conversational forums. If people desire knowledge that others control, they are attracted to participate in the events that deploy such knowledge, whether these are debates, ritual assemblies, or schools. Presence both permits access to circulating statements, and evinces a person's acceptance of attendant relations of conversational exchange. Those present in a village or at kava ground debates consume the knowledge and public consensuses of local leaders; those present at ritual assemblies and school forums consume the wisdom of doctrinal leaders.

Conversely, a withdrawal of physical presence has an opposite symbolic value. Absence signals the termination of knowledge consumption and, therefore, the severing of relations of conversational exchange. If a person no longer supports a group, or finds himself in conflict with its members, he avoids forums in which group knowledge is broadcast. People may refuse to live with local leaders if they come to doubt their wisdom. A person's withdrawal beyond hearing range breaks local conversational relations, and may also provide him access to some rival locus of knowledge statement circulation. Although a man's name—his geographic subjectivity—accords him a proper place of residence, he may choose instead to live elsewhere in order to take part in alternative conversations.

In the early days of the Christian regime of truth, missionary Frank Paton noted of one homecoming convert: "When Iakar came they did not want him, but as he was one of the owners of the land they could not prevent him from settling among them" (1903:205). Most of the small villages of southeast Tanna still tend toward doctrinal homogeneity. People generally avoid living with others who subscribe to different truths. If they are confronted by a co-resident's anomalous consumption of rival knowledge, they may physically withdraw in order to avoid talking seriously with him, and to avoid hearing his statements. This sort of retreat occurred at Iakar's return home:

> His tribe are bitterly opposed to the Worship, and with the exception of Siak and his family, not one of them would have anything to do with him. In fact, as they could not drive Iakar out, they left the village themselves. Lomai asked them where they could go to escape the Worship, as it was now all over Tanna (1903:237).

Withdrawal of physical presence also marks other conversational disagreements besides the doctrinal. In the heat of some village argument, one party may grab a faggot from a fire and rush off to burn down his house. Satig, enraged by her brother's criticism, for example, once had to be grappled to the ground as she tried to set her house on fire. Torching one's house is an icon of co-residential discord, as well as a person's manifest disengagement from a village conversational locus.

Schwartz, in his analysis of the Paliau movement on Manus, observed a similar Melanesian equation of hearing, knowledge consumption, and acceptance of conversational relations of inequality: "Paliau in his speeches stressed the principle of 'hearing the talk.' 'Hearing the talk' meant discipline and obedience" (1962:263). On Tanna, a man's presence at doctrinal events, such as Friday John Frum rituals, or Sunday Christian masses, likewise signals his willing consumption of circulating knowledge statements, by virtue of his participation there in conversational relations of doctrinal exchange. Those people, contrarily, who deny the authority of some body of doctrinal knowledge shy away from the forums (debates, doctrinal events, schools) in which they suspect those statements will be broadcast. Some leaders of Christian organizations have not been to Sulphur Bay in decades, although they live only a ridge away. They thus avoid being unwilling participants in some unwelcome knowledge exchange. They negate by their absence doctrinal truth claims, and also the conversational authority of knowledge producers.

Bonnemaison (1987:555) provides a description of a case of doctrinal avoidance by means of conspicuous silence, a discursive strategy that is typically Tannese. This strategy allows two sides to get along with the business of whatever needs to be done together, while each maintains a posture of disengagement from the political wisdom and doctrinal associations of the other. The refusal to listen and thus to consume knowledge is here absolutely clear. Some John Frum supporters of Ituga village, as they customarily should, invited their kin from a neighboring hamlet to celebrate the naming of a child by drinking kava together and spitting the dregs to inform local ancestors (a ritual act of ancestral communication called *tamafa*). These neighbors, however (the mother's brothers of the child named that day), were supporters of the Vanuaaku Party, not John Frum. Nevertheless, one of these men must spit a *tamafa* message of support to the ancestors after the father has revealed the child's name. Bonnemaison describes the two sides exchanging roots of kava, preparing and drinking the drug, spitting *tamafa*, and leaving several hours later for home hamlets—all without a word being exchanged between the two opposed doctrinal camps.

During electoral campaigns, similarly, political party leaders convene rallies at which they frequently address only the already committed (Lindstrom 1982a). For example, at one such rally that the leaders of the Vanuaaku Party purposely convoked in a village inhabited by supporters of the Moderates, campaigners arrived to find the place deserted. Its residents had fled south to their own hastily scheduled conclave in order to avoid hearing rival political statements, and participation in distasteful conversational exchange.

By arranging his presence or absence at those events and forums where knowledge circulates, a person can regulate his consumption of statements, and his position within local conversational orders. Conversely, the conversationally powerful attempt, where possible, to restrict personal mobility (of women, of children, of the faithful) in order to hinder their consumption of rival knowledge, so to protect existing discursive regimes of truth. During the nineteenth century, in this fashion, pioneer missionaries attempting to deploy Christian knowledge often had hotly to pursue elusive islanders. They had a tough time attracting an audience. Given the symbolic importance of presence in conversational modes of information, a polite but noncommittal attendence on someone else's words is less an option than it is in the West. To reject fully any message, the locally correct response is to run away. These nineteenth century island truants were newfangled "traditionalists" attempting, by putting themselves out of hearing, to avoid emerging relations of conversational domination, as the Tannese today continue to avoid rival political rallies. Mrs. Watt describes doctrinal didactic tactics:

> [Matthew] is a most faithful itinerant preacher; and when lately he and our cook went to hold a service inland at a new village, and only saw the backs of the fleeing people, he followed them. Meanwhile the fugitives had laid a barrier of wood on the way, warning them not to go beyond. When he came to it he gave a look to his neighbour and said, "Let us be strong and go." They removed the

obstruction and walked on. When they reached the public square they found all the men gathered inside the kava-house. One entered at one door and the other at the other, and so cut off all way of escape. The fugitives, feeling safe from all interruption, seeing they had laid down the barricade, which they judged sufficient to deter the preachers, had gone into the kava-house to rest and twist their hair. Fancy their amazement when these two men confronted them! Neither party spoke for a considerable time, and the fugitives looked very angry, but Matthew broke the silence by saying, "We are ready to die if you like to kill us, but we are come here to have Worship." One, more hardened than the rest, replied, "You cannot have worship here, and hinder us from getting on with twisting our hair. You drove us out of our own village, and now you follow us here." The silence thus broken down, Matthew discoursed on the vanity of all earthly things; especially what was purely heathenish. The result was, worship was conducted, although some showed ill-feeling by refusing to close their eyes during prayer. They asked Matthew what he meant by thus hunting them; did he mean to drive them to the other side of the island? It is a common thing on Tanna when you arrive at a village to see numbers vanish into the bush rather than endure worship (1896:289–290).

The silence thus broken down, the conversation began.

Given the conversational nature of discourse on Tanna, people pursue other strategies—besides disengagement, refusing to close one's eyes, and withdrawal of presence—to avoid knowledge consumption, and the communicative ratios of inequality this consumption sustains. Some resistant tactics work by causing "noise" in the material channels of information transmission. Mary Matheson, with her husband John a missionary at Imoa from 1858 to 1862, despaired of the failure of one attempt at Christian broadcasting:

They could not hear either the voice of prayer or of praise, owing to the fiendish yells of our enemies and the incessant noise which they kept up by chopping and beating with their clubs upon trees, old logs, etc. (Patterson 1864:493; see Adams 1984:121).

Similarly, when McLeod attempted itinerant preaching to John Frum supporters in 1945–1946, he discovered "there was always a great deal of spitting during these services" (1951:6)—spitting that would both reaffirm people's restatement of the truth about ancestral authority during the early John Frum years, and their desire not to hear Christian knowledge. An earlier anti-Christian ploy, noted above, was the burial of Christian texts. For a time, resistant traditionalist spokesmen stymied the consumption of Christian knowledge by insisting that people bury the pamphlets and translations the missionaries were attempting to deploy within Tanna's conversational marketplace. One can occasionally evade relations of conversational domination in this fashion, by disrupting the media of information transmission and restoring a silence of a sort.

When people *desire* to consume knowledge statements, and not abstain, they may nonetheless not occupy the necessary discursive positions to do so. Similarly, there are patterned inequalities in the number of statements and in the content of knowledge any person can hear. To consume culture, in addition to personal opportunities to travel, and access to clear audio channels, an islander must also command the skills required to decode linguistically encoded messages. Island speakers phrase statements in several locally available languages. Depending on one's measure of linguistic boundaries, the Tannese speak from three to six indigenous languages and supplement these with Bislama, English, and French.

A given mode of information reproduces itself through time inasmuch as educative practice both advances and limits individual access to requisite linguistic and other decoding skills. Those people who have a weaker command of one or another of the island's languages depend on linguistically informed conversational middlemen in order to hear some of the encoded knowledge that circulates in the information marketplace. In textualizing modes of information, similarly, "large cleavages" exist in the social appropriation (or consumption) of statements (Foucault 1981:64). Inequalities in personal access to education, and to knowledge of decoding skills, maintain these invidious cleavages.

On Tanna, apart from the colonially imported languages, linguistic education is not institutionalized. People learn local languages as they do any other available body of information on the island. Informal, perceptive learning practices, however, also work to reproduce certain personal inequalities in linguistic ability. Those men who travel widely to attend debates and other knowledge broadcasting forums frequently cross the island's linguistic boundaries. Many adult men are thus actively or passively multilingual (see Lindstrom 1983). Other islanders, less subjectively qualified to travel, have fewer linguistic skills. Most older women, for example, have an inferior command of Bislama, compared to men and younger women who have enjoyed greater opportunities to interact with linguistic outsiders.

Those people without linguistic decoding skills lack the requisite knowledge to consume directly some of the statements that spokesmen circulate at debates and doctrinal events. Although they may be present at a broadcasting forum, to the extent that the statements circulating there are coded in a language they do not know, their opportunity to converse is impaired. Their access to circulating knowledge is thus often indirect. They depend on the mediation of others who provide for them knowledge translations, or "restatements." Similarly, in the case of imported, alien knowledge coded in English or French (languages the recently educated young more commonly command), older islanders depend, for their consumption, on the mediation of these younger translators.

Restrictions on travel, educationally patterned personal abilities in linguistic decoding skills, and differential access to and control of clear channels of information transmission bring into being hearing inequalities within the local mode of information. These consumption control procedures limit a person's conversational scope. Not everyone possesses equivalent qualifications and opportunities to hear, or to otherwise receive circulating knowledge statements. If those people whose access to the information market is in some way impeded desire to learn, they must listen to others who possess greater conversational opportunities. Because of their personal rights to travel or their linguistic faculties, those islanders who can hear are also empowered to mediate, translate, and possibly restate knowledge statements for popular consumption. Spokesmen who have attended some broadcasting forum, and have heard the statements deployed therein, for example, usually take the opportunity to restate what they have heard on their return to home villages and kava clearings. This restatement enacts at least temporary inequalities within local conversational relations; primary statement consumers instruct the stay-at-home and the linguistically ignorant.

These are conversational inequalities both in hearing and in personal abilities to decode or restate the meaning of what is heard. Unequal hearing results from differential personal access to the information market, and to the statements circulating therein. Those people who lack such access can only hear if they conversationally relate with more successful knowledge consumers. These consumers, the conversationally "rich," repackage knowledge for further exchange with the interested "poor."

A second sort of inequality in knowledge consumption is differential personal management of "received" statement meaning. This inequality adheres less in knowledge reception (everyone in a conversation may, in fact, hear the same statement) than in the determination of an authentic public hearing. This is an interpretive rather than a repetitive restatement of knowledge. Beyond simple translations, the powerful also dominate conversation by *editing* the knowledge that others consume.

EDITING

As Raymond Williams has noted, "editing" is not only a matter of excision and selection:

> New positive relations of a signifying kind can be made by the processes of arrangement and juxtaposition, and this can be true even in those unusual cases in which the original primary units are left in their original state (1980:60).

Although Williams is principally concerned with the electronic media of knowledge circulation, editing procedures exist as well within modes of information in which the "original primary unit" is the spoken statement. Editing control procedures affect both statement *interpretation* (by means of arrangement, juxtaposition, and restatement) and statement *selection* (by means of evaluation and censorship). As such, some of the knowledge statements that people consume have been "transformed by further intermediate labour, in which the primary communicative means have become material with which and on which another communicator works" (Williams 1980:60).

The Tannese follow a number of obvious editorial strategies to package knowledge for public consumption. Although the primary statement unit may be itself unaltered, producers can arrange and shape the context of stating. They may improve or depreciate the exchange value and authority of a knowledge statement by regulating the timing of its formulation; by selecting for it an advantageous enunciatory position within a statement sequence; by providing, in addition, a further statement of its authorizing source as well as the speaker's own qualifications to know; or by assuming an appropriate and expected conversational demeanor, posture, tone, code, and channel.

Here is the importance of oratorical eloquence within conversational modes of information. The importance of grandiloquence, haranguing, and stump oratory has often been noted in societies throughout Melanesia (see, for example, Brenneis and Myers 1984). Fine words add value to statements. If the form of a knowledge statement excites an interest to hear, it entices people to listen and consume its content. Serious talking is thus often shamelessly seductive, although this conversational courtship may take different forms, given the polymorphous stylistic desires of people within different modes of information (for example, see Rosaldo 1973:222). Some truths require plain speaking. Others parade in a shimmery fancy dress of ostentatious metaphor. Tannese debaters, in this regard, often pose their statements in attractive figures of speech in order to capture and seduce hearers. Some examples from the debate statements presented in earlier chapters include metaphoric descriptions of knowledge as a *hat*, as *voes* (voice), and as *paoa* (power); the figurative representation of good relations as "calm seas"; the claim to a leading spokesman position phrased as "to speak the banyan tree here"; and so on. Insofar as this rhetorical manipulation of the shape and context of a knowledge statement informs its content, spokesmen propose how knowledge consumers ought appropriately to take what they say.

A second, more consequential, form of conversational editing that affects knowledge consumption is the restatement of primary statements. Here, primary units are *not* left in their original produced state, whether figuratively dressed up or not. This sort of editing is different from that "self-editing" that occurs at the moment of statement production. (In conversational discourse where people orally formulate and repeat primary statements, people self-edit as they speak.) Rather, this is conversational "other-editing." Once a primary knowledge statement exists in the information market, powerful conversationalists appropriate this to give it some secondary hearing. They produce "commentary" around it, and so provide listeners an interpretative restatement. This triadic structure of knowledge stater, knowledge editor, and knowledge consumer, here, recalls Tannese patterns of knowledge production, in which a spokesman mediates between an external authority and an audience. In this case, however, editors restate what other *people*—and not their dreamed ancestors—have said. They represent others in serious talk. The conversational powers of this editorial discursive position are even more obvious than that of the inspired spokesman.

Editorial commentary is a discourse control procedure that, in rephrasing circulating knowledge statements, works to sustain existing ratios of conversational domination, although perhaps not always the details of some knowledge content itself. In restatement, this content may slip (see Barth 1987:30). In textual Western discourses, commentary repeats what is already known, and thereby rehearses a discourse's constituative knowledge statements. It smooths out chance inconsistencies within the already known, and inhibits the emergence of alternative knowledge out of internal discursive contradictions (Foucault 1981:57–58).

But commentary's function in Tannese discourse is inverted. Although islanders comment voluminously within their disciplines and doctrines, these comments go beyond mere repetition and rehearsal of core knowledge statements. In repeating knowledge, they often revise, rather than reproduce, this: "Each reciter is an author, though some are more creative than others" (Goody 1977:29). No material text exists that might freeze the content of knowledge, or anchor this content to some essential sameness the secret of which commentary attempts to unravel. Instead, every comment potentially restates. Like the game in which a child at one end of a line invents a statement, and whispers this into his neighbor's ear, who whispers it into that of the next, and so on until the end of the line, commentary on Tanna functions to restate discourse, not repeat it. John Frum's original statements of customary revival, for example, in his spokesmen's commentaries, have now been stretched so far as to condemn today's disco clubs.

Editorial opportunity (access to the discursive function of "editor," and to editorial control procedures such as commentary) is restricted. In the main, only those people who already enjoy personal rights to produce and circulate knowledge within serious talk have much opportunity to edit circulating, primary statements for public consumption. They already command an audience of knowledge consumers. The conversationally dominated, on the other hand, possess fewer opportunities to externalize or inflect the public meaning (hearing) of primary knowledge statements—even those statements they themselves produce.

Statements coded in an opaque language, such as (*mhen parori*), a portion of the song that heads this chapter, particularly invite secondary editorial commentaries. As discussed in Chapter Four, an opacity of language characterizes many traditional island songs. Some of this nonsense, singers claim, is the language of their ancestors. People attribute other nonsense words to the languages of neighboring or distant lands. Gray, the first missionary at Weasisi, noted: "A native, we know, readily uses the preformatives of his own dialect with the stem root words of another dialect. I have found these corruptions and foreign words in all native songs I have examined" (1894:43; see Bonnemaison 1987:356). Malinowski, encountering similarly senseless words in Trobriand Island garden spells, described this problem as "the meaning of meaningless words" (1935:213).

Semantic opacity in songs, and in other more prosaic knowledge statements, accords spokesmen a conversationally powerful editorial function. Those pundits who decode nonsense statements, that they or others produce, prescribe their public meanings. Thus, Malinowski relied on a "wise" informant who interpreted the semantic blanks in a number of Trobriand Island garden spells: "In some formulae we are able to translate the words clearly and satisfactorily after our magically illumed commentator has given us their esoteric meaning" (Malinowski 1935:219). To interpret Gnau songs, Lewis relied on senior men who "would give the statement of what the verse was about with fair confidence, and then after that, in response to further questions, say what particular words they could interpret" (1980:60; see also Barth 1975:17; Codrington 1891:335–336; Fortune 1932:257–258). Consumers depend on these editorial readings (that is, hearings) in order to achieve some understanding of the songs they sing, and the spells they utter.

On Tanna, conversational editors either themselves may produce opaque statements, or they may appropriate nonsense statements enunciated elsewhere, in order to provide hearings. Nikiau's senseless songs of the early John Frum period, and Nampas' daughter's new nonsense language she teaches to her scholars both furnish material for interpretive editing and restatement. In particular, partially opaque doctrinal songs, such as the following two, one of which chronicles the recently deployed name of John Frum's language, *Tumorumo*, provide this kind of opportunity for conversational exegesis:

Semsemu man Amerika	Semsemu [a local spirit] is an
Hawaii Honolulu	American
Hawaii Honolulu	Hawaii Honolulu
Semsemu man Amerika	Hawaii Honolulu
oriorau e oriorau e.	Semsemu is an America
	[nonsense].
Iou Tomi Timi	I Tommy Jimmy
kaoboe Tina	okay okay
oke oke	[nonsense].
uel Tumorumo	
iso soera tieni tenama.	

Those people who are conversationally situated to produce secondary restatements of opaque primary statements rehearse both specific and general cultural knowledge. This commentary maintains the viability of cultural claims and propositions that circulate within the island's information market, and also supports existing ratios of conversational domination.

Conversational pundits edit other circulating statements besides the referentially opaque. These statements may be dreamed messages that a person takes to a "clever" for a hearing. Clevers sometimes can provide interpretations of particular troubling or notable dreams. More commonly, editors go to work on statements that are circulated by gossip, or broadcast at more public forums, such as a doctrinal school or assembly. John Frum songsmiths from across Tanna produce new cult hymns; but doctrinal leaders at Sulphur Bay reserve the right to edit these songs before they are publicly performed (Wilkinson 1979:192). Powerful editors select among and interpret other people's primary statements.

Perhaps the most important, and the most institutionalized, edi-

torial position within island conversation is that which people nowadays label debate "witness" (or, alternating their oral stops, "wik-
ness"). Although repetitive copyrights and representative limitations
on speaking for others protect some circulating knowledge from editorial appropriation, qualified spokesmen who witness a debate are
able to restate many of the statements broadcast in serious talk there.
Witnesses edit for public consumption the debate statements that
others formulate. They restate some of the knowledge enunciated by
those people with less personal qualification than themselves to
mean what they say. Although any knowledge statement may invite
a number of private, possible readings (hearings), the powerful editorialize how this is to be understood in serious, public conversation.
Powerful editors also manage the production of a summary debate
statement that, if all has gone well, enunciates the larger consensual
agreements achieved by the day's talk.

When people meet to debate a conflict, a decision, or a public
stance or interpretation, those men who attend to witness this serious
talk speak little until the end of the day. If they take to their feet in the
early going, it is usually to admonish or to instruct other speakers in
conversational custom and decorum. This speaking demonstrates both
their knowledge and their conversational power so to admonish; here,
they answer unasked questions. When discussion climaxes, powerful
witnesses rise to their feet to enunciate their hearing of the general
sense of the meeting (see also Brenneis 1984:75; Firth 1975:42;
Goldman 1983:172; Lederman 1984:97; Weiner 1983:163).

The parties who convene a debate may invite particular witnesses from neighboring groups, or a person may on his own volunteer editorial commentary that restates the knowledge statements
deployed in debate. In the land dispute between Uiuai and Iati, at
which neutral parties were scarce, for example, one man in this
fashion nominated himself to witness ("judge"):

Oraet kimri jaj me nepwun	All right, one should appoint
hakure mhakiri nagkiariien.	some judges to sit and weigh
Mhakiri nagkiariien sakimirau	the debate.
mhata poen sakimirau	Weigh the debate of you two
mua sapaku poen rasori si poen	to determine
savani rouihi.	whose position is strong (large)

In nah tukwata amwhen ia and whose is weak (small).
kwopun nah. This is what we will determine
Mhata reraha u kitaha pam sav- here.
ehe mhagkiari mhagkiari ianhu It is wrong for all of us to
mua si nah tro jaj? come and talk
Nagkiariien ro ianha i. for who will judge?
Na hatui nermama nepwun Debates are like this.
iraha hakure. One should appoint some people to sit back (and witness).

Witnesses are invariably mature spokesmen who have secured, over time, numerous relations of conversational inequality with knowledge consumers. If a debate aims to resolve a dispute, each side may bring along witnesses it knows are sympathetic to the knowledge statements it asserts. The editorial discursive function, however, demands that witnesses assert an apparent impartiality for their commentary:

Sore iakamagkiari ahavin Sorry I am interrupting the
nagkiariien naha debate
mata iahakure u rerim ro ting but we perceive your feeling
ianhu mua kimaha wan saed sai that we are all on Uiuai's side
Uiuai naha takwtakwnu iahamo as we judge.
jaj. No it isn't thus.
Rekim ripiko mha ro ianha i. A custom meeting's fashion is
Kastom miting iti wei savani thus:
naha ro ianha i: we sit and weigh your two
tahakure mhata amwhen poen positions.
sakimirau me ianha i ua. It isn't that we only support
Na ripiko mha iahavahi apa ti Uiuai there.
Uiuai naha. We are here for both sides.
Saed saed peri mi nah
iahamakure minrau nah.

A second self-selected witness supported this spokesman's claim to editorial impartiality:

Pwiak mi tika rerinrau rirhi	My two younger brothers
mua iakvehe mua takasitu ia	might think that I come to
Uiuai mua takasitu ia kimirau,	help Uiuai or I come to help
mata iakvehe mua takatirig ia	you two,
nagkiariien sakimirau.	but I come to listen to the talk
	of both of you.

Importantly, the enunciation of debate consensuses requires an editorial voice. Someone must state what the emergent decision is in order to make this public—in order to circulate an authoritative version of meeting results within the island's information market, and store this in people's memories. Here, the powerful do represent and speak for silent women, children, and conversationally insignificant men, who rarely talk, and even more rarely editorialize during public meetings.

Summary editorial commentary of this sort "externalizes" conversationally produced meaning, in Berger and Luckmann's sense of the term: "Human existence is, *ab initio,* an ongoing externalization. As man externalizes himself, he constructs the world *into* which he externalizes himself. In the process of externalization, he projects his own meanings into reality" (1967:104). Inequalities of access to Tanna's discourse control procedures of editorial commentary, however, contrive inequalities among socially constructed meanings. Some externalized knowledge statements project more social meaning than do others, insofar as they dominate an information market. This is a conversationally unequal social construction of reality.

In addition to the summary, general sense of a debate, witnesses also editorialize many of the singular statements produced and circulated there by other people, especially if a statement's content touches on disciplinal or doctrinal knowledge. This representation is more than merely speaking for a silent other. Here, a witness edits a knowledge statement already broadcast for public consumption. For example, after an unusual statement an elderly woman produced in defense of a classificatory granddaughter, her son stepped in and hastened to edit her words:

Pwah iakni sanaha iakni sanaha	Let me say this, explain a little
kwopti sanaha rini.	about what she said.

He then proceeded to give a restatement about how his mother's statement ought publicly to be consumed.

Editorial commentary of this sort "exorcises the chance element of discourse by giving it its due" (Foucault 1981:58). Those commentators who are personally qualified to edit other people's talk help reproduce the existing mode of information by explaining away or accounting for any untoward statements. If women or other of the powerless produce some alternative, perhaps dangerous, knowledge statement that stands outside of admitted cultural truths, commentators edit these statements for public consumption. This restatement effectively censors or trivializes the statements of those people with less discursive qualifications to mean what they say.

The editing of single statements, or of the received (that is, heard) meaning of larger conversational events such as public debates, thus rehearses much of shared culture. The summary commentary of those editors who witnessed the land dispute between Uiuai and Iati, in addition to restating the final consensus of the meeting as a whole, also refreshed a number of locally known truths. One witness, for example, commented on the shared ethic of reciprocity:

Irau krouo lida ti narimnari me	They two lead everything
ianha ira.	about it [control the land].
Rouen a takwtakwnu krouni mua	They now say that you two
kimirau tirouaraka ia kwopun	must give up that land plot.
naha.	All right, it goes over there.
Oraet ruvahi pen safwe.	Now in my opinion,
Na kini ia saiou tingting,	because they say you must
iakata amwhen ira mua krouni	leave that place, give up the
mua tikier naha ia kwopun	plot,
naha, tirouier naha ikin,	they two have injured you
irau trouo nari riti rifam ruvahi	[given you something heavy].
pen mi kimirau.	They once told you that land
Mata in nah in nah irau krouni	was yours.
a imwam imwam naha ia	They should remedy their be-
kwopun naha. Na trouo nari	havior,
naha ia tafaga nah savanrau	they lied to you.

kirmini,	Now that they say you must
rouekua ianram.	get out,
Takwtakwnu naha krouni mua	they must give you something.
tikier,	
irau trouakeikei rouo nari riti	
rouvahi pehe mik.	

A second witness, similarly, called to public mind the recent revaluation of local traditions (*kastom*):

Mata savahi saed sai kastom ro.	Let us follow custom.
Kastom ruvni nife nari mua tro;	Custom has told us what to
kimirau irouatirig i.	do;
Mata kua samagkiari takwtak-	you two think about this.
wnu ia saed savai jif me mine ka-	Now we debate according to
stom.	the fashion of chiefs and
Kastom ravahi majoriti ti noien	custom.
nari riti mwi.	Custom governs the majority of
Rini pehe nagkiariien riti ti	what to do once again.
kitahar.	It speaks to us three.

Editorial commentaries restate disorderly and sometimes dangerous statements and bend these so that they support ruling discourse, or so that they at least make sense in its terms. Tanna's witnesses and other editorial discursive functions reflect and maintain interpersonal inequalities in people's rights to mean what they say.

In addition to interpretive commentary and restatement of broadcast knowledge for public consumption, conversational editors also sort, evaluate, and select among the knowledge statements a local information market has in stock. The discourse control procedures that regulate cultural production and circulation rarely contrive to censor completely all alternative and resistant knowledge. Those obdurant statements that manage to break through productive and circulatory barriers, however, encounter further discourse control procedures that limit and constrain their public consumption. Here, editing attempts to assign different conversational exchange values to statements in order to predispose knowledge consumption patterns. A primary knowledge statement often carries, alongside, parasitic secondary commentary, provided by island editors. This aims either to advance or depreciate its conversational exchange value. Although islanders may, in fact, hear a number of alternative or rival knowledge statements that circulate within the island's information marketplace, evaluative commentary makes many of these statements unattractive by distorting or disguising their message. These statements are harder to listen to, and harder to hear.

To some ears, island doctrines appear to entertain a hodgepodge of belief: Christians evoke ancestral authority; John Frum supporters discuss the significance of Jesus and Noah; traditionalists speak of the coming millennium; the island's educated avant-garde publicly expresses doubts about economic modernity. Nonetheless, local doctrines, although perhaps less given to totalitarian extremes than our religions and sciences of the textualizing West, still attempt to depreciate, explain, and thus encompass alternative and resistant knowledge. Most islanders would do away with heterodoxy if they could. People are not wholly comfortable with heterogeneous doctrinal truths (see Bonnemaison 1987:625). The existence of heterodoxy signals the existence of competing nexuses of conversational domination and, at the political level, also that of rival doctrinal organizations. The successful ascendancy of one hegemonic truth, on the other hand, would sustain a single totalitarian conversation, and a political order that organizes the knowledge universe—the island's information market.

To evaluate knowledge, conversational editors rank statements along several axes of value. The axis that perhaps most efficiently fixes knowledge's exchange value is truth/falsehood. A second, closely related axis is that of ordinary/absurd. Others axes include right/wrong, customary/novel, local/foreign, useful/not useful, and so on. On the first of these axes, commentary renders a threatening knowledge statement false; on the second, it ridicules it as absurd. Although production of formalized jokes is uncommon on Tanna, conversational editors do make considerable use of ridicule in their evaluative commentary. The heavy hand of this sort of commentary gives a speaker pause before he produces an untoward statement; and, if nevertheless rashly produced, serves to depreciate that statement's meaningful content and its value for consumers (see Borofsky 1982:121, 129). Bourdieu has described this sort of linguistic censorship (although he was writing of stylistic correctness): "By 'watching their tongues,' the dominated groups recognize in practice, if not the supervision of the dominant (though they 'watch themselves' most closely in their presence), then at least the legitimacy of the dominant language" (1977:656).

Terdiman (1985:76) identifies irony as the characteristic tone of counter-discourses: "Its function is to project an alternative through which any element of the here-and-now may be shown as contingent, and thereby to subject the whole configuration of power within which it took its adversative meaning to the erosive, dialectical power of alterity" (1985:76). Countering this erosive irony of counter-discourses is a blunter, more straightforward ridicule that the powerful use to editorialize and make fun of alternative knowledge.

Ridicule is a punitive editorial device by which people depreciate and thus attempt to incorporate and account for the primary knowledge statements of rival and alternative doctrines (see, for example, Eyre 1987:2–3). Ridicule beats down ironical discourse. "Ridicule," of course, labels and conflates a number of kinds of talk in which editors target different objects for abuse. Some editorial ridicule focuses on the absurdity of the statement. Thus, in response to a John Frum knowledge statement, doctrinal adversaries may editorialize: "John Frum is only the wind." Here, the statement itself is "crazy talk" (*nagkiariien ramamïri*).

Most Tannese ridicule, however, impugns the relationship between a knowledge statement and its producer. It targets the act of stating. Ridicule of this sort suggests that a person's production of a particular statement is absurd, in that it violates one or more of the rules of conversational practice (e.g., anomalous speaker claims to be a spokesman, weak speaker commitment, misplaced statement authority, etc.). In this fashion, early John Frum spokesmen ridiculed Christian missionaries' commitment to their message. They mocked missionaries for preaching brotherhood while refusing to eat at the same table with islanders (Guiart 1956b:168). Similarly, a debate witness scorned several men's statements that they would respond seriously to misuse of their narrowcasting exchange roads, because they had failed to act resolutely in the past:

Mata in nah kimirahar kapran-	You three are like women
mirahar, iakni ianhu i.	(female animals), I say.

Kimirahar kapranmirahar, iharo	You three are like women,
nari mhamarihekir.	afraid to do anything.
Pwah kimaha aga nepwun tah-	Let some of us do it.
amo.	Stop talking so much!
Ko ihapwah nini apuneien nari!	

This sort of editorial ridicule does not specifically target a knowledge statement's content. Secondary commentary does not attempt to silence or restate the primary statement itself. Instead, it devalues a statement by discrediting the act of stating, or the statement context. Ridiculous commentary depreciates a knowledge statement's exchange value by deriding some aspect of the stater/statement relation. A statement is absurd and out of place, given who is talking, or the events that surround that talk, or other contextual aspects of the conversation. The ridiculousness or truth of knowledge statement *content*, on the other hand, may pass unedited. Thus, in less polemical conversations, confirmed Christians admit the significance of John Frum (but ridicule his spokesmen), while John Frum supporters hardly question the existence of God (although His missionaries are absurd).

This same editorial targeting of the stater/statement relation, as opposed to a knowledge statement's meaningful content, also characterizes editorial evaluations of statement truth. Island commentators frequently dispute the "truth" (*niparhienien*) of knowledge statements. Truth on Tanna, as in Western modes of information, serves to repress the emergence of alternative cultural knowledge and desires. Truth is, in this regard, "a system of ordered procedures for the production, regulation, distribution, circulation and operation of statements" (Foucault 1980:133). Each society

> has its regime of truth, its general politics of truth: that is, the types
> of discourse which it accepts and makes function as true; the mech-
> anisms and instances which enable one to distinguish true and false
> statements, the means by which each is sanctioned; the techniques
> and procedures accorded value in the acquisition of truth; the status
> of those who are charged with saying what counts as true
> (1980:131).

Tanna's regime of truth differs somewhat from that which operates in other modes of information. To take "falsity" as truth's opposite mistranslates island evaluative sensibilities. Untrue statements are "lies" (*nekuaien, navsieteien, nos aiien*) more than they are false. *Nifefeien*, the term that comes closest to the objective falsity of Western, textualizing modes of information, builds on a semantic core meaning "hypocrisy."

People, of course, readily proclaim the truth and grumble, aghast, at the perfidies of others. Recalling and restating 26 years later his conversations with Nampas and also Tain and his official Americans, Vani was bemused when I suggested that they merely enjoyed joking. No, he answered, *in rarapi nekuaien* (he handled lies). This sort of truth/falsehood is less concerned with excluding wayward knowledge statement content than it is with disciplining the stater. Tannese truth governs who talks seriously, not so much what discourse says (see Foucault 1981:54). Truth regulates the act of stating, particularly the identities of a knowledge statement's producer and consumer. Falsity (whatever cannot be proved) is, in the island's mode of information, less powerful than falsehood (knowledge that implicates local subjectivity or personhood).

In that the truth value of a knowledge statement depends critically on aspects of the stater's identity and of his act of stating, conversational editors, to evaluate truth, pay more attention to the personalities of statement producers and to the facts of knowledge production and circulation than they do to established, discursive canons of proof that might discipline knowledge content. As a procedure of statement exclusion, Tannese falsehood thus implicates and accuses the person who makes a statement as much as it does knowledge content. In the island's mode of information, *both* the subjectivity and objectivity of knowledge are discursively controlled. Given the island's authority-principal, of course, the individual target of editorial commentary is not a transcendental, creative subject or author. It is, rather, the preposterous dreamer, the deceitful prophet, or the unjust spokesman.

Foucault points to a perhaps similar distinction between the current "will to truth" within Western textualizing discourses and earlier Greek forms. Whereas the earlier truth, that "inspired respect and terror, and to which one had to submit because it ruled, was the one pronounced by men who spoke as of right and according to the required ritual," (Foucault 1981:54) our more recent understanding of truth has shifted the focus from the person to his statement.

Foucault calls this "will-to-truth" where truth "no longer resided in what discourse was or did, but in what it said: a day came when truth was displaced from the ritualised, efficacious and just act of enunciation, towards the utterance itself, its meaning, its form, its object, its relation to its reference" (Foucault 1981:54).

If we, perhaps recklessly, carry to Tanna Foucault's distinction between two sorts of truth/falseness (within, to be sure, an alien mode of information), we might further distinguish here *falsehoods* from *falsities*. On Tanna, in that the truth of statements is particularly associated with details of the act of enunciation, and the personal qualifications of those talking, truth more directly and more obviously "exercises power" (Foucault 1981:56) over the people engaged in serious talk. The truth depends upon *who* talks and how he talks. The justly powerful, of necessity, speak the truth; conversely, those who state the truth have just power.

On Tanna, as a consequence, those people who successfully evade or abrogate relations of conversational domination manage to do so by accusing statement producers of lying. Recall Kafua's commentary on Reia's legend about Mwatiktiki's Imwai Nei: "I don't know if his story is truth or lies." And Tain and Nampas, trafficking in Americans, *rarapi nekuaien* (handled lies). But it was only when ruling relations of conversational inequality at Isina finally collapsed that Tain (with his hungry American) turned into a liar. Because he lies, a person has no power. Or, when he has no power, he lies. By denying the truth value of a knowledge statement, and refusing to consume this, people may disengage from ruling conversations, cut relations of knowledge exchange, and challenge the just, conversational rights of the powerful. No matter the referential truth of its content, in some mouths, for some consumers, a statement is always a lie.

Truth on Tanna, therefore, is an even sterner discourse control procedure of exclusion. Truth, whatever details of statement reference might be, validates the rights of the stater and the propriety of his act of stating. Conversely, when editorial commentators call a knowledge statement false, they simultaneously devalue the conversational rights of the person talking, and the justness of his act of stating. Truth and falseness, therefore, are always personalized. A person who is wrong is a liar. If being truthful is powerful, being wrong is shameful.

The compulsively familiar apparatus of objective, referential truth and falsity belong to other, textualizing modes of information, alien to the island. On Tanna, whatever knowledge a person agrees to consume is the truth, and (or because) its producers are wise. Those knowledge statements that circulate within rival conversations, on the other hand, are false, and (or because) their producers are liars (see Barth 1975:101–102, 219-222; D'Azevedo 1962:26; Watt 1895:226–227). This is an effect of an orientation towards knowledge source instead of knowledge content (see Schwartz 1962:296). Thus Iau, who spent some time railing at the cupidity of people foolish enough to buy the truth of John Frum knowledge, later that day listened to his son tell of how he had read, while in primary school, of a filial relation between Prince Philip of Great Britain and a mountain-dwelling Tannese culture hero. Given local conversational relations and the source of knowledge, Iau's response to his son was *parhien, parhien!* (true, true), it must be true!

The editorial evaluative axis of truth/lie, like ridicule, thus serves as a discourse control procedure that precludes some knowledge statements, staters, and statings from serious conversation. By editorializing the truth and the ordinariness of primary knowledge statements, editors either authenticate or devalue what is said, at the same time that they inform the personal conversational qualifications of the speaker. The truth and the lie regulate and maintain existing patterns of cultural consumption. By establishing the lie, editors make the consumption of some circulating knowledge statements less likely, and so protect their own truths. They retain a market for their own knowledge. Consumers are less inclined to abandon ruling truths, even if somewhat shopworn, for the unpalatable lie. The lie reduces that danger posed by alternative knowledge, and by rival knowers—their statements rendered false, their conversational power thus unjust.

These editorial control procedures, which regulate knowledge consumption by fixing the conversational exchange value of primary statements, are particularly important in light of the occasional failure of other discourse procedures to control fully cultural production and circulation on Tanna. An openness in knowledge production, in personal opportunities to repeat and formulate novel statements, potentially threatens existing regimes of conversational domination. Despite the apparatus of control, islanders have occasionally succeeded in producing and circulating untoward statements that challenge ruling knowledge. When external authorities can inspire new knowledge at any moment, the political threat of troublesome revelations must be met. If women or young men, for example, say something new that is dangerous to older men, this must be made to sound crazy or deceitful. An editorial function is thus absolutely essential. Secondary commentary and other consumption control procedures must act quickly to defuse ominous or unpropitious knowledge productions.

I suspect editorial functions of this sort are found in all modes of information where revelation is the basis of new and possibly legitimate knowledge, as it is still within some Western religious discourses. St. Paul, in this manner, established an editorial function for Christianity in Chapter Fourteen of his First Letter to the Corinthians. He distinguishes between those people who speak in tongues (knowledge producers), and those who interpret what is said (knowledge editors): "If anyone speaks in a tongue, two—or at the most three—should speak, one at a time, and someone must interpret" (14:27). "Therefore, my brothers, be eager to prophesy, and do not forbid speaking in tongues. But everything should be done in a fitting and orderly way" (14:39–40). Prophet interpreters, i.e., editors, by controlling secondary evaluative commentary, manage how a revealed knowledge statement is to be publicly consumed. They thereby have a final opportunity, through editorial restatement or by calling the producer a liar, to silence, deflect, or inflect any primary statement that threatens existing orders of truth and knowledge.

On Tanna, witnesses and editors similarly defuse dangerous knowledge statements and make these unpalatable for public consumption. They fix statement value. Editorializing excludes alternative knowledge statements, even if authentically authorized and inspired, from much of the conversational marketplace. Editors silence, co-opt, trivialize, make ridiculous, or falsify dangerous alternatives. Their production of secondary commentary, which informs linguistic opacity, restates other statements, or superimposes on knowledge an evaluation of its ordinariness and truth, fixes the conversational exchange value of local knowledge.

Editorial control procedures, and those people who qualify to serve this discursive function, never succeed completely in silencing all alternative and resistant knowledge. In modes of information where domination is marked, however, the powerful manage, more than elsewhere, to editorialize. Statement restatement is common. One also encounters here, more than elsewhere, the truth and the lie.

REGIMES OF TRUTH

In Vanuatu Pidgin English, "true" (*tru,* or *tru ia,* "true here") is a common conversational backchannelling device. A listener, to mark his willing consumption of some communicated statement, acknowledges its truth. Backchannelling *tru,* he also acknowledges his exchange relationship with the statement's producer within a shared conversational order. Consuming the statement as truth, he admits the personal wisdom of his interlocutor. The stater is not a liar. Together, both stand "in the true" (Foucault 1981:61).

Where editorial control devices successfully overcome, co-opt, or silence enough heterogeneous knowledge statements, these discursive procedures support a regime of truth: "'Truth' is linked in a circular relation with systems of power which produce and sustain it, and to effects of power which it induces and which extend it. A 'regime' of truth" (Foucault 1980:133). Evaluations of truth, discursively, are "the ensemble of rules according to which the true and the false are separated and specific effects of power attached to the true" (Foucault 1980:132).

The totality of knowledge statements circulating within Tanna's information market is diverse and multiple. If properly produced, any of these statements *might* be true: "The American ate the pig in his office," or is it "Nouata ate the pig in his office?" A statement may meet all established discursive requirements (e.g., it comes from an authoritative source, it is properly copyrighted, it follows the right roads, etc.). Even so, conversational editors may succeed in making it into a lie. They manage to expose and falsify dangerous and rival statings of alternative truths. So triumphant Christianity silenced customary veracities. So John Frum silenced deceitful Christian doxology.

Moreover, the power in truth is not only that of subjectification (a delineation of authentic personhood). It is also that of domination (unequal personal management of the truth, and of the conversational production of truthful commentary). A regime of truth excludes more than the false. It excludes liars. So Christians silenced sinful traditionalists. So John Frum silenced lying Christians.

On Tanna, people call their regimes of truth the "Law" (in Bislama, *lo*). They combine in this two of law's English meanings: law that states the true ordering and relating of known phenomena; and law that regulates personal behavior (cf. Sack 1985; Schwartz 1962:366). During the island's Tanna Law and America Law, the Law was thus both the true and the permitted. A Law organizes the island's information market and its conversational relations so that all people make and hear statements in terms of only one truth. A Law, furthermore, establishes and protects relations of conversational domination. Those who regulate truthful conversation take charge of truth-telling individuals as well. Tannese truths are thus doctrinal, in Foucault's sense; here, a Law "puts in question both the statement and the speaking subject" (1981:63).

Island Laws, which regulate conversational content, are regimes of limited and organized truth. Where the details of desire, and the variable success of discourse control procedures, accord one truth more exchange value than others, a doctrinal knowledge may establish a hegemony. Here, one discursive regime and the truths it deploys so dominate people's conversation that the circulation of other knowledge statements around the island is impeded or forestalled.

In cases where this truthful silencing is extreme, editorial commentary sustains a "central, effective and dominant system of meanings and values, which are not merely abstract but which are organized and lived" (Williams 1980:38). This conversational absolutism depends on the operation of discourse procedures of knowledge exclusion:

> from a whole possible area of past and present, certain meanings and practices are chosen for emphasis, certain other meanings and practices are neglected and excluded. Even more crucially, some of these meanings and practices are reinterpreted, diluted, or put into forms which support or at least do not contradict other elements within the effective dominant culture (Williams 1980:39; see Parenti 1978:216).

This is hegemony that "constitutes a sense of reality for most people in the society, a sense of absolute because experienced reality beyond which it is very difficult for most members of the society to move, in most areas of their lives" (Williams 1980:38; see Smart 1986:160–164).

A conversational hegemony has a history. Roughly speaking, it must begin, faintly, as a number of newly formulated and tentatively circulated knowledge statements. These, on Tanna, were the words that alien Christian knowledge brokers first enunciated, kneeling on the beach at Port Resolution, in 1839; or they were the messages that, in the late 1930s, cited a new authoritative source—the then unknown John Frum. These adventitious knowledge statements, given the existing configuration of personal interests and desires, realized significant exchange value in the local information market. They succeeded where many others undoubtedly failed. Conversational modes of information are unsparing of no-account statements. No literacy exists to textualize and store the isolated voicing of unpalatable statements in the far recesses of some musty archive, or in the forgotten scribblings of the insane or the heretical. If a spoken statement is heard and repeated on the island, however, it penetrates the informational universe and makes its way into shared memory.

Those knowledge producers whose statements acquire exchange value bring into being new and continuing relations of conversational inequality, insofar as others agree to consume their further knowledge productions. Here is the beginning of discursive domination and a new conversational regime. Within emergent relations of conversational inequality, the wise also appropriate and manage some of the discourse control procedures that regulate knowledge statement circulation and consumption. They also assume the local discursive functions of witness, teacher, and editor. Overvaluing their own knowledge and depreciating and silencing alternatives, they thus nourish and protect the emerging doctrinal order. Hegemony itself solidifies when circulating new truths begin to organize the details of personal desire itself. Here, consumed answers feed back to affect people's questions. Consumed knowledge, by reconstituting persons, objects, concepts, and strategies, restates locally known and felt realities.

By the knowledge each allowed, Tanna Law and America Law both reorganized the content of island conversation. For example, each restated and made sense of the new man, of *kastom*, of the place of Tanna in the midst of newly encountered foreigners, of God, Jesus, John Frum, Mr. World and other new authoritative sources, of desire for foreign goods and knowledge, and of strategies by which that desire might be served. The ruling doctrines thus enunciated new truths, and also restated existing cultural knowledge of the person and of the world.

Tanna Law elaborated, in particular, a notion of time structured by cyclical weeks, each beginning with a laborless holy day. People consumed Christian knowledge that transfigured local architecture. Houses with walls, carefully aligned, replaced customary wall-less women's houses and menstrual huts, and also men's kava houses. The emerging Law made false the discipline of magic, and also penetrated and reorganized those of medicine and geography. Dance stopped. Songs became hymns. First-fruit ceremonies transformed into Thanksgiving services. The new truths transfigured the body as well. Imported scissors and Christian zeal mastered the remarkable customary, twisted male hair style. Leafy penis wrappers and bark skirts gave way to cloth. Kava drunkenness resolved into sober prayer as the authoritative voice of God stilled, for a time, the murmurings of local ancestors.

America Law reappreciated some customary knowledge and practice, such as dancing, kava drinking, and magic; and it elaborated other island traditions. It drew on the wartime experience of many islanders who traveled north in 1942 to work at the American supply bases established on Efate and Espiritu Santo. John Frum spokesmen made sense of people's interests and desires by strategically manipulating various imported wartime symbols, including red wooden crosses copied from the uniforms of Army medics and the doors of ambulances. Whereas for Tanna Law the white shirt replaces the penis wrapper, for America Law it is the military uniform. Today, islanders prize uniforms and military insignia provided by passing yachtsmen and tourists. A few were foresighted enough to retain secretly the numbered dogtags issued to them during tours of labor duty for the U.S. military. The John Frum hymn repertoire includes many songs from the war. Some people can still sing credible renderings of "God Bless America" and the "Marines Hymn" (see Heinl 1944:240). A John Frum military drill team marches, during doctrinal events, carrying bamboo rifles. Each marcher bears the logo "USA" in red paint across his chest and back. A sergeant commands the team, barking out twisted but still recognizable field commands. The nonsense language, here, is U.S. military English.

The two conversational laws of Tanna's past century ultimately failed to establish a hegemonic reality that totalized the information universe and all knowledge consumption therein. In that some knowledge statements escaped the grasp of available discourse control procedures, so thus did a measure of known reality. Even so, Tanna and America Laws did fix extensive regimes of truth. These regimes temporarily dominated island conversation. Christian and John Frum talk penetrated the local information universe and became common knowledge, if not entirely true. Both regimes spoke to and reorganized subjective desire. Both established new truths and new lies.

Both regimes, moreover, established new truth-tellers and new liars. This is the second aspect of an emerging law: the restructuring of conversational relations. A regime of truth supports an order of conversational domination alongside that subjectification it establishes. The conversationally powerful, who speak the truth, attempt to silence both heresies and the heretics who spread these words. Within doctrinal organizations, they manage the discourse control procedures by which they are conversationally empowered, in order to protect their enunciatory, circulatory, and editorial functions. Tanna Law and America Law were thus more than an extensive deployment of serious new truth statements. Beyond this, each constituted a particular conversational regime, situating people as truth-tellers, truth consumers, or liars.

Doctrinal spokesmen manage conversation by articulating answers. The truth statements they produce enunciate and speak to people's interests to hear. The wise attract numerous knowledge consumers, and thus transcend the island's normal, local limitations of age and geography on the scope of ordinary personal authority. Spokesmen with a new truth found area-wide doctrinal organizations of upwards of several thousand consumers. They manage the inspirational means of access to revealed knowledge (e.g., dreaming, travel, literacy, etc.), and so reproduce their speaking function within conversation. They convene regular broadcasting ceremonies and forums in order to circulate more effectively their truth statements.

The genius of the men who made John Frum's law the Law was to use as their model the circulatory devices of the preceding Tanna Law. In particular, they institutionalized a series of periodic events and forums, including regular Friday night dances that correspond to regular Christian services. These forums for the deployment of knowledge mitigate some of the material limitations of conversational discourse. On Christian Sunday and John Frum Friday, the conversationally powerful are able to broadcast knowledge statements to an audience that has traveled to hear the truth. At these forums, moreover, doctrinal spokesmen have the opportunity to produce editorial commentary that ridicules or appropriates alternative knowledge, so to maintain or extend existing patterns of statement consumption.

In addition to editorializing talk, doctrinal leaders institute other, more obviously repressive procedures that silence rival staters, as well as their dangerous statements, in order to protect the Law. They appoint guards (in Bislama, *gat*) and police (*polis*) to defuse alternative knowledge statements and enforce doctrinal truths (Guiart 1956b:173; cf. Schwartz 1962:268–269). They also establish courts (*kot*) to chastise sinners. Tanna Law leaders first convened courts in 1906, with some assistance from foreign knowledge brokers (Guiart 1956b:142):

> It is said that some of the missionaries set up native courts. In one sense that is true; in another it is not. From time immemorial the natives had courts, i.e., they met to discuss whether certain individuals were guilty of crimes laid to their charge; to find out who were the offenders; and to determine the punishments to be inflicted. What the missionaries did was to use their influence to improve the constitution of these assemblies, and to eliminate from their decisions the partiality, vindictiveness and barbarity which so often characterised them (Watt 1908:21).

Tanna Law forbade all work on Sunday, drinking alcohol or kava, customary dress, dancing, swearing, and other known sins. Police roped and sometimes whipped law breakers with the dessicated penes of bulls. They brought the accused to court. Here, Christian elders tried conservatives and recidivists who refused to accept the truth of the new Law, still consuming instead customary knowledge.

Courts protected Tanna Law by repressing these liars and falsifiers. Imposed punishments included cash fines, which went to the Law's school supply budget, and enforced labor on a system of new island roads and horse tracks. Punishment of sinners, in this sense, fit the crime as it furthered the deployment of the truth in new Christian schools and by mounted, itinerating statement circulators. The courts also exiled some of the guilty from their home villages. This exile, by distance, silenced resistant talk about alternative knowledge.

Courts and police atrophied with the collapse of Tanna Law's hegemony at the end of the 1930s (Guiart 1956b:150). The breakthrough of John Frum truth statements into the once monopolized knowledge market overturned ruling relations of conversational domination. As this new talk itself established a near market hegemony, however, conversationally parvenu John Frum truth-tellers managed to establish their own silences. Over the years of the John Frum movement its doctrinal leaders, too, have recruited several armies, drill teams, police, and guards (see Bonnemaison 1987:559–562;O'Reilly 1949:194).

In the late 1970s, for example, men recruited from supporting village teams served rotating tours of duty to guard the United States flags flying at doctrinal headquarters. As did their Tanna Law predecessors, these knowledge police tied up and brought to court anyone who challenged established truths, or otherwise came to the unfavorable attention of the wise. (Guiart characterized similar actions during Tanna Law as "garrattage des prisonniers" (1956b:131).) Like Tanna Law, America Law's leaders attempted to regulate personal behavior, including conversational and other relations between men and women. John Frum police arrested accused adulterers and elopers and brought them to Sulphur Bay for trial. Young Wopu, for example, after two exciting days on the run with his girlfriend, was ambushed by doctrinal police, tied up, and lugged down to Sulphur Bay to be judged by John Frum leaders.

In court, John Frum leaders hear the crime and set punishment—typically, fines of pig and kava. These fines, like those of Tanna Law, also support doctrinal truths about the revitalized utilities of customary kava and pig exchanges. John Frum courts similarly exiled from home villages a few men accused of sorcery and magic that violated the doctrinal Law (Bonnemaison 1987:195, 560). Here, like Tanna Law, America Law also penetrated and reorganized disciplinal knowledge and practice of magic, medicine, and geography.

Courts, more obviously than neighborhood debates and school forums, regulate the conversational broadcasting and consumption of

truth statements. In the court, a development of the customary debate, conversational relations are redrawn. In a debate forum, only
adult men are personally competent to talk. In court, qualifications to
converse and to edit knowledge are even more rigorously restricted.
The wise here control both the content and the relations of conversation. The new discursive position "judge" commands much more
conversational power than that of spokesman, teacher, witness, or
even editor. Courts, which enunciate the truth and punish liars, reproduce orders of both discursive subjectification and domination.

A successful regime of truth makes these knowledge powers possible. Truth-tellers have the power to silence and chastise falsifiers
and heretics, because they manage the truth. And their application of
power (of courts, of police, of bulls' penes, of rope, and of exile) to
silence those who refuse the truth reproduces their personal qualifications and conversational opportunities to tell the truth.

Island regimes of truth—Tanna Law and America Law—thus
consist of an effective organization and regulation of knowledge consumption. This is a special case of doctrinal success. Where one doctrinal discourse hegemonically dominates an information marketplace, it alone addresses and enunciates personal interests and
desire and, in this, regulates both shared cultural questions and answers.

Whether hegemonic or not, regulatory procedures operate constantly within all modes of information to limit people's consumption
of alternative knowledge: to make accessible, positive, and desirable
the one while repressing all others. Conversational consumption procedures first ensure unequal personal access to the information marketplace. Given the materiality of island information circulation,
some people have better opportunities and qualifications to hear and
to decode more knowledge statements than do others. Personal mobility and linguistic skills accord them greater access to available cultural knowledge.

Second, consumption control procedures ensure editorial inequalities in knowledge statement interpretation and evaluation, as
well as statement reception. This, too, follows from a person's position in the information market. Editors produce secondary commentary that restates and fixes the value of primary statements. Commentators give readings of how a knowledge statement should be taken.
These statements may be linguistically or doctrinally opaque, or they

may be audible and accessible. Even if the latter, however, some people lack control of meaning, no matter if they themselves have produced the knowledge statement. The conversationally powerful appropriate and restate their knowledge to make this publicly "transparent." Conversational editing of this sort improves or depreciates the exchange value of circulating knowledge by further packaging this for public consumption. Knowledge is made to be ordinary or ridiculous; truth or lies.

Finally, where one knowledge conquers a market—where control procedures silence most alternative statements—a regime of truth organizes both the content and the relations of discourse. Here, procedures of truth do more than make a person conversationally deaf and dumb. They call into question his subjectivity as well as his statements and his statings. He must either be a serious truth-teller or a liar. The true lives by the lie. While hegemony persists, those people who control the truth inaugurate additional, more severe consumption control practices, such as police and court, to silence and repress the liar as well as his lies.

Tanna Law and America Law ruled the island's information marketplace for relatively short periods, each no more than a few decades. This sort of near conversational hegemony, along with its exceptionally repressive knowledge consumption policing mechanisms, break down together. The conversational regime dissolves; knowledge consumption broadens; alternative statements make their way back into the market. Over the last century, several apparent disjunctions have cut and shaped the deployment of talk in the island's information marketplace. The Law of *kastom* gave way to Christian Tanna Law which, in 1941, was itself silenced by the Law of John Frum. Discourse control procedures that regulate the conversational consumption of culture, that ensure the positivity, desirability, and transparency of a hegemony, and that repress and make opaquely distasteful other knowledges, have ultimately failed—at least in this island mode of information. Why do these disjunctive successions of unsettled lies and truths occur?

6

Changing Conversations

Kafikieri rerin ramamisa	My friend, his heart is sore
mamatui reraha ti nekuaien	grimfaced from the lies
iko sore auar a ipwet	you are sorry for nothing today
aue, aue: Nekuaien asori!	alas, alas: What big lies!

—STRING BAND SONG

Regimes of truth, such as Tanna Law and America Law, comprise a body of serious knowledge that conversation carries; a conversational subjectification of persons; an order of conversational domination; and a set of discursive control procedures that overcome or parry the dangers of alternative knowledge. But how useful is a conversational model of society like this? Does it forget that social life is more than conversation?; that there are realms of domination beyond the conversational?; that relations of power are not always coincident with relations of communication (Foucault 1983:217)? Significant bases of power stand outside conversation per se: the physical structures of village house and forest clearing mutely organize island talk; a perceptive student may learn canoe carving wordlessly; the landless may starve in silence; a person may suffer quietly a powerful physical beating. Just how "serious" itself is Foucault's implication that we can change reality, as known, merely by talking seriously about this in a different way? Or that we can escape the powers that hold us by inventing a new discourse in which they are ignored?

174

We might stretch the conversational metaphor by figuring that silent beatings and other wordless social activities and structures are nonverbal statements. Although nonverbal, these too are a kind of knowledge that people produce, circulate, and consume within and alongside their conversations. Bourdieu's (1977) term "habitas" describes some of the silent, but still learned, ways we have of knowing and acting. We might similarly approach physical forces and bodily powers over things, that give "the ability to modify, use, consume, or destroy them" (Foucault 1983:217), to be not so much outside of conversation as "infra-conversational"—both beneath and within a mode of information. This is, of course, one of anthropology's oldest messages. The world exists, but we can only know it culturally according to the ways we have of talking seriously about it. Or, to return to Foucault, "The operation of objective capacities in their most elementary forms implies relationships of communication" (1983:218). A physical beating may exert force, but it stands outside of and has no effect on social relations of power unless it is also interpreted and conversationally addressed. (Conversation, here, may rely upon words, or a simple nonverbal knowing glance.) Serious talk must, in the end, establish reality's truth.

Non-discursive powers and events are ultimately culturally interpreted and editorialized. Conversation, of course, is unsustainable without necessary material conditions and resources, but these conditions themselves mean nothing outside of conversation (Dreyfus and Rabinow 1982:66). The ubiquitous Melanesian pig is an example. Although pig production, in many Melanesian societies, is

> a necessary condition of domination . . . the capacity to produce pigs is more general (and hence conducive to equality) than the capacity to "produce" domination through persuasive speech. "Talk" appears as the final determinant (Modjeska 1982:101–102).

Infra-conversational forces and relations support and make practicable a mode of information, but that mode informs how people understand and value those objective forces and facts, whether of pigs or punches. Talk organizes the field of things and "the transformation of the real" (Foucault 1982:218). In this way, a conversational metaphor for social life speaks to how people know and experience reality through their serious talking.

It is in this sense that changing talk may change the world. When one regime of truth replaces another, things, persons, desires, strategies, and existing powers can all transform. Changing conversation, however, is more easily said than done. A mode of information asserts a self-protective "ignorance" as it furthers its own knowledge. For the world to remain known in one way, other ways must remain either hidden or distasteful.

Unstated ignorance, or what people do not or cannot talk about seriously, is a delimitation of the "subjects" of conversation—in both senses of that word. First, ignorance circumscribes the topics, or knowledge content, of conversation. At the simplest level, this is merely that it is impolite or inappropriate to talk about certain subjects. Foucault notes this kind of silence that spreads by the working of conversational exclusions or taboos: "We know quite well that we do not have the right to say everything, that we cannot speak of just anything in any circumstances whatever" (1981:52). On Tanna, people often attempt to silence each other by invoking conversational taboos of this sort. At a dispute-settlement meeting, for example, people met to discuss why Pirei had severely beaten his wife—to make sense of this act by talking about it. During debate, witnesses tried to shush Pirei's statements that his anger stemmed from his son and daughter-in-law's ungoverned and customarily misguided sexuality that had caused the death of his grandchild:

Navahagien nah Pirei ikni nari	That sort of advice Pirei is
ia nakwai nimwa.	something for inside the house.
Nari ia nakwai nimwa fwe;	Something inside the house;
ikamavahag mi saik me nikwar-	there you advise your children
akwara.	(not to have postpartum sex).
Ikakeikei mua tikavahi nari ia	You must bring that up pri-
nakwai nimwa; rapwah nam-	vately; it isn't seemly that you
whenien mua tikuvahi muvehe ia	bring it to the company here
kampani fa rife takwtakwni.	and reveal it now.
Ro naurisien i ua.	It causes shame.

Silencing of this sort, however, does not insure ignorance. If anything, conversational taboos do the opposite. They feed a desire to learn, to discover the unmentionable. There are, however, other more

profound connections between silence and ignorance. Here, people
do not discuss something not because it is impolite or unjust to do so,
but because discursive conditions have kept them ignorant. These
conversational silences work to make unshared culture. Or, at a
broader level, they work to produce cultural knowledge of certain
things, but cultural ignorance of others. A regime of truth, in addition
to fixing the truth and the lie, also studiously ignores the existence or
possibility of alternative knowledge. Statements once said but not
stored, or not yet said, or never said obviously do not circulate. The
topics of island conversations are "rarefied," in Foucault's word
(1981:58). "*Everything* is never said" (Foucault 1972:118).

Second, ignorance also circumscribes the people who talk. These
conversational subjects are likewise rarefied. Differential personal ignorance of the informational marketplace, and uneven access to the
regulatory procedures of discourse control, maintain relations of conversational domination. Ignorance, here, is an effect of patterns of
local knowledge distribution: of shared and unshared culture. *Mi mi
no save* (I don't know), perhaps the archetypical Pidgin English
riposte, acknowledges this sort of personal ignorance. Such acknowl-
edgement, however, is still a conversational response. Although some
people may remain partially ignorant, as part of a continuing conversation they still produce and consume statements—especially those
which admit that ignorance.

If one could be *entirely and totally ignorant* only then could one
elude a regime of truth's subjugations as well as its relations of domination. Power ends where perfect ignorance begins. Those who neither consume nor produce knowledge statements evade ruling discourses and regimes of truth. Those who cannot hear and cannot
repeat a discourse's truth statements, however circulated, stand outside its power. Those who do not know and cannot talk share no
culture.

Predatory discourses, such as many of our own Information Age,
as well as the doctrines of Tanna, have assaulted and broken down
resistant areas of ignorance or silence (where other discourses circulate), in order to expand their own markets. The powerless within
one regime of truth, conversely, may strive to change the way they
talk, and to replace one discourse with another, in order to escape
both ruling subjugations and ratios of conversational domination.
The Tannese, occasionally, have succeeded in this. Three thousand

islanders, for example, failed to attend church on May 11, 1941, and did not consume that week's supply of Christian knowledge. Their counter-discourse, in this case, was John Frum talk.

Can one, in this fashion, drop out of conversation? Or think outside of discourse? Islanders have succeeded, at least, in modifying their conversations of the past. Old ignorances, and also old knowledge, shift as people formulate, talk about, and consume new statements, and as they also forget and fall silent. The unknown or the once-ignored becomes the known; the once-known, contrarily, comes to several possible ends. It, particularly in a non-textualizing mode of information, may be forgotten. Knowledge drops from memory. Elsewhere, in modes of information where once-known texts continue to circulate in concrete, literary form, such residual knowledge may be ignored as trivial, or otherwise editorialized as archaic or primitive. Bygone knowledge might be taken as false, as the big lie, as simple ignorance, or as a necessary but rudimentary stage in the progression and development of the truth.

Silence, as the absence of discourse, of course does not exist. Silencing, however, as a discursive procedure works to produce and reproduce both knowledge and ignorance. If islanders have yet to dissolve society by smothering all conversational interaction, they have substituted their discourses, one regime of truth supplanting and silencing another, and thus several times have dislocated the centers of knowledge and ignorance. One established regime of truth gives way to a new. These are "disjunctions" in discourse. Here, the conversationally powerful, who by silencing others once aborted dangerous knowledge in order to protect their own speaking functions, may in turn find themselves silenced and unable to converse seriously. The facts of personhood change as new conversational positions, with new qualifications and opportunities, emerge and as old functions lose voice and drop out of the conversation. Discursive disjunctions make new ignoramuses as well as new ignorances.

DISJUNCTION

Considerable change has occurred in island conversations as regime of truth followed regime of truth in the years since Cook's 1774 landfall at Port Resolution. The volume of customary talk declined in favor of Christian, which itself was interrupted by John Frum conversations. The question arises, however, as to the degree of discontinuity between these island Laws. A simple modification of the inventory of circulating knowledge statements does not in itself necessarily imply a disjunction—a revolutionary new discursive practice. A disjunctive conversation is something more than the formulation of new statements: "A change in the order of discourse does not presuppose 'new ideas,' a little invention and creativity, a different mentality, but transformations in a practice, perhaps also in neighbouring practices, and in their common articulation" (Foucault 1972:209). A disjunction, or

> the appearance of a new positivity is not indicated by a new sentence—unexpected, surprising, logically unpredictable, stylistically deviant—that is inserted into a text, and announces either the opening of a new chapter, or the entry of a new speaker. It is an event of a quite different type (Foucault 1972:172).

This event is the replacement of one mode of information by another: the transformation of the discursive conditions and procedures under which people produce, circulate, and consume what they know.

Discursive succession on Tanna from customary truths, to Tanna Law, to American Law has not, in these terms, been entirely disjunctive. As noted, the genealogy of island knowledge is difficult to trace; conversational discourse is refractory to genealogical analysis. Even so, inspecting the few historic island statements that have been textualized by Mrs. Watt and others, and listening to people talking today, one overhears considerable similarities in discursive practice from Law to island Law. Many of the discourse control procedures that regulate serious talk—the conditions that govern the production, circulation, and consumption of knowledge—have apparently carried over from one regime of truth to the next. To date, the authorization-principle, copyright restrictions and geographic oeuvres, and the persistent oral media and forums of statement deployment and consumption have regulated all island regimes of truth.

It is thus difficult to locate, within a genealogy of island knowledge, discursive disjunctions as cutting as those Foucault has described elsewhere. A simple-minded structuralism, seeking continuity instead of discontinuity, might reconcile *Kastom* Law with Tanna Law with American Law as simple alternatives—reflexes of the same, underlying, and enduring conversational structures. These would be transformed sets of superficial knowledge statements that deeper, cultural structures have generated in succession.

Following Williams (1980:40), one might distinguish between merely alternative and truly oppositional knowledge. Alternative statements, even if unexpected, surprising, unpredictable, or deviant, nevertheless remain within the compass and oversight of ruling knowledge:

> Thus we have to recognize the alternative meanings and values, the alternative opinions and attitudes, even some alternative senses of the world, which can be accommodated and tolerated within a particular effective and dominant culture (Williams 1980:39).

Oppositional knowledge, on the other hand, cannot be so easily tolerated and accommodated. Rather, these statements make no sense in dominant cultural terms. Their successful deployment and consumption disrupt existing conversational relations. Perhaps Tanna's successive island Laws, in this sense, have been merely alternative rather than fully oppositional regimes of truth. They have all emerged within the island's mode of information, under the same basic conditions of discourse.

A person seeking continuities in the succession of customary, Tanna, and America Laws might also see in this a simple example of "personnel replacement." When one Law supplants another, new people merely appropriate the island's perennial discursive functions of spokesman, teacher, editor, witness, and so on. The young, perhaps, seizing upon a once marginal set of knowledge statements, successfully deploy these and make them into the Law and so displace their once-knowledgeable elders. The young are a common menace, in this way, in many modes of information: "Every birth or revival of an ideology is borne by a new generational wave: in its experience, each such new intellectual generation feels everything is being born anew, that the past is meaningless, or irrelevant, or nonexistant" (Feuer 1975:20; see Barnes 1977:50). The young might be wrong about this. Or, perhaps they occasionally do manage to escape a measure of their discursively established ignorance by ignoring the serious talk of their parents. Younger Christian converts, accordingly, dropped out of traditional conversations; younger John Frum consumers, similarly, silenced their Christian elders.

Not just any serendipity of knowledge statements can contend with the truth, let alone expect much exchange value in the information marketplace. And from where do the young acquire the desire to silence their parents by refusing to listen any longer to their statements? Instead of seeking cultural and historical continuities on Tanna, I suggest that the island's sequence of Laws did entail something more than a simple, generational replacement of conversational personnel, or the oscillation of structurally alternative surface knowledges that all share the same deep communication structures. Jumps from one island Law to the next, although not cleanly disjunctive, were still discontinuous in important ways (cf. Barth 1987:36).

First, the successful deployment of some new body of knowledge reforms relations of conversational domination. Although discursive discontinuities between one regime of truth and the next may not be absolute, these disjunctions do make powerful the once ignorant, and silence the once knowledgeable. Discursive conditions themselves also undergo some change. Both Christian and John Frum doctrines empowered new speaking functions (teacher, witness, and judge), as well as innovated new circulatory forums (schools, ritual assemblies, and courts) while nullifying others. These new discursive functions possessed powerful editorial opportunities to decide the truth and the lie, the good and the shameful. New knowledge not only makes the once-true into the big lie, it transforms conversational relations. In this manner, Tain at Isaina first gained, then lost his audience. The American was first true, but then became lies.

Second, changes in the knowledge statement inventory of Tanna's information marketplace have been much greater between regimes of truth than within them. The knowledge statements of America Law drove from the market and replaced many of the statements that circulated within preceding Tanna Law conversations. Kava drinking, for example, is good, then bad, then good again. Here, at least, there is a degree of disjunction in the *content* of circulating knowledge from one Law to the next.

Of course, some change in the information market's knowledge inventory takes place within existing regimes of truth. During the lifetime of a Law, doctrinal spokesmen can produce supplementary statements that become part of the Law's authorized knowledge. In that these statements are produced, circulated, and consumed within the same regime of truth, they cohere as a set or a body of knowledge. Identical discursive conditions, particularly the editorial, have regulated their deployment. Their appearance within an ongoing conversation connects them up with statements that already exist. The knowledge a new statement carries is thus usually recognizably customary, or John Frum, or Christian, or that of other island doctrines. This sort of renovative knowledge production is a continuous modification and development of a Law's truths (see Keesing 1982:215). Barth (1987:31), for example, has described processes of "incremental" change within the cosmology of one Papua New Guinea society.

John Frum doctrine, too, has shifted and reformed since its inception, as his spokesmen formulated emendatory and innovative statements. In his debut at Green Point, John Frum first instructed islanders to cooperate in everyday garden tasks, and to obey both government and mission authorities (Guiart 1956b:155). This message soon changed. His advocates next circulated dicta that instructed people to resume customary kava drinking and dancing. Tanna Law had made these, along with other traditional practices, both criminal and wicked.

John Frum spokesmen also circulated statements about expected millenial events, in addition to those of cultural revival. This talk proclaimed the new age, instructed people to discard their European money, kill their cattle and goats, and abandon gardens and houses. John Frum, according to the message, would soon provide new money and other supplies. Additional statements warned of coming cataclysmic events: the world would capsize, mountains become valleys, and Europeans depart (Barrow 1952:4). Many John Frum knowledge consumers did kill their animals, quit productive labor, and discard their money. Some threw this into the sea (Barrow 1952:4); others participated in runs on local trade stores, buying whatever was on the shelves (Guiart 1956b:159; O'Reilly 1949:195; see also Marsh 1968; Priday 1950).

Knowledge of America began circulating early within John Frum conversations. Three months before Pearl Harbor, colonial authorities intercepted a letter which stated that John Frum's son would fetch back to Tanna the King of America, and also described planes hidden in the bush (Guiart 1956b:410). Six months later, an American fleet anchored at Port Vila. Allied forces quickly established themselves near Vila, and later opened a second base on Espiritu Santo. These bases first served as frontline establishments supporting the battles of the Solomons and Coral Sea. As the war moved north, they became permanent repair, supply, and transit depots.

Half a million servicemen passed through these ports on their way to and from the front (Geslin 1956:257). Military authorities, rapidly expanding their operations, needed local labor to unload ships, grow food, move garbage, and work in mosquito abatement programs. Many of the islanders they recruited to serve in the labor corps came from Tanna. About 1,000 island men signed on and went to work for the U.S. military in 1942. Back on the island, reformed John Frum knowledge statements evinced a new concern with the arrival, and later return, of American servicemen by ship, by submarine, or out from the bowels of the southern mountains (Guiart 1956b:182). As now restated, from America would come knowledge, goods, and freedom from colonial domination (O'Reilly 1949:202). Tain's official American was a statement of this sort.

John Frum conversation, during succeeding years, has continued to shift as spokesmen produce supplementary, incremental knowledge statements that respond to new questions. Christian doctrine has likewise changed. After Tanna Law collapsed, for example, Christian elders and pastors revised their doctrinal statements to re-enfranchise traditional *nupu* dancing, ritual exchange, and even kava drinking and other once ignored customary practices. These continuous, incremental permutations within doctrinal knowledge inventories contrast with a more discontinuous change between one regime of truth and the next. Here, knowledge producers formulate statements that are substitutive rather than supplementary. This new knowledge competes in the market with rival sets of statements that it typically attempts to replace and silence.

Third, the discursive bases of subjectification also shift as a new regime of truth silences an old. For example, both Tanna and America Laws restated customary talk about age and gender, and thus transformed a number of everyday personal experiences and practices. The young now may take greater charge of the arrangement of their own marriages. Men no longer marry more than one woman. Women no longer share a husband. Nor do women any longer retire monthly to menstrual huts. Both women and the young, furthermore, have a

growing access to new knowledge production and circulation procedures, such as travel, language skills, and reading, and therefore
have more audible positions within today's serious conversation.

In particular, the island's regimes of truth have transfigured people's bodies (see Dreyfus and Rabinow 1982:111–112). Tanna Law,
although it accepted certain customary practices including circumcision, altered much of bodily experience. It sat island bodies in chairs;
regimented lines of male bodies and female bodies in opposing
church pews; washed bodies with soap; trained bodies to new tools
and concentrated new exercise (such as screwing out the meat of
hundreds of coconuts for copra production); cut the hair from bodies;
dressed bodies in cloth. Perhaps the most striking bodily transformation that Tanna Law demanded was the cessation of customary practices of warfare, killing, and cannibalism. Human bodies, discursively,
for the first time became known as inedible.

America Law, likewise, cut certain subjective disjunctions, and
transformed personal experiences and desire. It conjoined male
bodies and female bodies without shame in new dance figures;
trained bodies to drill and march in step; decorated bodies with
painted "USA" on chest and back; refused bodies nightly sleep. Each
island regime of truth has known a different body, a different subject.

In sum, although the replacement of one island Law by another
may not be cleanly disjunctive, as Foucault has discussed such episodic interruptions in the West, these discontinuities have changed
island conversations in three important ways: they overturn ruling
relations of conversational domination—different people appropriate
powerful discursive spokesman and editorial functions; they restock
the information market's statement inventory—new knowledge
takes the place of existing statements within serious talk; and, to the
extent that they bring into being new discursive positions, functions,
rules, and practices, they transform conversational subjectification—
discursive disjunctions have reformed islanders themselves. The sub-
stitution of one Law for another entails more than just a continuous,
incremental knowledge production and personnel replacement, the
newly wise appropriating established positions of conversational
domination once held by the newly ignorant. Conversational discontinuities affect subjective experience and desire as well.

Whatever the profundity of Tanna's conversational discontinuities, the question remains why such disjunctions should happen

at all. Why has there been a succession of Laws? What gives certain new and alternative knowledge statements the strength to penetrate the screen of discursive control procedures? How does a counter-discourse become a ruling discourse? A first move toward accounting for disjunctions is the assumption of a relation between knowledge and interest (Abercrombie 1980:141; Barnes 1977:10, 58). The exchange value of knowledge in the island's information market fluctuates according to the existing structure of personal desire and interest (see Sahlins 1981:68–69). The value of any serious knowledge statement depends on its possible uses within interested conversation. A statement's exchange value, thus, is "relative and oscillates according to the use that is made of the statement and the way in which it is handled" (Foucault 1972:104).

A discursive disjunction between two regimes of truth correlates, in this manner, with shifts and discontinuities in the constitution of interest. This interest is *personal*—that which motivates individuals to produce, deploy, and consume knowledge. Whether or not additional kinds of "interest" exist (e.g., of classes, of groups, of wider systems— whether these are social, technological, ecological, or otherwise) is conversationally irrelevant. Any interests that might be attributed to economic classes and broader systems must also be recognized, filtered, and articulated in conversational practice. Barnes has summarized this point:

> The processes where knowledge is evaluated, changed, and revaluated will involve continuing reference to shared goals and interests. Note, however, that among such goals are specific, socially situated, predictive and technical requirements: it is not that agents operate by reference to goals and interests instead of to considerations of technical and empirical adequacy; rather it is that the sense of technical and empirical adequacy is itself intelligible only in terms of contingent goals and interests (1984:202).

Or, more succinctly, "desire is part of the infrastructure" (Deleuze and Guattari 1983:104).

Although interest is always personal, it is nonetheless defined within wider, conversational relations (Parenti 1978:11). I am broadening, here, the claim about reality made above. Just as we can only know the world and its natural forces through the ways we have of talking seriously about this, so can we only know our own interests and desires in social conversation. Desire makes us want to talk seriously in order to know; but it is only in social conversation that we are also led to know those desires themselves.

Any person has a range of interests, often contradictory, as may be the knowledge statements he consumes. All interests, whatever their orthodoxy, coherence, consequence, or functions, are conversationally interpreted. Even deviant and uncommon desires are expressed and realized socially. Of course, much of what we know does not result from specific questions, stimulated by our own singular desires. Rather, the greatest interest is a diffuse need just to take part in available local conversations. In so doing, we consume shared culture that we never knew we wanted. This cultural knowledge consists of answers to unasked (by us) questions.

From this perspective, there can be nothing like a subjective "false consciousness"—knowledge that distorts or disguises a person's "true" interests, which to him remain yet unknown. Although our interests are defined within personally unequal conversations, they are nonetheless neither false nor unreal for the particular individual concerned (cf. Lewy 1982:118). False consciousness, were it to exist, would presume the existence of its opposite: some real knowledge that chronicles true, but unknown, hidden, or unrealized interests (see Abercrombie 1980:15–16; Barnes 1977:49). A person's knowledge, although unavoidably limited, can only be taken as false within the terms of some other, contending discourse. But we can only know what we desire, just as we can only desire what we know. We can have no interest in what we ignore. A regime of truth, therefore, is all there is. It neither is nor disguises the real truth.

Knowledge and serious talking change when desires change. There are counter-discourses because there are counter-desires. A discursive disjunction, in these terms, is loss of control of the questions. The knowledge of island regimes of truth maintains exchange value insofar as it addresses people's interests. When these interests change, or if alternative knowledge appears in the marketplace that provides more compensatory answers, so does ruling knowledge. The Law, in its dual aspect of fixed truth and conversational inequality, collapses. The circulation of alternative, more satisfying knowledge statements devalues that truth which once dominated the marketplace. People drop out of one conversation to take part in another. They spread new knowledge in serious talk. These new statements are "revolutionary ideas" (Therborn 1980:117; Weiss 1984:314) in the sense that they alter both the content and the relations of local conversations.

For desire to get out of hand in this way, such that the mode of information is transformed, several things must happen. The procedures that regulate discourse, averting its dangers, obviously go amiss. No matter existing personal restrictions on knowledge production, and discourse control procedures that silence and editorialize, some people manage successfully to acquire or formulate new truth statements that find a market. An emerging discourse puts into words those individual desires that first gave it exchange value. In more closely expressing and satisfying an altered desire to know, the new discursive order also makes possible its own reproduction. During the past century on Tanna, for example, a growing desire for exotic knowledge provided Christian Tanna Law statements much of their exchange value. Later John Frum spokesmen, formulating new knowledge like that of American office construction, seized upon this serious question and addressed it more directly and satisfactorily. Newly formulated John Frum answers broke through Tanna Law's regulatory procedures, into common island conversations.

Regimes of truth, therefore, are never so hegemonically efficient as to organize and align completely all subjective desire (see Terdiman 1985:56). Some people have little interest in anything but orthodox discourses; but others develop a desire to overturn ruling conversational relations and existing ignorances and silences. Various heterodox, resistant, or persistent interests manage to form and hide within hegemonic orderings of knowledge and desire. "Dominant discourses always have a guilty conscience" (Terdiman 1985:64; see Jameson 1981:288). If knowledge statements that address and promote these fugitive questions break through discursive control procedures, a regime of truth may be transformed. The counter-discourses and desires that form within an existing regime of truth "are the odd term in relations of power; they are inscribed in the latter as an irreducible opposite" (Foucault 1978:96). Because circulating knowledge may express resistant as well as safe desires, discourse often endangers itself:

> We must not imagine a world of discourse divided between accepted discourse and excluded discourse, or between the dominant dis-

course and the dominated one; but as a multiplicity of discursive
elements that can come into play in various strategies . . . Discourse
transmits and produces power; it reinforces it, but also undermines
and exposes it, renders it fragile and makes it possible to thwart it
(Foucault 1978:100–101; see 1983:225).

Tanna's mode of information, for example, unavoidably subverts
itself in the conversational value it places on controlled knowing.
People desire both to learn each other's secrets, and to keep and tell
their own. This desire for secrets gives life to counter-discourses. The
simple mystery and exclusiveness of a counter-discourse attracts consumers, who perhaps only want to know something of which others
remain ignorant. The small talk and the harmless frissons of a new
mystery, however, sometimes get out of hand. Whispers about John
Frum amplified so fast that the noise of this talk destroyed mission
and administrative structures 40 years in the making.

Within one regime of truth, resistant knowledge mostly survives
as scattered, nearly silenced statements. Some of these address equally fugitive desire. By locating marginal statements and practices "that
are already present but do not count as real" (Dreyfus and Rabinow
1983:263), we can overhear incipient discourses that, perhaps,
soothsay new regimes of truth, just as Mrs. Watt's old woman clever
in 1882 foretold the John Frum of 1941. "Thus only if one is prepared
to study not only systems of thought and the human reality they
constitute, but also those practices which persevere even though they
seem to be trivial and even subversive can one understand how a new
ethical system emerges and focuses human reality in a new way"
(Dreyfus and Rabinow 1983:263). When these once marginal, once
quiet statements find a newly desiring audience, conversation transforms, sometimes disjunctively.

One might also look for the potential conversational discontinuities hiding in the internal contradictions of a discourse (Foucault
1972:155). A genealogy of John Frum doctrine, for example, would
probe its self-presentation. Some of the pressure for incremental
change within John Frum Law perhaps resulted from internal knowledge dissonances. Contradictions certainly inhere in the doctrine's
truth statements about America. When America remains at a distance, the authority of these statements is safe. When America initiates new, diplomatic and other relations with the national govern-

ment in Port Vila that escape Tanna's control, however, a nearing
authority dissipates and talk can become lie.

Another kind of contradiction existed in the mix of statements
about chiliastic catastrophe and statements of customary revival that
were both deployed early in John Frum conversations. Some John
Frum statements dissembled themselves as extensions, develop-
ments, or revivals of the old, while others proclaimed a new, dis-
joined, millennium. Both these temporal poses are known throughout Melanesia. Some island discourses make themselves a past that
they then are able to continue; but others state time to be disjunctive
and episodic, and so assert their new purity (see, for example, Errington 1974:257; Kahn 1983:110). The New Age, the New Man, the
New Life, the New Way, and the New Law have often been proclaimed in these islands. These Melanesian doctrines, perhaps, are
more honest than our own historical discourses in that they do not
continually struggle to patch together stories of continuity, of development, of origin, and of eventual fulfillment in the fullness of time.

The Tannese, too, typically represent their past as consisting of a
series of disjunctions. An initial period of peace and harmony (called
Niprou) collapsed into an era of dualistic hostility (the moieties
Numrukwen and Koiameta), which itself was remade as Sipi versus
Manuaua within historic times, only to dissolve before the triumph of
Christian Tanna Law (Bonnemaison 1987:146, 423–424). These eras
all have sharp edges. People talk about each as a replacement rather
than an outgrowth of the one before. John Frum doctrine is complicated by joining together typical statements of historic disjunction
(the new America Law) with talk about the past and a return to
customary continuities.

Finally, contradiction may also exist within the arsenal of local
discourse control procedures themselves. As noted, Tanna's
authority-principle, which allows anyone who can claim a source to
formulate new knowledge, does not always fit well with copyright
restrictions upon statement repetition. Thus, John Frum's initial
spokesmen from west Tanna failed to copyright their authority, and
failed to silence rival revelations of competing John Frum knowledge
at Sulphur Bay and elsewhere on the island.

Discursive disjunctions, in sum, happen when some once marginal knowledge, which addresses once marginal desires, floods an
information marketplace. A new regime of truth makes new igno-

rance. Although a new Law may answer certain questions that were muffled or unaddressed during a previous regime, the victorious substitutive conversation is ultimately as rarefied as the one it supplants. It ignores and mutes other interests. "A new 'solution' carries its own dangers" (Dreyfus and Rabinow 1983:263). After a discursive disjunction, conversation is simply otherwise ignorant.

The procedures of discourse regulation and control are perhaps *most* liable to break down in some conjunction of local and exotic knowledges. An existing rarefication of ignorance and subjective desire is hard put to maintain itself when faced with ingressive knowledge that carries alongside its own regulatory practice, including locally unknown media of statement production and deployment. Customary discourses on Tanna thus came face-to-face with Christian literacy, school, and books, not to mention money and guns. This sort of ingressive, subversive, and countering knowledge is more than just the trivial or the marginal, hiding inside people's normal feelings and everyday talk; rather, it comes from over the horizon. Conversational conjunctions are, in this regard, particularly dangerous.

CONJUNCTION

Until the nineteenth century, Tanna's was a rather isolated mode of information. During the past hundred years, however, numerous exotic knowledge statements have penetrated the island's information market. This discursive conjunction poses large threats to the stability of ruling conversational regimes. An infiltration of alien statements and exotic discursive practices potentially induces disjunctions in conversation. Exotic knowledge statements may encourage existing subjective interests or awaken new. They may give voice to fugitive interest, or address common desire in some more satisfying manner.

In a discursive conjunction, two rarefied ignorances intersect. Here, there is no guarantee that "the response of the 'generalized other' of human discourse, having also his or her own cultural standpoint, [will] correspond to the suppositions of one's own intentions and conceptions" (Sahlins 1981:67). Discursive conjunctions may thereby turn into disjunctions, as new knowledge—either imported or engendered within conjunctional conversational misunderstandings—begins to circulate for public consumption, and as intrusive

spokesmen and knowledge brokers attempt to enter into and dominate local conversations.

Furthermore, existing regimes of truth may lack effective discursive control procedures to impede the circulation of exotic knowledge, or to edit this safely for local consumption. Successive Laws on
Tanna correlate, in this manner, with the island's aggravating incorporation into the world information market. Alien statements, deployed by new circulatory procedures such as literacy, schools, and
magic lantern shows, seep into the local market. Those who dominate local conversation may, of course, successfully silence, appropriate, or edit incursive exotic knowledge: recall that mid-nineteenth
century islanders, for a time at least, buried the texts that circulated
Christian statements in order to protect customary truths. In other
instances, they may not. Christian statements eventually flooded and
conquered the island's information market, and restated local truths.
New spokesmen appropriated transformed dominant positions within island conversation.

A genealogy of island knowledge would necessarily pursue these
conversational conjunctions. World War Two, for example, vastly in-
creased opportunities for travel, as men set off to join military labor
corps. This practice invested young islanders, finding themselves
novel external authoritative sources, with new opportunites to formulate inspired knowledge statements. More recently, the introduction of radio and occasional video-viewing similarly undercuts local
conversational orders, in that the island's discursive control procedures ineffectively silence electronically circulated knowledge. No
one, yet, has buried his radio, his telephone, or his video cassette
player.

The penetration of Tanna by exotic discourses, and their conjunctions with local conversation, has quickened the succession of
Laws and truths on the island. Although exotic knowledge has ever-
ted local relations of conversational domination, the conjuncture of
island and foreign discourses is yet incomplete. Tanna's mode of information is still largely vocal. The discourses that rule the world
information market, on the other hand, are significantly textual as
well as oral.

Procedures that regulate knowledge production in conversational modes of information enforce different requirements on serious
talk than do those of Western, textualizing modes. The one compels a

tyranny of creativity; the other a tyranny of inspiration. In textualizing orders, most knowledge—including the scientific—is authored.
Apart from certain revealed religious discourses, a subject of the information age must exhibit recognized attributes of creativity in order
to formulate authentically new knowledge statements, and in order
to talk seriously. On Tanna, where doctrinal and disciplinal knowledge commands greatest conversational exchange value, most statements are authorized. The authority-principle obliges people to serve
as ancestral spokesmen, or as the proxies of other external knowledge
sources. Only those islanders with acknowledged access to such
sources are thus qualified to produce serious knowledge.

The diversity of control procedures that regulate the storage and
circulation of knowledge correlate, in part, with the different materiality of the statement in textualizing versus conversational modes of
information. These procedures qualify people unequally to deploy
knowledge. Differential access to stored (memorized, on Tanna) statements supports uneven patterns of knowledge distribution within the
information market. Only those islanders with rights to a road, moreover, have market access to narrowcast knowledge statements. Similarly, only those who are personally qualified to travel to broadcasting forums have the opportunity to deploy knowledge widely.

In both modes of information, a person must possess linguistic
and other encoding skills, having had access to educative institutions,
in order to transmit and receive coherent knowledge statements. In
textualizing orders of discourse, people must have additional access
to literacy and, more recently, to the electronic media in order to
deploy knowledge. Those individuals who own or operate the various media of information transmission obviously have better opportunities to reproduce their discursive and social positions within a
cultural order.

To consume knowledge, people must finally possess requisite
decoding skills, linguistic and otherwise, as well as access to knowledge reception devices. On Tanna, where reception is hearing, this is
the personal right to travel to forums where statements are circulated.
In textualizing modes of information, accessing devices include
books, and the various mechanical receivers of electronically broadcast knowledge. Unequal personal opportunity to edit primary statements for public hearing also supports conversational relations of
domination. On Tanna, editors appraise a statement in the terms of

several currencies, the most powerful of which is truth. Unlike the falsity of textual orders, the truth of island doctrinal discourses opposes itself to falsehood. Island falsifiers lie rather than misstate.

Given these differences in procedures of discourse control, and in the materiality of knowledge statements, it may be that oral and textualizing modes of information are differentially subject to disjunctions. On Tanna, where written texts hardly exist, knowledge imperceptibly slips from one conversational event to the next. According to the procedures that govern statement repetition, the representation of others, and editorial commentary, islanders restate as they state. Conversely, insofar as written, printed, and electronically stored texts ensure some measure of constancy in statement form, textual discourses are more firmly rooted than are conversational ones.

Furthermore, the various conversational control procedures that avert the dangers of discourse are not all equally efficient. On Tanna, for example, the authority-principle and other conditions of knowledge production often *fail* to control fully the formulation of new and rival knowledge. Dreams are harder to regulate than is access to computer skills, for example. A broad range of islanders can claim roads to one authoritative voice or another, and they produce whatever knowledge statements this source inspires. Although travel and road restrictions constrain knowledge deployment on the island, many narrowcast statements are often inadvertently popularized. In addition, gossip permits the silent, who do not possess good qualifications to broadcast knowledge at recognized circulatory forums, to hear and deploy statements in informal talk.

The most effective island devices for policing discourse, in this regard, are those procedures that control knowledge consumption. Although some new voice may produce an unexpected or untoward statement and successfully deploy this in the information market, as long as the conversationally powerful reserve the right to edit this statement for public consumption by fixing its ridiculousness or its truth, it loses its dangers. It no longer threatens established relations of conversational domination.

In textual modes of information, on the other hand, perhaps the most significant locus of discourse control is the circulatory. Given the written, printed, or electronic materiality of much of serious talk, access to stored knowledge, and management of the discourse control procedures that regulate knowledge deployment are expensive. Not everyone is economically or otherwise qualified to operate within a textualized information market. A person may easily produce a dangerous statement, but still have no qualification or opportunity to broadcast this.

A person, more so than on Tanna, may therefore freely determine and consume his own individual truths, but these remain his own only. His personal consumption of peculiar or heterodox knowledge statements does not necessarily provoke harsh policing mechanisms that undermine his discursive function, remove him from conversation, or question his subjectivity in general—at least up to a point. Western discourses, too, recognize the ridiculous, the liar, the crazed, and the mad. But here, falsity, not falsehood, opposes truth. A person's production or consumption of alternative or counter knowledges has, in this regard, a disciplinary effect of less subjective magnitude. The West's "will to truth" specifically ignores (as merely subjective) the subject's own truths. Where the circulation of dangerous statements in a market is expensive, sluggish, and partial, neither truth-tellers nor liars need much fixing. A deviant, individual voice is overpowered and lost in an informational marketplace filled with the racket of television, newspapers, books, videos, computer terminals, and satellites. Because most people lack a working access to important mechanisms of knowledge deployment, their personal construal or hearing of statements is less threatening to those who dominate the reproduction of our own shared culture. Most of our own lies are small.

Whether the main locus of control is knowledge production, circulation, or consumption, modes of information that empower their subjects differentially to know may suffer disjunction when discursive procedures fail to regulate practices of knowledge and constrain individual desire. Shared culture, at this point, begins to fail. When both the questions and the answers get out of hand, dangerous knowledge takes on exchange value, and dangerous speakers assume emerging positions of conversational prominence.

On Tanna, a discursive conjunction followed the importation of exotic knowledge from alien, textualizing orders of discourse. The storage procedures of textual modes of information, compared with vocal, are more durative than memory; their circulatory procedures, compared with face-to-face conversing, are more expansive and permeating. These statements travel. Those island spokesmen who today continue to appropriate and deploy exotic knowledge statements, and to import new discursive control procedures, endanger and challenge local conversational relations of domination (see Hamelink 1983:22). They also further strengthen the bonds of Tanna's discursive conjunction with the world information market.

SILENCE

The vectors of this discursive enchainment point also in the other direction. To conclude, what of the power of anthropological knowledge statements to conjoin—and thereby threaten—disparate conversations? A dictum: the island's Local Government Council Executive Committee

> said that journalists, anthropologists and travel writers should not be permitted to write about Tanna. It has happened that some writers have published contradictory stories about Tanna in the past which were inaccurate (Vanuatu Weekly/Hebdomadaire 1984:14).

What big lies! Anthropologists and other knowledge brokers who formulate and circulate knowledge statements that describe the island also take part in the conjunctive absorption of local ways of knowing by the world information market. As the inversion of local statement importers, anthropologists and other textualizing spokesmen who occupy this discursive position export knowledge that, in telling the truth of Tanna, subverts its protective silence.

These exported knowledge statements, deployed by literate means, circulate in information markets that dwarf cramped island conversations. They present a double danger. In general, local spokesmen lose control of more widely circulating truths. Alien discourses, not local, fix what is to be known about Tanna and the Tannese (including, here, what is to be known about the official events at Isina). Once anthropology and other textualizing discourses, such as journalism and travel-writing, penetrate and appropriate the island's conversational field, vast editorial procedures go to work assiduously performing their task of restating island statements. These restatements account for, understand, or trivialize local truths that no longer can have the last word.

Second, the island's conjunctive appropriation by alien discourses threatens, at the same time, the conversational powers of local truth-tellers. Given strengthening worldwide communicative conjunctions, both of knowledge content and of information deployment media, more and more of the statements about Tanna that presently circulate within the world information market find their way back to the island with increasing facility. These statements, which edit local truths, potentially undermine the existing conversational justness of local power relations.

Insofar as Tanna is yet only partially absorbed by alien modes of information, however, it remains disengaged from some of the relations of discursive domination that govern the wider world market. Protected by marginal silence, resistant local modes of information persevere. "Silence and secrecy are a shelter for power, anchoring its prohibitions; but they also loosen its holds and provide for relatively obscure areas of tolerance" (Foucault 1978:101). Whereas silence, in this manner, shelters island discourses from external seizure, silencing as a procedural tactic endeavors to protect local relations of conversational domination.

The stated attempt in the Local Government Council's proclamation is thus to disjoin from alien conversations that threaten local orders of conversational domination, as well as subjugation. Should a Law encounter journalism, or travel-writing, or anthropology, its local advantage is no longer assured. Textually augmented opportunities for new knowledge consumption on Tanna potentially undermine ruling regimes of local truth. When truth gets out of hand, people's conversational powers are endangered; islanders who no longer tell the truth forfeit their dominant conversational functions. Those who lie are unjust.

Both discursive control procedures of silence and of silencing have served well within local regimes of truth: silencing to protect and reproduce conversational domination; silences to shelter resistant island knowledge from textual appropriation by outsiders. Over the past century, however, some islanders who themselves assumed conversationally dominant functions within emergent regimes of truth have done so precisely by organizing Tanna's penetration by alien knowledge statements. Young Christians imported Christianity; more recently, young politicians have imported a version of Western democracy. These spokesmen are managing the distension of the discursive conjunction between Tanna and the outside world. These new elites, whose conversational positions have thus now come to depend on their control of the importation of exotic knowledge statements, by silencing anthropologists and other textualizing rivals, would regulate knowledge exports as well.

But why anthropological exports? One might presume much more pressing and sinister dangers from other outsiders who gather, textualize, and export economic, political, strategic, military, and the kinds of knowledge that have far more lucrative exchange value within the world information market than anthropology's stale and mannered ethnographies. What about the dangers of the agents of multinational mining, fishing, and timber corporations, international economic consultants, overseas aid and development disbursers, itinerant foreign affairs specialists, earnest missionaries, occasional spies, and military attaches?

The point is that rights to talk about and define oneself seriously are nowadays more and more conflicted. Beyond raw information itself, now there is also a recognition of the powers and dangers inherent in serious talk. Tanna either defines itself, or powerful outsiders provide an alien reading of the island—a reading that seeps back into islanders' own conversations about themselves. Culture has become a strategic zone in the new information age. Whose definitions will travel? Whose truths will become the Law? Whose Law will silence whose lies? In Melanesia especially, where young elites have legitimized their political power and position by pointedly citing customary authority and their reliance upon the guidance of tradition, it is not surprising that there is a suspicion of anthropological knowledge productions. These ethnographies present a reading of tradition, of *kastom*, that can challenge, undermine, and trivialize local interpretations. In so doing, ethnography also challenges the authority of the powerful. Vanuatu is not the only Pacific country that has attempted to exclude anthropologists, and silence exotic and competing talk about local customs.

An anthropologist's mere presence can also subvert the powers of local elites—whether ensconced in the Executive Committees of Local Government Councils, or in national capitals. By going into bush villages, anthropologists offer themselves as external sources and as friendly roads. People may attribute to them inspirations of new knowledge that perhaps threatens ruling powers. Anthropologists, at least, if not authorities themselves are routes along which valuable knowledge might be both exported and imported. Ordinarily, local councils and national governments set themselves up as "gates" on roads that lead to the outside world. If rural islanders want outside knowledge and exotic goods, they must deal with local elites, with their own governments. Anthropologists, however, are conduits through which villagers can contact the external world without the necessity of traveling on government roads. Ruling elites whose political powers may be unstable, and whose relations with rural peoples are uneasy, are justifiably suspicious of errant anthropologists who evade their controls.

Some of the discourse control procedures that regulate conversation at the island level are also at work in Vanuatu's national political arena. For example, the authority-principle can be recognized in political rhetoric's legitimating emphasis on Christianity and generalized custom, as two inspirational guides. National leaders account for much of what they say by citing both these external sources. Likewise, Vanuatu's nonaligned stance perhaps reflects people's interests in contacting every available, potentially useful external authority (including Libya, Vietnam, and Cuba). Discourse control procedures on knowledge circulation are also discernable at the national level. Approaching a decade of independence, Vanuatu's government nearly collapsed as contending factions attempted to silence one another. The symbolic importance of physical presence and absence appeared as Moderate parties boycotted Parliamentary sittings; and then appeared again as the ruling Vanuaaku Party ejected the entire opposition from Parliament. These conversational absences and silences shelter rival political doctrines and organizations. Circulatory controls on alternative voices are also noticeable in the disappearance of the Letters to the Editor column in the country's only, and government run, newspaper. A more ominous form of conversational control is apparent in locally infamous "green letters"—deportation orders the government uses to silence its most prominent, expatriate critics. Finally, like Tanna Law and America Law leaders on Tanna, the national government also makes good use of its police force, its courts, and its prisons in order to regulate knowledge consumption. It took an internationally constituted Supreme Court to release from prison Vanuatu's first president and its leading opposition party members who had been accused of treason, of acting against the Law.

Vanuatu's discourse control procedures, however, only reach so far. They have little efficacy beyond island conversations. Tanna Law silenced a good many customary truth statements. America Law disengaged island conversation from ruling Christian knowledge. Presently, local regimes of truth, likewise, are hard pressed to censor all the dangerous knowledge statements of external textual discourses that restate those same island truths. The conversational conjunction may be out of local control. Increasing numbers of exotic knowledge statement imports potentially unsettle constituted subjective desire. And they threaten the conversationally powerful, insofar as their control of people's questions slips away, with new disjunctions.

In the contest between island and alien truth regimes, spokesmen from each mode of information editorialize the other. The one, attempting to silence dangerous talk with locally available discourse control procedures, brings to the front its most powerful weapon: indictment of the big lie. At least on Tanna, this strategy subjectively disciplines and silences. The other's will to truth, however, cares little for falsehoods; its control procedures, contrarily, indict falsity. In our terms, Tain's official pig-eating American was not a lie, merely a false statement. The subject, for us, is discursively inconsequential; you can believe and talk as you like. Impeaching liars is thus unlikely to silence external discourses; anthropology merely edits and restates the statement of impeachment, and absorbs this as part of its "data."

Anthropologists and others from the textualizing West can laugh off evocations of geographic copyright over local knowledge, like this copyright proclaimed by Tanna's Local Government Council. Rather, our own discourses empower us to formulate and repeat any knowledge not already under a *creative* copyright. Tanna appears, thus, an open field despite its local network of copyrighted geographic oeuvres. Our creative copyrights overpower their geographic copyrights. Without effective devices to control alien talk that both accounts for and penetrates Tanna's conversational marketplace, local regimes of truth lose ground against external, more massive hegemonies.

Silence is tough to remake, no matter the growing risks that ingressive, textual discourses pose for local relations of conversational domination. The control procedures of alien textualizing discourses protect and reproduce new subordinate as well as new dominant speaking positions with an emerging world information system, along with the ruling international knowledge itself. Foucault's comment on the disengagement of an individual from ruling discourses may be applied also to this attempt to disengage Tanna's conversations from their global communicative conjunctions: "I have not denied—far from it—the possibility of changing discourse: I have deprived the sovereignty of the subject of the exclusive and instantaneous right to it" (1972:209).

Our external, totalizing, textualizing mode of information with a discursive will to truth continues to penetrate and absorb resistant pockets of silence, even on distant Pacific Islands as remote as Tanna. Western discourses themselves, of course, have no guaranteed, continuous future (Dreyfus and Rabinow 1983:263). Islanders have blocked exotic and distasteful knowledge, and disengaged from external conversational conjunctions, in order to protect local truths by burying Christian Bibles, by throwing European money into the sea, and by silencing anthropologists. Still, expansion of the world information market follows advances in the electronic technologies of statement circulation. These technologies engender as well more trenchant productive and consumption procedures of discourse control. It is not anthropological knowledge alone that threatens Tanna's mode of information, its truths, and its ruling conversational relations of subjugation and domination. On Tanna, as everywhere else, the new ignorances of the information age are none too distant. The silence thus breaking down, the conversation begins.

References

Abercrombie, Nicholas
    1980   *Class, Structure, and Knowledge: Problems in the Sociology of Knowledge.* New York: New York University Press.

Adams, Ron W.
    1984   *In the Land of Strangers: A Century of European Contact with Tanna, 1774–1874.* Pacific History Monograph No. 9. Canberra: Australian National University Press.

Allen, Michael R.
    1981   Innovation, Inversion, and Revolution as Political Tactics in West Aoba. In *Vanuatu: Politics, Economics, and Ritual in Island Melanesia,* M. Allen, editor, pp. 105–134. Sydney: Academic Press.

Ashbrook, T.
    1986   Islanders Await American Dream. *The Boston Globe* (October 3):2.

Barnes, Barry
    1977   *Interests and the Growth of Knowledge.* London: Routledge and Kegan Paul.
    1984   The Conventional Component in Knowledge and Cognition. In *Sociology and Knowledge: Contemporary Perspectives in the Sociology of Knowledge,* N. Stehr and V. Meja, editors, pp. 185–208. New Brunswick, NJ: Transaction Books.

Barrow, G.L.
    1952   The Story of John Frum. Unpublished report to the Western

Pacific High Commission. Port Vila: Vanuatu Government Archives.

Barth, Fredrick
1975   *Ritual and Knowledge Among the Baktaman of New Guinea.* Oslo: Universitetsforlaget.
1987   *Cosmologies in the Making: A Generative Approach to Cultural Variation in Inner New Guinea.* Cambridge: Cambridge University Press.

Bastin, Ronald
1980   Cash, Calico, and Christianity: Individual Strategies of Development on Tanna, New Hebrides. Doctoral dissertation. Department of Anthropology, University of Sussex.
1985   Weasisi Mobility: A "Committed" Rural Proletariat? In *Circulation in Population Movement: Substance and Concepts from the Melanesian Case,* M. Chapman and R. M. Prothero, editors, pp. 175–190. London: Routledge and Kegan Paul.

Bedford, R.D.
1973   *New Hebridean Mobility: A Study of Circular Migration.* Dept. of Human Geography. Research School of Pacific Studies Publication HG/9. Canberra: Australian National University Press.

Berger, Peter L., and Thomas Luckman
1967   *The Social Construction of Reality: A Treatise in the Sociology of Knowledge.* Harmondsworth: Penguin Books.

Bonnemaison, Joël
1979   Les voyages et l'enracinement: Forms de fixation et de mobilité dans les sociétés traditionelles des Nouvelles-Hébrides. *L'Espace Géographique,* 8:303–318.
1984a   Les jardins magiques: Le géosystème de l'horticulture vivrière dans une île Mélanésienne du Pacifique Sud (Vanuatu). In *Le Development Rural en Questions: Paysages et Spaces Rureaux et Systemes Agraires, Mahgreb-Afrique Noire-Mélanésie,* C. Blanc-Pamart, J. Bonnemaison, J. Boutrais, V. Lasailly-Jacob, and A. Lericollais, editors, pp. 461–482. ORSTOM Collections Mémoires 106. Paris: ORSTOM.
1984b   The Tree and the Canoe: Roots and Mobility in Vanuatu Societies. *Pacific Viewpoint,* 25:117–151.
1985   Territorial Control and Mobility within Vanuatu Societies. In *Circulation in Population Movement: Substance and Concepts from*

the Melanesian Case, M. Chapman and R. M. Prothero, editors, pp. 57–79. London: Routledge and Kegan Paul.

1987   *Tanna: Les Hommes Lieux. Les Fondements d'une Identité: Territoire, Historie, et Société dans l'Archipel de Vanuatu (Mélanésie): Essai de Géographie Culturelle* (Livre II). Collection Travaux et Documents No. 201. Paris: Editions de l'ORSTOM.

Boon, James A.
1982   *Other Tribes, Other Scribes: Symbolic Anthropology in the Comparative Study of Cultures, Histories, Religions, and Texts.* Cambridge: Cambridge University Press.

Borofsky, Robert Alan
1987   *Making History: Pukapukan and Anthropological Constructions of Knowledge.* Cambridge: Cambridge University Press.

Bourdieu, Pierre
1977   The Economics of Linguistic Exchange. *Social Science Information,* 16:645–668.

Bourdieu, Pierre, and J. Passeron
1977   *Reproduction in Education, Society, and Culture.* London: Sage.

Brandt, Elizabeth
1980   On Secrecy and the Control of Knowledge. In *Secrecy: A Cross-Cultural Perspective,* S.K. Tefft, editor, pp. 123–146. New York: Human Sciences Press.

Brenneis, Don
1984   Straight Talk and Sweet Talk: Political Discourse in an Occasionally Egalitarian Community. In *Dangerous Words: Language and Politics in the Pacific,* D. Brenneis and F. Myers, editors, pp. 69–84. New York: New York University Press.

Brenneis, Don, and Fred R. Myers, editors
1984   Dangerous Words: Language and Politics in the Pacific. New York: New York University Press.

Brunton, Ron
1979   Kava and the Daily Dissolution of Society on Tanna, New Hebrides. *Mankind* 12:93–103.
1981   The Origin of the John Frum Movement: A Sociological Explanation. In *Vanuatu: Politics, Economics, and Ritual in Island Melanesia,* M.R. Allen, editor, pp. 357–377. Sydney: Academic Press.

1990   *The Abandoned Narcotic: Kava and Cultural Instability in Melanesia.* Cambridge: Cambridge University Press.

[n.d.]   Tradition and Power in Melanesia. Unpublished ms.

Burridge, Kenelm
1969   *New Heaven, New Earth: A Study of Millenarian Activities.* New York: Schocken Books.

Calvert, Ken
1978   Cargo Cult Mentality and Development in the New Hebrides Today. In *Paradise Postponed: Essays on Research and Development in the South Pacific,* A. Mamak and G. McCall, editors, pp. 209–224. Rushcutters Bay, NSW: Pergamon Press.

Camden, Bill
1977   *A Descriptive Dictionary: Bislama to English.* Port Vila: Maropa Bookshop.

Campbell, F.A.
1873   *A Year in the New Hebrides, Loyalty Islands, and New Caledonia.* Geelong: George Mercer.

Campbell, Shirley
1978   Restricted Access to Knowledge in Vakuta. *Canberra Anthropology,* 1(3):1–11.

Carney, S.N., and A. MacFarlane
1979   *Geology of Tanna, Aneityum, Futuna, and Aniwa.* Port Vila: New Hebrides Geological Survey, New Hebrides Government.

Carrier, James G.
1984   *Education and Society in a Manus Village.* Educational Research Unit Report No. 47. Waigani: University of Papua New Guinea.

Clifford, James
1983   On Ethnographic Authority. *Representations,* 1:118–146.

Codrington, R.H.
1891   *The Melanesians: Studies in Their Anthropology and Folklore.* Oxford: Clarendon Press.

Collins, Randall
1975   *Conflict Sociology: Toward an Explanatory Science.* New York: Academic Press.

Crowe, Peter
    1986   'Pince son ombilic et le mien vibrera:' Chant muet, kava, et
           rêves dans la musique Mélanésienne. *Anuario Musical*
           39/40:217–238.

d'Azevedo, Warren L.
    1962   Uses of the Past in Gola Discourse. *Journal of African History,*
           3:11–34.

Deleuze, Gilles, and Felix Guattari
    1983   *Anti-Oedipus: Capitalism and Schizophrenia.* Minneapolis: University of Minnesota Press.

Derrida, Jacques
    1976   *Of Grammatology.* Baltimore: Johns Hopkins University Press.

Dreyfus, Hubert L., and Paul Rabinow
    1983   *Michel Foucault: Beyond Structuralism and Hermeneutics* (second edition). Chicago: University of Chicago Press.

Elias, Norbert
    1984   Knowledge and Power: An Interview by Peter Ludes. In *Society and Knowledge: Contemporary Perspectives in the Sociology of Knowledge,* N. Stehr and V. Meja, editors, pp. 251–292. New Brunswick, NJ: Transaction Books.

Epstein, A.L.
    1969   *Matupit: Land, Politics, and Change Among the Tolai of New Britain.* Berkeley: University of California Press.

Errington, Frederick
    1974   Indigenous Ideas of Order, Time, and Transition in a New Guinea Cargo Movement. *American Ethnologist,* 1:255–267.

Eyre, Stephen L.
    1987   Knowing and Not Knowing: A Matter of Fact? Paper presented at the 86th annual meetings of the American Anthropological Association, Chicago, November 18–22.

Fardon, Richard
    1985   Introduction: A Sense of Relevance. In *Knowledge and Power: Anthropological and Sociological Approaches,* R. Fardon, editor, pp. 1–20. Edinburgh: Scottish Academic Press.

Feuer, Lewis S.
    1975   *Ideology and the Ideologists.* New York: Harper and Row.

Firth, Raymond
   1975   Speech-Making and Authority in Tikopia. In *Political Language and Oratory in Traditional Society,* M. Bloch, editor, pp. 29–43. New York: Academic Press.

Fortune, Reo
   1932   *Sorcerers of Dobu.* New York: E. P. Dutton.

Foucault, Michel
   1972   *The Archaeology of Knowledge.* New York: Pantheon Books.
   1977   *Language, Counter-Memory, Practice: Selected Essays and Interviews.* Oxford: Basil Blackwell.
   1978   *The History of Sexuality, Volume 1: An Introduction.* New York: Vintage Books.
   1979   What Is an Author? In *Textual Strategies: Perspectives in Post-Structuralist Criticism,* J. Harari, editor, pp. 141–160. Ithaca: Cornell University Press.
   1980   *Power/Knowledge: Selected Interviews and Other Writings 1972–1977.* New York: Pantheon Books.
   1981
   [1970] The Order of Discourse. In *Untying the Text: A Post Structuralist Reader,* R. Young, editor, pp. 48–78. Boston: Routledge and Kegan Paul.
   1983   The Subject and Power. In *Michel Foucault, Beyond Structuralism and Hermeneutics,* H. Dreyfus and P. Rabinow, editors, pp. 208–226. Chicago: University of Chicago Press.

Frake, Charles O.
   1980   *Language and Cultural Description: Essays.* Stanford: Stanford University Press.

Frater, Alexander
   1980   Pandemonium Beneath the Palms in the Isles of Bali Ha'i. *London Observer Magazine* (June):38–59.

Geertz, Clifford
   1973   *The Interpretation of Cultures.* New York: Basic Books.
   1983   *Local Knowledge: Further Essays in Interpretive Anthropology.* New York: Basic Books.

Geslin, Yves
   1956   Les Américains aux Nouvelles-Hébrides. *Journal de la Société des Océanistes,* 12:245–286.

Godelier, Maurice
   1982   Social Hierarchies Among the Baruya of New Guinea. In *Ine-*

quality in New Guinea Highland Societies, A. Strathern, editor, pp. 3–34. Cambridge: Cambridge University Press.

Goldman, Laurence
    1983   *Talk Never Dies: The Language of Huli Disputes.* London: Tavistock.

Goodenough, Ward H.
    1964   Cultural Anthropology and Linguistics. In *Language in Culture and Society,* D. Hymes, editor, pp. 36–39. New York: Harper and Row.

Goody, Jack
    1977   *Domestication of the Savage Mind.* Cambridge: Cambridge University Press.

Government of Vanuatu
    1984   *Statistical Indicators, Third Quarter (Ref 2.1).* Port Vila: National Planning and Statistics Office.

Gramsci, Antonio
    1971   *Selections from the Prison Notebooks of Antonio Gramsci,* edited and translated by Quintin Hoare and Geoffrey Nowell Smith. New York: International Publishers.

Granero, Fernando Santos
    1986   Power, Ideology, and the Ritual of Production in Lowland South America. *Man,* 21:657–679.

Gray, William
    1894   A Song of Aniwa. *Journal of the Polynesian Society,* 3:41–45.

Gregory, Robert J., and Janet E. Gregory
    1984   John Frum: An Indigenous Strategy of Reaction to Mission Rule and Colonial Order. *Pacific Studies,* 7:68–90.

Gregory, Robert J., Janet E. Gregory, and John G. Peck
    1978   The Relationship of Kava to a Cultural Revitalization Movement. Final report to the National Institute of Drug Abuse, Project DA01129. Washington, DC: National Institute of Drug Abuse.
    1981   Kava and Prohibition in Tanna, Vanuatu. *British Journal of Addiction,* 76:299–313.

Grimshaw, Beatrice
    1907   *From Fiji to the Cannibal Islands.* London: Thomas Nelson and Sons.

Guiart, Jean
  1952   John Frum Movement in Tanna. *Oceania*, 22:165–177.
  1956a Culture Contact and the "John Frum" Movement on Tanna, New Hebrides. *Southwestern Journal of Anthropology*, 12:105–116.
  1956b *Un siècle et demi de contacts culturels à Tanna (Nouvelles-Hébrides)*. Publications de la Société des Océanistes, No. 5. Paris: Musée de l'Homme.
  1975   Le mouvement 'Four Corner' à Tanna (1974). *Journal de la Société des Océanistes*, 46:107–111.

Guy, Jacques B.M.
  1974   *Handbook of Bichelamar*. Pacific Linguistics C-34. Canberra: Department of Linguistics, Research School of Pacific Studies, Australian National University.

Hall, Stuart
  1979   Culture, the Media, and the "Ideological Effect." In *Mass Communication and Society*, J. Curran, M. Gurevitch, and J. Woollacott, editors, pp. 315–347. Beverley Hills: Sage Publications.

Hamelink, Cees J.
  1983   *Cultural Autonomy in Global Communications: Planning National Information Policy*. New York: Longman.

Hamilton, Peter
  1985   Editor's Foreword. In *Michel Foucault*, B. Smart, pp. 7–9. London: Tavistock Publications Ltd.

Harrison, Simon
  1986   Laments for Foiled Marriages: Love-Songs from a Sepik River Village. *Oceania*, 56:275–293.

Hau'ofa, Epeli
  1981   *Mekeo: Inequality and Ambivalence in a Village Society*. Canberra: Australian National University Press.

Heinl, Robert D.
  1944   Palms and Planes in the New Hebrides. *National Geographic*, 86:229–256.

Herr, Barbara
  1981   The Expressive Character of Fijian Dreams and Nightmare Experiences. *Ethos*, 9:331–352.

Hours, Bernard
  1974   Un mouvement politico-religieux Neo-Hébridais: Le
           Nagriamel. *Cahiers ORSTOM, Séries Sciences Humaines,*
           11:227–242.

Howes, Michael
  1980   The Uses of Indigenous Technical Knowledge in Develop-
           ment. In *Indigenous Knowledge Systems and Development,* D.
           Brokensha, D.M. Warren, and O. Werner, editors, pp. 335–
           351. Washington, DC: University Press of America.

Humphreys, C.B.
  1926   *The Southern New Hebrides: An Ethnological Record.* Cam-
           bridge: Cambridge University Press.

Hutchins, Edwin
  1980   *Culture and Inference: A Trobriand Case Study.* Cambridge, MA:
           Harvard University Press.

Inglis, John
  1854   A Missionary Tour in the New Hebrides. *Journal of the Eth-
           nological Society of London,* 3:53–85.

Jameson, Fredric
  1981   *The Political Unconscious: Narrative as a Socially Symbolic Act.*
           Ithaca: Cornell University Press.

Jupp, James, and Marian Sawer
  1979   New Hebrides 1978-1979: Self-Government by Whom and
           for Whom? *Journal of Pacific History,* 14:208–223.

Kahn, Miriam
  1983   Sunday Christians, Monday Sorcerers: Selective Adaptation
           to Missionisation in Wamira. *Journal of Pacific History,* 18:96–
           112.

Kay, John, editor
  1872   *The Slave Trade in the New Hebrides: Papers Read at the Annual
           Meeting of the New Hebrides Mission, 1871.* Edinburgh: Ed-
           monston and Douglas.

Keesing, Roger M.
  1982   *Kwaio Religion: The Living and the Dead in a Solomon Island So-
           ciety.* New York: Columbia University Press.

Kristof, N.
    1987   Space Age Succeeds Stone Age on Pacific Isle. *New York Times*
            (July 19):1, 6.

Lawrence, Peter
    1964   *Road Belong Cargo: A Study of the Cargo Movement in the South-
            ern Madang District, New Guinea.* Manchester: Manchester
            University Press.

Lawrence, Peter, and M.J. Meggitt
    1965   *Gods, Ghosts, and Men in Melanesia: Some Religions of Aus-
            tralian New Guinea and the New Hebrides.* London: Oxford
            University Press.

Lederman, Rena
    1984   Who Speaks Here? Formality and the Politics of Gender in
            Mendi, Highland Papua New Guinea. In *Dangerous Words:
            The Politics of Language in the Pacific,* D. Brenneis and F. My-
            ers, editors, pp. 85–107. New York: New York University
            Press.

Lévi-Strauss, Claude
    1966   *The Savage Mind: The Nature of Human Society.* Chicago: Uni-
            versity of Chicago Press.

Lewis, Gilbert
    1980   *Day of Shining Red: An Essay on Understanding Ritual.* Cam-
            bridge: Cambridge University Press.

Lewy, Guenter
    1982   *False Consciousness: An Essay on Mystification.* New Brunswick,
            NJ: Transaction Books.

Lindstrom, Lamont
    1980   Spitting on Tanna. *Oceania,* 50:228–234.
    1981a   Achieving Wisdom: Knowledge and Politics on Tanna (Van-
            uatu). Doctoral dissertation. Department of Anthropology,
            University of California, Berkeley. [Available from University
            Microfilms International.]
    1981b   Big-Man: A Short Terminological History. *American An-
            thropologist,* 83:900–905.
    1981c   Cult and Culture: American Dreams in Vanuatu. *Pacific Stud-
            ies,* 4:101–123.
    1981d   Speech and Kava on Tanna. In *Vanuatu: Politics, Economics,
            and Ritual in Island Melanesia,* M.R. Allen, editor, pp. 379–
            393. Sydney: Academic Press.

1982a   Cultural Politics: National Concerns in Bush Arenas on Tanna (Vanuatu). In *The Politics of Evolving Cultures in the Pacific
Islands*. Proceedings of a Conference Sponsored by the Institute for Polynesian Studies, Brigham Young University—
Hawaii Campus, February 1982. pp. 232–246. Laie, HI: Institute for Polynesian Studies.

1982b   Grog Blong Yumi: Alcohol and Kava on Tanna (Vanuatu). In
*Through a Glass Darkly: Beer and Modernization in Papua New
Guinea*, M. Marshall, editor, IASER Monograph No. 18, pp.
421–432. Waigani, PNG: Institute of Applied Social and Economic Research.

1982c   Leftamap Kastom: The Political History of Tradition on Tanna
(Vanuatu). *Mankind*, 13:316–329.

1983   Say What? Language and Political Boundaries on Tanna,
Vanuatu. *Anthropological Linguistics*, 25:387–403.

1984   Doctor, Lawyer, Wise Man, Priest: Big-men and Knowledge
in Melanesia. *Man*, 19:291–309.

1985   Personal Names and Social Reproduction on Tanna. *Journal
of the Polynesian Society*, 94:27–45.

1986   *Kwamera Dictionary/Nikukua Sai Nagkiariien Nininife*. Pacific
Linguistics C-95. Canberra: Dept. of Linguistics, Research
School of Pacific Studies, Australian National University.

1987   Drunkenness and Gender on Tanna, Vanuatu. In *Drugs in
Western Pacific Societies: Relations of Substance*, L. Lindstrom,
editor, pp. 98–118. Assn. for Social Anthropology in Oceania
Monograph No. 11. Lanham, MD: University Press of America.

Luhrmann, T.M.
1989   The Magic of Secrecy. *Ethos*, 17:131–165.

Lynch, John
1978   *Grammar of Lenakel*. Pacific Linguistics B-55. Canberra: Dept.
of Linguistics, Research School of Pacific Studies, Australian
National University.

MacClancy, Jeremy V.
1981   From New Hebrides to Vanuatu, 1979–80. *Journal of Pacific
History*, 16:92–104.

1983   Vanuatu and Kastom: A Study of Cultural Symbols in the Inception of a Nation State in the South Pacific. Doctoral dissertation. Dept. of Anthropology, Oxford University.

1984   Vanuatu Since Independence: 1980-83. *Journal of Pacific History*, 19:100–112.

Macmillan, E.M.
    1924   *Children of the New Hebrides.* Melbourne: Brown, Prior, and
            Co.

Macmillan, Thomson
    1935   Koukarei: An Old Warrior of East Tanna, His Fighting Days
            and His Christian Life. *Quarterly Jottings from the New
            Hebrides,* 167:14-16.

Malinowski, Bronislaw
    1935   *Coral Gardens and Their Magic,* volume 2. New York: Ameri-
            can Book Co.

Marsh, D.
    1968   The Surprising Gospels of John Frum: He Who Swept Sin
            Away. *Pacific Islands Monthly,* 39(10):83–90.

McArthur, Norma, and J.F. Yaxley
    1968   *Condominium of the New Hebrides: A Report on the First Census
            of the Population, 1967.* Sydney: Government Printer, New
            South Wales.

McLeod, Charles
    1951   The Work at White Sands. *Quarterly Jottings from the New
            Hebrides,* 229:4–7.

Meek, V.L.
    1982   *The University of Papua New Guinea: A Case Study in the Sociol-
            ogy of Higher Education.* St. Lucia: University of Queensland
            Press.

Meggitt, Mervyn J.
    1962   Dream Interpretation Among the Mae Enga of New Guinea.
            Southwestern Journal of Anthropology, 18:216–229.
    1968   Uses of Literacy in New Guinea and Melanesia. In *Literacy in
            Traditional Societies,* J. Goody, editor, pp. 300–309. Cam-
            bridge: Cambridge University Press.

Meillassoux, Claude
    1960   Essai d'interpretation des phénomène economique dans les
            sociétés traditionnelles d'auto-subsistence. *Cahiers d'Études
            Africaines,* 4:38–67.

Meleisea, M.
    1980   We Want the Forest Yet Fear the Spirits: Culture and Change
            in Western Samoa. *Pacific Perspective,* 9:21–29.

Modjeska, Nicholas
  1982   Production and Inequality: Perspectives from Central New
          Guinea. In *Inequality in New Guinea Highland Societies,* A.
          Strathern, editor, pp. 50–108. Cambridge: Cambridge Uni-
          versity Press.

Myers, Fred R.
  1986   Reflections on a Meeting: Structure, Language, and the Polity
          in a Small-scale Society. *American Ethnologist,* 13:430–447.

Nabanga, Hebdomadaire d'Information
  1979   String Band Competition 1979: La Musique et l'Esprit d'un
          Peuple. 139 (December 22):5.

Nisbet, Henry
  1840–
  1851   Diary. In *Journals and Other Papers, 1836-1876.* Microfilm, Pacif-
          ic Manuscripts Bureau No. 417, Australian National University.

Ong, Walter J.
  1971   The Literate Orality of Popular Culture Today. In *Rhetoric, Ro-
          mance, and Technology: Studies in the Interaction of Expression
          and Culture,* W.J. Ong, editor, pp. 284–302. Ithaca: Cornell
          University Press.
  1982   *Orality and Literacy: The Technologizing of the Word.* London:
          Methuen.

O'Reilly, Patrick
  1949   Prophetisme aux Nouvelles-Hébrides: Le mouvement
          JonFrum à Tanna. *Le Monde Non Chrétien,* 10:192–208.

Parenti, Michael
  1978   *Power and the Powerless.* New York: St. Martin's Press.

Paton, Frank
  1903   *Lomai of Lenakel: A Hero of the New Hebrides, A Fresh Chapter
          in the Triumph of the Gospel.* London: Hodder and Stoughton.

Paton, John
  1890   *John G. Paton, Missionary to the New Hebrides: An Autobiogra-
          phy.* London: Hodder and Stoughton.

Patterson, George
  1864   *Memoirs of the Rev. S.F. Johnston, the Rev. J.W. Matheson, and
          Mrs. Mary Johnston Matheson, Missionaries on Tanna.* Phila-
          delphia: W.S. and A. Martien.

Poster, Mark
    1984   *Foucault, Marxism, and History: Mode of Production Versus Mode of Information.* Cambridge: Polity Press.

Price, C.
    1976   Origins of Pacific Islands Labourers in Queensland, 1863-1904: A Research Note. *Journal of Pacific History,* 11:106–121.

Priday, H.
    1950   JonFrum is New Hebridean Cargo Cult. *Pacific Islands Monthly,* 20(6):67–70; 20(7):59–64.

Rice, Edward
    1974   John Frum He Come: A Polemical Work About a Black Tragedy. New York: Doubleday and Co.

Rosaldo, Michelle
    1973   I Have Nothing To Hide: The Language of Ilongot Oratory. *Language in Society,* 2:193–223.

Rubinstein, Robert L.
    1981   Knowledge and Political Process on Malo. In *Vanuatu: Politics, Economics, and Ritual in Island Melanesia,* M.R. Allen, editor, pp. 135–172. Sydney: Academic Press.

Ryan, Dawn
    1969   Christianity, Cargo Cults, and Politics Among the Toaripi of Papua. *Oceania,* 40:99–118.

Sack, Peter
    1985   Bobotoi and Pulu, Melanesian Law: Normative Order or Way of Life? *Journal de la Société des Océanistes,* 41:15–23.

Sahlins, Marshall
    1981   *Historical Metaphors and Mythical Realities: Structure in the Early History of the Sandwich Islands Kingdom.* Assn. for Social Anthropology in Oceania Special Publication No. 1. Ann Arbor: University of Michigan Press.
    1983   Other Times, Other Customs: The Anthropology of History. *American Anthropologist,* 85:517–544.

Salmond, Anne
    1982   Theoretical Landscapes: On a Cross-Cultural Conception of Knowledge. In *Semantic Anthropology,* D. Parkin, editor, pp. 65–87. London: Academic Press

Sankey, Ira David, James McGranahan, and George C. Stebbins
1896   *Sacred Songs, No. 1: Compiled for Use in Gospel Meetings, Sunday Schools, Prayer Meetings, and other Religious Services.* New York: Bigelow and Main.

Schütz, Albert J.
1968   *Nguna Texts: A Collection of Traditional and Modern Narratives from the Central New Hebrides.* Honolulu: University of Hawaii Press.

Schwartz, Theodore
1962   *The Paliau Movement in the Admiralty Islands, 1946-1954.* Anthropological Papers of the American Museum of Natural History, volume 49(2).
1973   Cult and Context: The Paranoid Ethos in Melanesia. *Ethos,* 1:153–174.

Shapiro, Michael J.
1984   Literary Production as a Politicizing Practice. *Political Theory,* 12:387–422.

Shineberg, Dorothy
1967   *They Came for Sandalwood: A Study of the Sandalwood Trade in the Southwest Pacific, 1830-1865.* Melbourne: Melbourne University Press.

Smart, Barry
1986   The Politics of Truth and the Problem of Hegemony. In *Foucault: A Critical Reader,* D. Hoy, editor, pp. 157–174. Oxford: Basil Blackwell.

Stephen, Michelle
1979   Dreams of Change: the Innovative Role of Altered States of Consciousness in Traditional Melanesian Religion. *Oceania,* 50:3–22.
1982   "Dreaming is Another Power!:" The Social Significance of Dreams Among the Mekeo of Papua New Guinea. *Oceania,* 53:106–122.

Sturrock, John, editor
1979   *Structuralism and Since: From Levi-Strauss to Derrida.* Oxford: Oxford University Press.

Taylor, Charles
1986   Foucault on Freedom and Truth. In *Foucault: A Critical Reader,* D. Hoy, editor, pp. 69–102. Oxford: Basil Blackwell.

Terdiman, Richard
1985   *Discourse/Counter-Discourse: The Theory and Practice of Symbolic Resistance in Nineteenth-Century France.* Ithaca: Cornell University Press.

Therborn, Goran
1980   *The Ideology of Power and the Power of Ideology.* London: NLB.

Tonkinson, Robert
1979   Divination, Replication, and Reversal in Two New Hebridean Societies. *Canberra Anthropology,* 2:57–74.
1982   National Identity and the Problem of Kastom in Vanuatu. *Mankind,* 13:306–315.

Tryon, Darrell T.
1976   *New Hebrides Languages: An Internal Classification.* Pacific Linguistics C-50. Canberra: Dept. of Linguistics, Research School of Pacific Studies, Australian National University.

Turner, George
1845   *Nakukua Kamauseni Nankerian ia Tanna Asori.* Samoa: London Missionary Society Press.

Tyler, Stephen
1986   Post-Modern Ethnography: From Document of the Occult to Occult Document. In *Writing Culture: The Poetics and Politics of Ethnography,* J. Clifford and G. Marcus, editors, pp. 122–140. Berkeley: University of California Press.

Van Trease, Howard
1982   Before Vanuatu: Anatomy of the French Plan to Hang Around Forever. *Pacific Islands Monthly,* 53(7):31–35; (8):27–29; (9):27–30.

Vansina, Jan
1985   *Oral Tradition as History.* Madison: University of Wisconsin Press.

Vanuatu Weekly/Hebdomadaire
1984   Tanna Says 'No' to TV Cameras. 2(August 11):14.

Wagner, Roy
1972   *Habu: The Innovation of Meaning in Daribi Religion.* Chicago: Chicago University Press.

Waiko, John
1986   Oral Traditions Among the Binandere: Problems of Method in a Melanesian Society. *Journal of Pacific History,* 21:21–38.

Walzer, Michael
1986   The Politics of Michel Foucault. In *Foucault: A Critical Reader*, D. Hoy, editor, pp. 51–68. Oxford: Basil Blackwell.

Watt, Agnes
1896   *Twenty-five Years Mission Life on Tanna, New Hebrides*. Paisley: J. and R. Parlane.

Watt, William
1895   Cannibalism as Practiced on Tanna, New Hebrides. *Journal of the Polynesian Society*, 4:226–230.
1908   Missionaries and Native Courts. *New Hebrides Magazine*, (January):21–23.

Wawn, William T.
1893   *The South Sea Islanders and the Queensland Labour Trade: A Record of Voyages and Experiences in the Western Pacific from 1875 to 1891*. London: Swan Sonnenschein.

Weeks, Sheldon G., editor
1977   *The Story of My Education: Autobiographies of Schooling in Papua New Guinea*. Educational Research Unit Occasional Paper No. 5. Waigani: University of Papua New Guinea.

Weiner, Annette
1976   *Women of Value, Men of Renown: New Perspectives on Trobriand Exchange*. Austin: University of Texas Press.
1983   From Words to Objects to Magic: Hard Words and the Boundaries of Social Interaction. *Man*, 18:690–709.

Weiner, James F.
1986   Men, Ghosts, and Dreams Among the Foi: Literal and Figurative Modes of Interpretation. *Oceania*, 57:114–127.

Weiss, Johannes
1984   Radical Ideas and Power. In *Society and Knowledge: Contemporary Perspectives in the Sociology of Knowledge*, N. Stehr and V. Meja, editors, pp. 311–328. New Brunswick, NJ: Transaction Books.

Wilkinson, Julia
1979   A Study of a Political and Religious Division on Tanna. Doctoral dissertation. Dept. of Anthropology, Cambridge University.

Williams, Raymond
1980   *Problems in Materialism and Culture: Selected Essays*. London: NLB.

Worsley, Peter
    1968   *The Trumpet Shall Sound* (second augmented edition). New York: Schocken Books.

Yamamoto, Yasushi, and Matori Yamamoto
    1985   Broadcasting in a Traditional Society: A Case Study on Radio in Western Samoa. *Proceedings of the Department of Social Sciences, College of General Education, University of Tokyo*, 34:169–193.

Young, Michael W.
    1983   *Magicians of Manumanua: Living Myth in Kalauna.* Berkeley: University of California Press.

Young, R.E.
    1977   Education and the Image of Western Knowledge in Papua New Guinea (Part 1). *Papua New Guinea Journal of Education,* 13(1):21–35.

Index